Moving Up in the New Economy

Moving Up in the New Economy

CAREER LADDERS FOR U.S. WORKERS

Joan Fitzgerald

A CENTURY FOUNDATION BOOK

ILR Press
AN IMPRINT OF
Cornell University Press
Ithaca and London

THE CENTURY FOUNDATION

The Century Foundation, formerly the Twentieth Century Fund, sponsors and supervises timely analyses of economic policy, foreign affairs, and domestic political issues. Not-for-profit and nonpartisan, it was founded in 1919 and endowed by Edward A. Filene.

Copyright © 2006 by The Century Foundation, Inc.

First published 2006 by Cornell University Press

Printed in the United States of America

Library of Congress Cataloging-in-Publication Data

Fitzgerald, Joan, Ph. D.
   Moving up in the new economy : career ladders for U.S. workers / Joan Fitzgerald.
      p. cm.
   "A Century Foundation book."
   Includes bibliographical references and index.
   ISBN-13: 978-0-8014-4413-5 (cloth : alk. paper)
   ISBN-10: 0-8014-4413-6 (cloth : alk. paper)
   1. Career development—United States.   2. Occupational mobility—United States.   3. Occupational training—United States.   I. Title.
   HF5382.5.U5F54   2006
   331.702'0973—dc22

                                                       2005025048
Cornell University Press strives to use environmentally responsible suppliers and materials to the fullest extent possible in the publishing of its books. Such materials include vegetable-based, low-VOC inks and acid-free papers that are recycled, totally chlorine-free, or partly composed of nonwood fibers. For further information, visit our website at www.cornellpress.cornell.edu.

Cloth printing   10 9 8 7 6 5 4 3 2 1

*To the memory of Robert Mier and Bennett Harrison,
whose love, courage, and integrity will always guide me*

Contents

Foreword

By global standards, Americans of all classes are rich. At the same time, inequality in the United States is very high, as measured by either income or wealth. At the top of the income scale, the best off among us, of course, are fabulously rich, but most of us have lagged behind because of several decades of relatively slow growth in wages. In fact, since 1973, except for a relatively short period during the 1990s, inequality has increased steadily.

There have been many explanations for this pattern. Economists, statisticians, labor leaders, businessmen, politicians, and pundits argue continually about the relative importance of a variety of factors, including automation, the introduction of computers, changes in trade policy, changes in labor law, international competition, outsourcing, the new information economy, the decline of manufacturing relative to its share of overall employment, and lagging productivity. Indeed, the most thoughtful analysts have pieced together a likely tale involving a number of these factors. From the perspective of an individual worker, however, increased insecurity coupled with a lack of upward movement has meant several things at once: a growing amount of personal debt, a sense of increasing powerlessness, and confusion about how to choose a successful career path. These issues are especially acute for the majority of Americans who do not graduate from college.

For this large group of Americans, the most important pieces of their lives are family and work. Like many other features of American society—indeed world society—these central relationships have been changing rapidly. Not so long ago, most jobs involved heavy labor on the farm or in a factory. Women ran the household and, on farms, helped with the crops. Today, at least in modern nations such as the United States, that pattern amounts to ancient history. Few work on the farm at all, and women are a normal part of the workforce. Along with farmwork, manufacturing employs a sharply lower percentage of all workers. The service sector has come to dominate the economy. As it has done so, education has become more and more important for job seekers, and any differences between the physical capacities of men and women have become less and less relevant to the demands of the workplace. Increasingly, families rely on the wages and salaries of wives as well as husbands to make ends meet, and distinctions between the roles of women and men are diminishing. Now the norm is the two-earner family, with both earners working in white-collar jobs.

Business organizations have changed at least as much as the workforce. Big American employers of the past were relatively secure in their economic dominance, and their security translated into job security for their employees. In 1950, Bethlehem Steel, the Baltimore and Ohio Railroad, Pan American Airlines, and General Motors all enjoyed protected oligopoly status with big markets and secure sales. Since then, domestic and international competition have increased the economic pressure on almost all firms. As firms have lost market share and profits, their employees have lost job security, fringe benefits, and even basic wages.

These change have been particularly hard on the relatively poorly educated. As competition has carved leaner and meaner corporations, those without the skills to jump to alternative employment have often found themselves tossed onto the scrapheap of obsolete labor.

No longer can unskilled men follow in their father's footsteps and find good factory jobs. And on the other side, no longer do employers make the same effort to build a loyal workforce. Jobs and workers stay together only as long as both parties find the arrangement convenient, with a diminished sense of long-term responsibility.

In the context of these changes in work and the workplace, Joan Fitzgerald, associate professor and director of the Law, Policy, and Society Program at Northeastern University, explores the possibility of encouraging employers to play a larger role in the process of improving the skills and the job prospects of their employees. Potentially, both sides could benefit, with employees looking forward to upward mobility within the same organization, and employers looking forward to increased loyalty and effort among their workers. Fitzgerald refers to such opportunities for mobility and training within the firm as "job ladders."

At a practical level, programs designed to move workers along in their careers, raising them to higher pay levels and greater responsibility, if successful, obviously are good for everybody. They provide more productive workers for industry, they provide higher incomes for workers and their families, and, inevitably, they provide more tax revenues and fewer public burdens in the government sector. Thus, at a time when wage stagnation and economic insecurity have become persistent problems for Americans, the work of Joan Fitzgerald and others who examine such programs is particularly welcome.

Given the importance of this subject, The Century Foundation has been supporting major examinations of this problem for more than a decade, resulting in books such as *Created Unequal* by James Galbraith; *Top Heavy* by Edward Wolff; *Securing Prosperity* by Paul Osterman; *Growing Prosperity* by Barry Bluestone and Bennett Harrison; *The New Ruthless Economy* by Simon Head; *No One Left Behind*, a report of our task force on retraining America's workforce; Joan Lombardi's *Time to Care*, as well as ongoing work, such as Edward Wolff's forthcoming book on skill, work, and inequality, Amy Dean's new look at unions, and Timothy Smeeding's examination of the costs and consequences of economic inequality in America.

By exploring career ladders in a number of important industries—health care, child care, education, manufacturing, and biotechnology—Fitzgerald spans the U.S. labor market, from traditional manufacturing, through the rapidly growing human services sectors, into the rarified realm of high technology. In each case, she is intent on finding how workers without college education can be given more opportunity to learn and advance within the sectors in which they are employed.

Fitzgerald also enhances our understanding by making more concrete the dilemma that faces the unskilled or semiskilled worker in today's demanding and unforgiving labor market. It is not clear how much of this challenge can be met through improving career ladders. A cold reality of our new global economy is that there is little room for sentiment and charity. If it is profitable to train and promote workers from within, job ladders have a better chance to succeed than if it is not. The market will certainly let us know the answer. Even in the public sector, voter pressure for lower taxes makes it difficult to both deliver services and deliver job skills training in the same organization unless it is an efficient combination.

For those of us who believe in the power and the responsibility of the public sector to promote opportunity and mobility, Joan Fitzgerald has produced a stimulating book that makes clear the challenges we face in the evolving labor markets of the twenty-first century. She points out that investment in worker-advancement systems is much more effective if it is part of a larger strategy to provide reasonable compensation and advancement opportunities for workers. Surely these goals are among the middle-class values that all American politicians claim to embrace. But there has been little systematic effort to build on the best examples of such systems.

The need, as she points out, is not evidence that workers can be made more productive and achieve increased earning power. That much is clear. The need rather is to overcome the critical shortage of public and private policies intended to provide such opportunities for advancement. This shortfall is alarming, given not only the reality of millions of so-called working poor but also because the United States has always been thought of as the leader in upward mobility. Our experience over the past generation, however, has shaken our confidence in that vision of opportunity. Wages are not growing fast enough, except for the very well off, and even college is an increasingly difficult goal for the children of working-class families.

In other words, the topic of this book is important in ways that go well beyond the small world of experts on worker training. It touches on a central question facing us today: how can we restore the ideal of rising productivity and widespread upward mobility? For her contribution to answering this important question, I thank Joan Fitzgerald on behalf of the Trustees of The Century Foundation.

RICHARD C. LEONE, PRESIDENT
The Century Foundation
April 2005

Acknowledgments

In the three years it has taken to complete this book I have been supported by many people and organizations.

Funding for the research was provided by the John D. and Catherine T. MacArthur Foundation, The Century Foundation, and the Annie E. Casey Foundation. I thank Debra Schwartz, Greg Anrig, and Bob Giloth, the respective program officers, and Century Foundation president Richard Leone for their support for the project.

In the process of determining which sectors to include and understanding how career ladders work, I interviewed at least one hundred people, many who are named in the book. Several people spent a considerable amount of time explaining their work or leading me to key people for my research. They include John Burbank, Steve Dawson, Cheryl Feldman, Barbara Frank, Bob Ginsburg, Mishy Lesser, Lori Lindburg, Eric Parker, Jim Ryan, and Dan Swinney. I much appreciate their taking time out of their very busy schedules to provide the richness of detail needed to really understand how particular programs work.

Many others have contributed to this book in different ways. Virginia Carlson coauthored the *American Prospect* article with me that got the book started. Susan Christopherson and Kathy Van Wezel Stone were the sounding board for many of my conclusions during summer "ladies' labor market lunches" in Wellfleet. Nancy Mills, the executive director of the Working for America Institute, helped me think through the sectors to include. Paula Rayman generously shared insights from her research on biotechnology. Valora Washington, the consulting program director at the Schott Foundation, provided insights on child care. As an editor, Rhea Wilson's deft pruning and shaping and sometimes brutal clearcutting of text made this a much more readable book. I also thank Fran Benson at Cornell

University Press for her enthusiastic support of the book. The attention to detail provided by research assistants Daphne Hunt and Alexandra Curley was extraordinary. I am greatly appreciative of their efforts and of Crystal Meyers, who prepared the bibliography.

I started this book soon after moving to Boston and Northeastern University. My friend and colleague at the Center for Urban and Regional Policy at Northeastern University, Barry Bluestone, has been a source of enthusiastic support throughout the project. He, along with the Center's executive coordinator, Heather Seligman, and associate director David Soule have created a work environment with an abundance of warmth and good humor. Mary Lassen, the president and CEO of the Women's Union, and Laurie Sheridan, former director of the Boston Workforce Development Coalition, provided forums for discussing my research and invited my participation in their organizations. The friendship of Robin Parker and the late Susan Eaton made my transition to Boston easier.

I have had the extraordinary good fortune to be blessed with an amazing extended family that makes it all worthwhile. Thanks especially to LaVerne Hufnagel, Shelly Fitzgerald, and Nell Newton for love, support, and advice. And above all, where would I be without my husband, Bob Kuttner, my biggest champion and soul mate in this cruel, crazy, beautiful world.

Abbreviations

AAS	Associate in Applied Science
ACDS	Apprenticeship for Child Development Specialists
AFSCME	American Federation of State, County, and Municipal Employees
AFT	American Federation of Teachers
ATE Center	Advanced Technological Education Center
BBRI	Biomedical/Biotechnology Research Institute
BEST	Building Essential Skills Training
BLS	Bureau of Labor Statistics
BRITE	Biomanufacturing Research Institute and Training Enterprise
BWP	Biotechnology Workforce Project
CARES	Compensation and Retention Encourage Stability
CAEL	Center for Adult and Experiential Learning
CBEST	California Basic Educational Skills Test
CCSF	City College of San Francisco
CDA	Child Development Associate
CEEC	Center for Education, Employment, and Community
CFL	Chicago Federation of Labor
CGMP	Current Good Manufacturing Practices
CHCA	Cooperative Home Care Associates
CLCR	Center for Labor and Community Research
CNA	certified nurse assistant
CORE	Coalition to Reform Elder Care
COWS	Center on Wisconsin Strategy
CUNY	City University of New York
DACUM	Developing a Curriculum

xvi ABBREVIATIONS

DHS	Department of Human Services
DOE	Department of Education
ECCLI	Extended Care Career Ladder Initiative
EDC	Education Development Center, Inc.
ELMS	entry-level manufacturing skills
EOI	Economic Opportunity Institute
ESEA	Elementary and Secondary Education Act
ESL	English as a Second Language
FDA	Food and Drug Administration
FY	fiscal year
GED	Graduation Equivalency Diplomas
GDP	Gross Domestic Product
GPA	grade point average
HR	Human Resources
ICIC	Initiative for a Competitive Inner City
IWPR	Institute for Women's Policy Research
JARC	Jane Addams Resource Corporation
JPNDC	Jamaica Plain Neighborhood Development Corporation
LAUSD	Los Angeles Unified School District
L.I.N.C.	Ladders in Nursing Careers
LPN	licensed practical nurse
MATC	Milwaukee Area Technical College
MCDP	Military Child Development Program
MTEL	Massachusetts Test for Educational Licensure
MSSC	Manufacturing Skill Standards Council
NACFAM	National Council for Advanced Manufacturing
NAEYC	National Association for the Education of Young Children
NAICS	North American Industry Classification System
NCBC	North Carolina Biotechnology Center
NCCU	North Carolina Central University
NCSU	North Carolina State University
NEA	National Education Association
NICHD	National Institute of Child Health and Human Development
NIMS	National Institute for Metalworking Skills
NSF	National Science Foundation
ORCE	Observational Record of the Caregiving Environment
PHI	Paraprofessional Healthcare Institute
PET	ParaEducator to Teacher

Project CARRE	Creating Access, Readiness, and Retention for Employment
PTTP	Paraprofessional Teacher Training Program
QCCI	Quality Child Care Initiative
RN	registered nurse
SANDAG	San Diego Association of Governments
SEIU	Service Employees International Union
SIC	Standard Industrial Classification
SVP	Social Venture Partners
TANF	Temporary Assistance to Needy Families
TIF	tax increment financing
WAGES Plus	Wage Augmentation Funding for Entry-level Staff Plus
UC	University of California
UFT	United Federation of Teachers
UI	unemployment insurance
VESL	vocational ESL
WIA	Workforce Investment Act
WMEP	Wisconsin Manufacturing Extension Partnership
WRTP	Wisconsin Regional Training Partnership

Chapter 1

The Potential and Limitations of Career Ladders

The United States used to be a country where ordinary people could expect to improve their economic condition as they moved through life. For millions of us, this is no longer the case. Many American adults have a lower standard of living than they had as children in their parents' homes. As they move into midlife, fewer now see the dramatic income gains that characterized the World War II generation. On the contrary, job insecurity has become common across the economic spectrum. Layoffs, once thought to be a risk only for blue-collar workers, now frequently hit managers and technical workers (such as engineers). In the service sector, precarious employment is endemic. We have come to accept as the norm that people will change jobs and even careers several times in a lifetime—and not necessarily for the better. For the most educated and well connected, these transitions may offer opportunities, though even for the elite they sometimes result in downward mobility. For those in low-skill jobs, opportunities for advancement at one's place of employment—or in the move from one employer to the next—are increasingly rare. In the context of welfare reform, this means that few of the millions of people who have moved from welfare to work have moved out of poverty.

This book is about restoring the upward mobility of U.S. workers. Specifically it is about the one workforce-development strategy that is currently aimed at exactly that goal—the strategy of creating (or re-creating) not just jobs but also career ladders. Career-ladder strategies aim to devise explicit pathways of occupational advancement.

The challenge is more complex than it may seem. Although job responsibility and earning levels tend to correlate roughly with skills, enabling people to move up from entry-level jobs is not just a matter of educating and training them. Often there is no pathway for low-wage workers to advance through a progression of more responsible and better-paid jobs as they gain skills and experience, for the simple reason that there are no more intermediary jobs for them to advance into. In many industries the middle rungs of what ought to be or used to be a career ladder are simply missing; there are well-paid professional or managerial jobs at the top and dead-end jobs at the bottom—and few if any positions in between. Elsewhere, work that could be defined as professional or paraprofessional, with skills, salaries, and career trajectories to match, has been broken down to be performed instead by low-wage, high-turnover employees. As a result, career-ladder programs usually must be directed as much toward encouraging employers to restructure the workplace as toward helping workers obtain needed training.

Moreover, since employers organize the workplace the way they do in response to a variety of factors, any attempt to create career ladders must take account of those factors—from the competitive environment in which an organization does business to the labor shortages, skills mismatches, and geographic limitations that constrain it.

Thus the success of career-ladder strategies is far from a sure thing. Whether a career-ladder strategy will have the impact its advocates hope for on the national economy as a whole, and on the earnings of American workers overall, is even less certain. This book explores the promise and limitations of current career-ladder programs in the hope that a greater understanding of both will bring us closer to solving the problems these programs mean to address.

Career-ladder programs can increase wages and create more satisfying jobs for low-wage workers. But to succeed, they need to be supported by complementary regulatory and workforce development policies and income subsidies. Further, significantly more employers need to be convinced that this approach is in their self-interest. So far, the nation's job-training and worker-education programs only minimally support career advancement as a goal. From employers to local, state, and national economic development policy, we have a long way to go in creating opportunities for all workers to move up in the new economy.

Dozens of career-ladder programs have started up around the country over the last ten years or so. All attempt to counteract the national trend toward low-skill, low-wage jobs by identifying pathways people might follow to gradually advance into better jobs. The programs clarify what training or education is required to move to the next step on the ladder, and they provide workers with the support services and financial aid they need to complete the training. For example, career-ladder programs are helping nurse aides to become licensed practical nurses, clerical workers to become information technology workers, and bank tellers to become loan officers. In some cases the ladders existed already, but employees and potential employees needed assistance in using them. In other cases new positions had to be created to fill in gaps between rungs, and employers had to be educated about the advantages of doing so. In all cases the programs are providing crucial links between employers and workers—and usually links to the community beyond. Most career-ladder programs are partnerships involving some combination of community colleges, unions, community organizations, and employers. Some also receive a great amount of support from government workforce-development agencies, while others operate independently.

The programs, indeed, are often monuments to cooperation. Nonetheless their task can fairly be described as overcoming the resistance of employers, the barriers in the way of employees, and the inadequacies of existing workforce-training institutions. A few words about each of those challenges follow:

If career ladders are to be established, employers must be willing to create jobs with advancement potential and to think explicitly about their company's internal labor market. But many are not. Many put cost-cutting ahead of investment in their workers and accordingly have downsized their labor forces and outsourced their work. Some employers simply find it more cost-effective to rely on a casual, high-turnover, low-wage workforce. In addition, employment practices in some industries exhibit distinct biases against advancing women or African Americans, Latinos, or other minority group members. Such companies rarely want to look too hard at their own personnel practices. Other companies, with even the best of wills, are too small to have real career ladders; and in industries dominated by small firms, deliberate multi-firm efforts are required to create pathways for advancement among firms. These are no small feat to sustain. In summary, both entrenched hiring practices and industry structure may make it difficult to establish career ladders.

Professional and individual barriers also come into play. In the nursing field, for example, registered nurses (RNs) with four-year college degrees often resist efforts to make the RN credential more accessible to experienced health workers via on-the-job training. At the same time many would-be ladder climbers face serious obstacles to advancing. Progress often requires workers to hold jobs, manage home and family responsibilities, and go to school simultaneously. Holding one's own on all three fronts is not easy for the most advantaged workers and is even more problematic for poor people. Unless time off, financial subsidies, and social and emotional support are available, many workers will be unwilling to start or unable to complete the training programs that can get them to the next rung of the career ladder. (The same cluster of family demands and transportation problems that make continuing education difficult may produce a spotty work history as well, which also militates against advancement.)

The number of American workers in this predicament is large. Today's economy is often characterized as one that demands and rewards high-tech, high-skilled workers. And so it does. But at the same time slightly more than two-thirds of the American labor force does not have a college degree.[1] During the nation's longest period of economic growth in the late 1990s, over one-fifth of male and almost one-third of female full-time workers earned wages that economists consider poverty-level.[2] These are circumstances that cry out for a strong federal job-training system, but instead, the one we have, despite every congressional attempt to improve it, remains inadequate to the task.

Since the 1960s the federal government has provided job training for the poor and for displaced workers, but most of these programs—including Manpower Development Training Assistance, Comprehensive Employment Training Assistance, and the Job Training Partnership Act—have failed to do much more than subsidize low-wage jobs. Experts in the field have offered several explanations: the failure to coordinate job training and other adult education programs; the overwhelming focus on the poor, which stigmatizes clients in the eyes of employers; the penchant for training people in skills for which there is little demand; and the frequent failure to deliver the skills that are promised.[3]

Congress enacted the Workforce Investment Act in 1998 to improve this situation by consolidating programs in federal job training, adult education, literacy, and vocational rehabilitation into a more streamlined and flexible workforce development system.[4] The core of this legislation was the creation of One-Stop Employment Centers, a centralized point of access for all federally funded employment programs. But the primary goal of the One-Stops is to place people in jobs first and to provide limited training only after placement efforts have failed. Thus, while the new legislation attempts to fix the the fragmentation of the previous system, it has not changed the orientation of workforce development from placement with as little training as possible to providing enough training so that people can enter occupations with advancement potential. In fact, it provides less funding for actual skills training than did its predecessor program, the Job Training Partnership Act.[5] But even if it were funded at higher levels, the present system still would not be set up to provide or support the ongoing training—the lifelong learning—that workers need to advance beyond an initial job placement.

The resistance of employers, the barriers faced by workers, and the inadequacies of existing training programs are a lot to overcome, and the ability of career-ladder programs to do so is the key issue this book explores. That exploration ultimately takes the book in two directions. The chances of success of the career-ladder strategy depend in part on the quality of the programs themselves and, perhaps to an even greater degree, on the larger economic forces they are up against.

In the field of workforce development, there is considerable excitement about workforce intermediaries—independent organizations that take on the task of establishing connections between employers, job seekers, educators, and other service providers. Intermediaries are expected to have far more success in obtaining good jobs for low-skilled workers than traditional job-training providers have had. This is largely because intermediaries attend to the needs of employers as well as to the requirements of job seekers. Most researchers and advocates in the field hold that a union, a community college, a community-based organization, or a government-sponsored entity can be an effective intermediary, and a growing literature addresses the question of how such organizations can best create and maintain the necessary links among the key workforce-development parties.

Career-ladder programs, which are also designed to make connections among these parties and are run by the same cast of workforce intermediaries, can certainly benefit from the lessons of that literature. But if career-ladder programs are to be more than just job-training and placement facilitators, if they are to succeed as well at influencing how employers structure work and how government workforce policies support lifelong learning and advancement opportunities, then there's more about the practices of existing programs and the possibilities of future programs that needs to be unraveled and reported. That is the task of this book, and I will come back to it—and to the whole notion of intermediaries—shortly.

However, probably more important than the quality of certain programs and the capacities of particular intermediaries, the potential of career ladders depends on economic forces that are beyond any program's control. A study of the career-ladder strategy must examine what latitude employers actually have to create or re-create paths of advancement. Indeed, given an economy of 142 million workers, driven mostly by market forces, it is important to ask whether the potential impact of career-ladder programs can, under any circumstances, add up to more than a drop in the bucket.

In the remainder of this chapter, I turn to a more detailed discussion of these issues and present the plan of the book.

The Economic Trends of the New Economy: Making Career Advancement Harder

Several trends in the new economy are making good jobs scarcer. First, the decline of unionization has dismantled old-style job security and advancement systems.[6] Second, increased competition in product markets has put pressure on companies to cut costs, especially labor costs. Third, employment has shifted from manufacturing to service industries, which tend to have more earnings disparity and fewer prospects for advancement. The consequences of these trends have been wage polarization (the increasing gap between the incomes of America's richest and poorest people) and a loss of upward mobility. Although they are interconnected, I discuss each separately below.

Wage Polarization and the Persistence of Low-Wage Work

The United States has the highest level of earnings inequality of all industrialized nations.[7] In the mid-1980s the economists Bennett Harrison and Barry Bluestone characterized the distribution of wages as an hourglass, with fewer and fewer families earning "middle-class" wages.[8] Since then, wage polarization has only increased.[9] Between them, top- and bottom-income jobs account for nearly 60 percent of recent job growth.[10] In the 1990s only about 6 percent of job growth was among jobs in the middle quintiles of the income distribution.[11] At the same time the pay of top and bottom jobs was growing further apart. From 1970 to 2000 the top 10 percent of earners realized a 30 percent increase in earnings, while the bottom 10 percent experienced a 20 percent loss. (Real wages for workers at the bottom began to rise in the late 1990s, but by 2000 were falling off again.) These findings, cited in a study completed by the Aspen Institute's Domestic Strategy Group, led the authors to conclude that the trend, if it continues, will slow economic growth and potentially increase current tension around immigration, ethnicity, and race.[12]

As mentioned earlier, one-fifth of male and almost one-third of female workers earn not just low but poverty-level wages, and this is not merely a reflection of more people working part-time.[13] Forty-four and a half percent of poor people have at least one member of their family working full-time.[14] The official government poverty level is set so low that the government itself now typically uses 200 percent of the poverty level as the cutoff for its aid programs; and using that threshold, 16.7 percent of non-elderly Americans live in working poor families.[15]

Several trends are behind the persistence of low-wage jobs in a full-employment economy. Trade patterns, immigration, the weakening of wage regulations, and declining unionization all have made a difference. The shift from manufacturing to services, however, is probably the most important factor.[16] It is worth recalling that the manufacturing sector used to have a highly unionized labor force with predictable terms of employment regularized in negotiated contracts. Public policies also sheltered this sector from low-wage foreign or out-sourced competition. These factors kept wages relatively high and the earnings distribution within industries relatively equal. Career ladders were not a big part of this reality. In semiskilled work, such as auto assembly, some career ladders existed (from assembly line to skilled trades), but they did not affect most workers. Nonetheless basic wages were sufficient to support a middle-class living standard. From the postwar period through the late 1970s manufacturing provided middle-class pay for people with relatively low educational levels. As these jobs declined, they were replaced by lower-paying service-sector jobs, which were the largest contributors to employment growth between 1984 and 2000.[17]

From a human capital perspective, there is nothing inherent in service jobs to suggest that they should pay wages significantly lower than manufacturing paid in its heyday. According to the U.S. Bureau of Labor Statistics, there is little difference in the overall skill requirements of the manufacturing and the service sector.[18] It is higher levels of unionization in the manufacturing sector that have been chiefly responsible for its relatively high wages compared to other sectors. (When manufacturing unions were at their peak, even non-union shops, if only to deter unionization, paid close to union wages.)[19] Conversely, lower rates of unionization in the service sector partially explain its lower wages and higher levels of wage variation.[20] The economist Richard Freeman has calculated that declining rates of unionization account for about 20 percent of the rise in low-wage work in the 1980s and 1990s.[21]

In other words, more and more Americans are stuck in low-wage jobs not just because we are not providing enough education and training to move people into well-paying jobs but also because we are not producing enough well-paying jobs. Studies from 1984 to 1996 show that the U.S. economy paid a living wage for only about a quarter of workers.[22] Wage growth for workers in the 90th and 95th percentile of wages grew considerably faster, at 27.2 and 31.1 percent, respectively, than for those in the bottom 10 and 20 percent (.9 and 7 percent, respectively).[23]

The Decline in Upward Mobility

The disappearance of middle-class jobs also means that there are fewer opportunities for advancement for those in low-wage jobs.[24] In recent years the most extensive employment growth has occurred in occupations that pay below-average earnings. According to the Economic Policy Institute's review of Census and Bureau of Labor Statistics (BLS) data, between 2000 and 2003 the only private-sector industry with above-average compensation that expanded employment was Finance, Insurance, and Real Estate (and, of course, there are plenty of clerical jobs in that sector that pay below-average wages). But nearly all the well-paying sectors experienced a reduction in employment share, most notably manufacturing, information, utilities, wholesale trade, and professional business services.[25] The structure of employment has racial dimensions, since the bottom quintile of the labor market is disproportionately occupied by blacks, Hispanics, and immigrants.[26]

An individual's opportunities for wage gains over time are diminishing. In one study Annette Bernhardt and her colleagues compared the growth of wages over a fifteen-year period in two sample groups of men, one starting in 1966 and the other starting in 1979. The study found 21 percent less wage growth in the later group, meaning that about 40 percent fewer workers were moving into the central part of the wage distribution.[27] Comparisons of baby boomers (those born between 1946 and 1964) and the "baby bust" generation (born between 1965 and 1976) also reveal that earnings growth is lower in the younger group.[28]

The Panel Study of Income Dynamics (PSID) is a national sample of about five thousand families, with low-income families overrepresented. Greg Duncan of Northwestern University and his colleagues at the Center for Policy Research at Syracuse University have been using the PSID to follow upward-mobility patterns of men from the age of twenty-one, comparing those who entered the labor market in 1968 to those who entered after 1980. They analyzed how long it took for labor market entrants to earn an annual income sufficient to support a family of three at the official poverty line, and then how long to move into the ranks of the middle class.[29] They, too, found that people who entered the labor market in 1980 took longer to reach middle-class earnings levels—if they reached them at all. Only 55 percent of the later group reached the poverty level by age twenty-five compared to 70 percent for the earlier group. Only 17 percent of the later cohort reached middle-class status by age twenty-five compared to 34 percent of the earlier group. Education and race factor into these results but do not explain them. Duncan and his colleagues conclude, "The lower level and slower growth of earnings, even among the college educated, belies the American dream of income mobility and increasingly better standards of living for all."[30]

Employers and Precarious Employment

The decline of manufacturing and growth of service industries, like the increase in global competition and the resulting pressure on companies to cut labor costs, are economic forces to be reckoned with. But how industries respond to competition and how service-sector jobs are organized are the result of deliberate choices that employers make. Thus the effects of these economic forces on the labor force—the polarization of incomes and persistence of low-wage work over the last twenty-five years, as well as the decline in upward mobility—are consequences of the larger economic trends but are not the only possible consequences. They are the result of how employers structure work.

In the postwar period the employment relationship was typically organized around narrow job descriptions, lifelong employment, and seniority-based wage increases.[31] In the 1970s and 1980s firms in many industries moved to more flexible and "lean" production systems in response to increasing global competition, the need to be more responsive to markets, and the fact that deregulation allowed them to treat most of their employees as casual labor.[32]

As recently as the 1970s several major industries were regulated with respect to the prices a company could charge and the competition it faced. These included telephone companies, gas and electric companies, airlines, interstate trucking firms, and natural gas companies. Because firms in these industries were guaranteed a fixed rate of return, they did not attempt to compete based on labor costs. Not surprisingly these industries tended to be bastions of good, secure, blue-collar jobs, and strong unions. Every one of these industries was deregulated. A new world of price competition produced competition to lower labor costs. By the same token, hospitals formerly were regulated with regard to the prices they could charge and were assured a fair return. This also made hospitals a congenial venue for union organizations. And, like other industries, hospitals have been gradually deregulated since the 1970s, with consequences for casualization of all but the most highly skilled of medical occupations.

A related change was a flattening of organizational structures, which reduced opportunities for advancement within firms.[33] In *Lean and Mean* (1994), the late economist Bennett Harrison provided convincing evidence that much of the supposed prowess of small businesses as job generators in the 1980s and early 1990s was actually a function of vertical disintegration, as large businesses contracted out goods and services formerly produced in-house. The reality was less a burgeoning of jobs in new and dynamic small businesses than the fact that very large firms, once the heart of the high-wage and secure labor market, were now outsourcing more work. Many of the supposedly new ventures were satellites of large companies whose internal labor markets had been hollowed out as a cost-saving measure. In this kind of downsizing, firms rely on subcontractors and temporary workers to perform tasks that formerly were performed internally.[34] The motivation, of course, is to be "poised for contraction" rather than supporting a pipeline of workers advancing on a career ladder.[35] IBM, for example, was known for its no-layoff policy until the 1990s, when the company restructured employment by reducing its workforce, staffing less-skilled jobs (including clerical jobs) through employment agencies, and rehiring laid-off workers on a temporary basis as consultants.[36]

The new flexibility is often advertised as a benefit to workers, but in reality it is defined and contoured mainly for the convenience of management. UCLA law professor Katherine Stone argues that this brand of flexibility has created an economy of precarious employment, a category that extends beyond the contingent employment of temporary or subcontracted workers to include those with steady, full-time jobs but no promise of long-term job security.[37] In contrast, from the end of World War II through the early 1970s, far more people could assume that their jobs were long-term and, if they worked hard, they could advance in the same company. Many firms had established career ladders, often requiring only on-the-job training for advancement. Others had contractual seniority systems that increased pay with experience. The system kept employers and workers happy—turnover was low, and advancement and reimbursement systems seemed fair—at least in manufacturing and regulated industries in the utilities and transportation sectors.[38]

Today's system of precarious employment operates under what Stone calls a "new psychological contract," which differs markedly from the mindset that dominated in the postwar period (see table 1.1). One big difference is job security. Nowadays two-thirds of employers do not assure job security to their employees.[39] Jobs are defined more broadly in many industries, so workers must acquire more skills for any particular job. And rather than expecting to be promoted within one firm, most workers expect to have to change jobs, making networking more important. Because unionization has declined and workers change employers more frequently, wages are based

TABLE 1.1
Expectations about employment, then and now

Old Psychological Contract	New Psychological Contract
Job security	Employability security
Firm-specific training	General training
De-skilling	Up-skilling
Promotion opportunities	Networking opportunities
Command supervision	Microlevel job control
Longevity-linked pay and benefits	Market-based pay
Collective bargaining and grievance arbitration	Dispute resolution procedures for individual fairness claims

Source: Stone 2000, 572.

on what the competitive market will bear and dispute resolution replaces collective bargaining.[40]

Although many of those who were part of the labor force prior to 1980 see the new policy as a loss, younger workers do not remember things being any other way. When I was explaining the concept of precarious employment to two software executives in Seattle, one of them, a twenty-something woman, looked at me quizzically, and said, "Why would I want a job to last more than five years?" This woman sees herself as a free agent and values freedom more than stability and security.[41] But while this new freedom may benefit those nimble enough to take advantage of it, it leaves countless others vulnerable to business cycles and random shifts in the employment structure of the economy.

Nowadays, neither high levels of education nor employment in growth sectors insures against precarious employment. In the 1990s many large companies eliminated entire layers of management, laying off thousands of college-educated workers.[42] Almost 40 percent of Silicon Valley's labor force works under "flexible" (i.e., temporary) agreements related to specific projects, rather than in stable employment with one company over an extended period of time.[43] Even among those with "permanent" jobs, turnover is high.[44] Independent contractors in information technology have "boundary-less" careers, their advancement taking place in hops among organizations rather than within a single hierarchical organization.[45] In a system of such careers, people are not long-term employees; they are owners of human capital, which is used by employers over undefined time periods.[46] As the Hewlett-Packard cofounder William Hewlett used to advise people, "If you want to succeed here you need to be willing to do three things: change jobs often, talk to your competitors, and take risks—even if it means failing."[47]

Rosemary Batt and Jeffrey Keefe have documented the decline of upward job mobility in the telecommunications industry since the deregulation and breakup of the formerly integrated Bell Telephone system.[48] Under the old Bell system, employees were assured of continued employment and the company's ongoing investment in training them. It was understood that some women could advance from clerical to management positions, and even those who remained in the heavily female occupation of telephone operator had job security and decent wages and benefits. Accompanying deregulation of the Bell monopoly has come competition and declining profit margins, and telecom companies have organized themselves to minimize fixed costs and labor costs generally.

The Wharton School professor of management Peter Cappelli describes how the new labor relationship works at AT&T:

> AT&T has experienced one of the most dramatic changes in its employee relationships and has introduced a series of new policies to help define the new deal. AT&T executives described the old deal as one in which "the employee provided a fair day's work and a tremendous sense of loyalty, commitment, and dependability. For its part, AT&T rewarded most employees with a fair day's pay, a secure future, and an opportunity to rise through the ranks. Managers and professionals were virtually assured of lifetime employment." With the breakup of the Bell Systems and the competition of deregulation, an AT&T executive noted, "the company moved to encourage entrepreneurship, individual responsibility, and accountability. Rewards were more closely tied to performance, and most dramatically, surplus employees were let go. Thus, AT&T's psychological contract died in the 1980s." When security ended, loyalty and commitment became casualties as well.[49]

Batt and Keefe relate how women's upward mobility within telecommunication firms has eroded as the companies have segmented their customer markets to gain a competitive edge, separating high- and low-end residential customers, as well as those in small and large businesses, and often housing them in different cities or states. Nowadays telephone-operator jobs are often contracted out and pay just above minimum wage. Firms have also replaced company-provided training with tuition-reimbursement programs, which leave it to employees to arrange for their own acquisition of skills and to front the money for it. For low-income employees, the reimbursement programs are virtually useless.

Similar changes in the organization of work are being made throughout the service sector. Customer segmentation is becoming a norm in these industries. Services are tailored, for instance, for customers of small- and large-businesses, as well as for those living in high- and low-end residences. Better customers get better services. The strategy allows the companies to maximize profit using the least possible number of skilled workers and expending more effort where it will produce more business. But when a company's functions are thus divided and separated geographically, then upward advancement within the firm becomes almost impossible.

One common response to these changes is that American workers are becoming more attached to their occupations than to their employers.[50] With declining returns to seniority, employer-employee relations are becoming less important than they used to be in determining an employee's long-term advancement potential.[51] In the new economy, building a career requires moving repeatedly from one organization to another.[52] A study of the career trajectories of biotechnology workers suggests that advancement resembles a game of hopscotch more than a traditional career ladder.[53]

Like other manifestations of the new flexible labor market, playing hopscotch—switching from one employer to the next and trading bouts of unemployment for periodic entrepreneurial opportunity—sometimes works for highly skilled workers. But for those with lower levels of skill and education, the new flexibility often creates a paradox. These workers are more likely to be both overworked and underemployed. As the economists Barry Bluestone and Stephen Rose put it, "They work as much as they can when work is available to compensate for short work weeks, temporary layoffs, or permanent job loss that may follow."[54] In this "feast or famine" cycle, precarious employees work more hours when they can, simply to maintain their standard of living, not to increase it. Rather than enhancing freedom, for many people, the new system of boundaryless careers increases employment insecurity.[55]

The Question of Employer Latitude

If the new economy is creating more precarious jobs, can public policy influence the rules of the game or can career-ladder programs influence employer choices so as to increase the number of well-paying jobs and the potential for advancement? At first glance the answer seems to be no, not likely. Employers structure work to maximize profits in a highly competitive global economy, and that is not going to change. However, in an earlier era, when domestic competition between manufacturers was quite high, employers also structured work to maximize profits. What made it possible for workers to gain higher wages and better working conditions in the textile, apparel, auto, and steel industries in that era were government policies that boosted minimum wages, mandated overtime pay, encouraged unionization, and led to more highly structured labor markets generally.

These policies served industry's competitive needs as well, by giving no competitor an edge and all a steady supply of laborers. In the new economy another set of public policies may well be able to maximize the benefits of flexibility for employers and workers, and create a new form of security for workers. In fact, the promotion of new kinds of career ladders—with some form of portability built into them—could be just the ticket.

In any case, heightened competition does not have to erode wages and job stability. Profitability does not always require a company to adopt a low-wage, low-skill, low-security workforce strategy. Indeed, *within* industries employers already pay different wage rates and employ different technologies. Both high-road and low-road choices can be profitable.[56]

Research by the Russell Sage Foundation suggests that employers have significant discretion to organize the workplace either on a model of low skills and wages, or on a model of high-performance work practices, investment in worker training, and explicitly structured career paths. The proof of that discretion is the considerable variation in the ways that employers currently deploy technology and worker skills. In plastics production, total compensation among workers in the same occupation varies by as much as $7.00 per hour, depending on whether the firm is a low-road or high-road producer.[57] Sometimes the nature of the product determines how production is organized. In medical equipment production, technology can be used in ways that produce good jobs for workers (with opportunities, skills, and decent wages) or crummy ones. In the manufacture of low-tech medical products such as syringes and catheters, high-volume production, in fact, relies on advanced technology and highly skilled workers. Conversely, in the manufacture of some custom-made, high-tech products such as electro-surgical equipment, the technology is embedded in the product, which, paradoxically, can actually be produced with lower-skilled workers.[58] How jobs are structured in any given industry varies over time, among firms, and even among occupations within an industry.

Decisions to restructure employment are themselves subject to ongoing restructuring. It is not uncommon for employers to restructure in order to tear down internal labor markets, or to de-skill jobs and rebuild them later if cost reductions or other desired goals are not realized. For example, in response to shortages of registered nurses and pressures from HMOs to reduce costs, many hospitals in the 1980s and 1990s experimented with increasing the ratio of nurse aides to registered nurses. This required a redesign of how nursing services were delivered. The strategy did reduce direct labor costs, but many hospitals found that it increased care costs, because patient problems were not caught as early under the new structure and required more drastic and costly interventions in the end.[59] A study of the relationship between levels of RN staffing, patient outcomes, and costs in more than one thousand hospitals revealed that, overall, higher levels of RN staffing decreased complications and costs.[60] It is not accurate to conclude that hospitals will or will not rely on lower-skilled staff to cut costs. At different points in time, in response to different circumstances, hospitals change staffing patterns.

Likewise, some firms in the insurance industry have lately reversed decisions to locate customer service centers in remote geographic areas with low prevailing wages. Case studies in these industries found that when employers discovered that the cost savings were not as great as anticipated, they chose to reintegrate their operations, and they re-created some parts of their internal labor markets—thus re-creating more advancement opportunity.[61] Both the remote-location operations and the returned operations turned out to be comparably profitable and efficient.

As illustrated in these examples, some employers are finding that driving down wages and eliminating pathways to mobility may be counterproductive, or less profitable than they had hoped. But that does not foreshadow a general trend toward re-created career ladders. Career-ladder advocates suggest two circumstances under which employers would be particularly interested in career ladders—when they are experiencing either high turnover or shortages of adequately skilled workers—but even these circumstances do not guarantee that a career-ladder strategy will be chosen.

Turnover has become a major problem for low-wage employers.[62] With little reason for loyalty and little actually at stake, low-wage workers often quit after relatively short periods to take better jobs or for other reasons. Turnover is so high in the eleven fastest growing low-skill occupations that only about one in six job openings represents a new job, as opposed to a replacement job.[63] The annual rate of turnover for tellers at many banks is between 65 and 80 percent.[64] The rates are even higher for certified nursing assistants working in nursing homes.

High turnover does not automatically mean that an employer's response will be to improve working conditions. Some employers have learned to manage turnover when a ready supply of replaceable workers is available. Many banks use college or even high school students as tellers, knowing they will only stay on the job for a year or two, because they are reliable workers during this time. United Parcel Service manages a 400 percent turnover rate in truck-loading positions by hiring college students.[65] But other employers—health care providers, child care centers, and schools, for instance—cannot provide quality service with a managed turnover strategy. These employers are likely to be interested in promoting career ladders to improve morale, productivity, and job satisfaction.[66]

Employers experiencing shortages of skilled workers along with high turnover may have even more reason to invest in training for their lower-skilled workers—and to create a career path of higher-wage, medium-skill jobs along which employees can advance.

Employers do not have unlimited latitude to structure the work of their organizations, and the constraints facing particular employers in particular industries remain to be considered. But it is important to acknowledge that, even under the constraints of profitability, employers generally do have choices about how to structure the workplace. They often have the option to choose a path that provides good jobs with good pay and advancement opportunities. That does not mean they will see it for themselves, choose it if they do, or create career ladders that entry-level workers can conveniently use. Nor do most low-wage workers know how to navigate the education and training system to find the programs that will allow them to take advantage of the advancement opportunities that employers might create. But for that, as mentioned earlier, we have intermediaries.

Workforce Intermediaries: Connecting Work, Education, and Career Advancement

The concept of the "workforce intermediary" has been popularized by foundations, advocacy groups, and academic researchers (myself included). The idea is that some outside group, neither worker nor employer, is needed to maximize the opportunities workers have to advance in their skills and careers. In the standard account, these intermediaries should serve three distinct functions that are quite similar to those served by career-ladder programs. They provide labor market services to both employers and job seekers—particularly low-wage, low-skilled job seekers. They organize partners and funding streams toward common goals. And they "mobilize other institutions in the community to join efforts to create a more efficient and equitable regional labor market with varied advancement paths for low-skilled workers."[67] In principle, intermediaries are needed to bridge a structural gap: employers may not appreciate the value of providing training opportunities for their incumbent or prospective workforce, and workers may not know how to find and make use of career opportunities.

Workforce intermediaries address obstacles that prevent people from holding a steady job and those that keep employers from providing jobs that people want to hold onto. Intermediaries provide a combination of job training, education, and soft skills (e.g., time management, workforce etiquette, communication, and conflict resolution) to prepare their clients for the labor market. They also coordinate a range of social support services (e.g., drug treatment, psychological counseling, child care, and transportation).[68] Further, they resolve problems that arise between clients and employers. Some offer longer-term career guidance to help people continue their education while working so that they can move into better jobs.

Since most middle-class people have ready access to education and the social networks through which jobs are found, intermediaries work mostly with low-income groups. Many community-based organizations (CBOs) have become quite effective in this arena. A large literature identifies the specific program elements and documents how organizations have networked to provide the comprehensive set of services needed to move people from welfare to work, often into living-wage jobs.[69] An often cited example is the Jane Addams Resource Corporation (JARC), a nonprofit community development corporation at the center of a regional training alliance in Chicago. JARC was organized in 1985 to provide technical assistance and job training to manufacturers as part of a broader industrial retention strategy in the Ravenswood community on Chicago's northwest side.[70] JARC has expanded its job training services to metalworking firms throughout the region and is a founding member of a regional consortium, the Regional Manufacturing Training Alliance, organized to increase productivity among manufacturers in the Chicago metropolitan area. As a workforce intermediary, JARC has influenced how employers hire and promote workers in order to create more job opportunities for city residents, particularly for low-income populations.[71]

Among intermediaries pursuing career-ladder strategies, a few are nationally based organizations trying to deal with dire worker shortages. The VHA Health Foundation, for example, is funding career-ladder initiatives in several cities to enable entry-level workers in hospitals and other health care institutions to advance into technical positions. There are also unions that promote career ladders and provide continuing education for their members. Transportation Workers of America locals in San Francisco and New York, for example, are developing career ladders so that workers can advance from traditional mass transit system maintenance jobs into jobs associated with maintenance of intelligent transportation systems.

Many community colleges are designing certificate and degree programs that facilitate advancement in particular industries. These programs start with basic skills and provide continuing upgrade training once people are employed.[72] Some of these colleges also provide support services for nontraditional students or network with CBOs and social service agencies to provide these services.[73] For example, Shoreline Community College in suburban Seattle is working with employers and people moving off welfare to create career ladders in four occupational clusters. Students go through an initial assessment and are then placed in a pre-employment program, remedial classes, or ESL (English as a Second Language) classes. As soon as students have enough skills to begin an entry-level job in one of the target occupations, they combine work and continuing education to advance into better jobs. Students develop a career plan early on and work with a counselor to keep moving ahead on their career goals. A retention specialist, who serves as the liaison between students and employers, works with students in choosing a career pathway.[74] The community college acts as an intermediary: college staff provides or refers students to support services to make sure that they complete their training or academic work, and college staff also works with employers to identify advancement opportunities and to help them understand the problems workers may be facing on the job.[75]

As these brief examples illustrate, workforce intermediaries facilitate the partnerships that are necessary to create effective career ladders, and a number of intermediaries are interested in pursuing career-ladder strategies. Numerous studies have identified the specific program elements needed to provide the comprehensive set of services that can move people from entry-level to living-wage jobs.[76] This is valuable information. But to move beyond matching people to existing jobs—to begin to change the kinds of jobs the country produces—is a much taller order. Which intermediaries in which circumstances might be up to the challenge is a question for further examination.

The Plan of the Book

Three main questions about career ladders frame this book. The first, at the most programmatic level, is what it takes for a career-ladder program to succeed in helping particular employers to restructure work and helping particular employees to advance. The second is how much difference even the most successful career-ladder programs can make, given the macroeconomic forces that are driving the economy. The third is whether there are federal, state, and local workforce-development policies that, if adopted, could favorably change the odds, namely, public policies in support of lifelong learning and advancement, which might improve the prospects for restoring the upward mobility of the American worker.

In each of the following chapters I examine the labor market of a specific industry and the extent to which workforce intermediaries have been able to change how employers hire and advance employees. Each chapter focuses on a different sector of the economy where there is potential for building more advancement opportunities for entry-level workers. The various economic sectors were chosen to illustrate the unique set of challenges that intermediaries face in constructing career ladders in different sectors. The sectors are health care, child care, education, biotechnology, and traditional manufacturing.

The first three sectors—health care, child care, and education—are domestic service industries in which government essentially sets wages either directly through salaries or indirectly via reimbursements. A key concern in all three is the quality of service. An examination of career ladders in each reveals debates over how to improve the quality of service and the quality of jobs (including pay levels). These sectors are dominated by women (although this has become less pronounced in the teaching profession). In direct health and child care, workers are unable to move out of poverty even if working full-time. Child care and health care have traditionally been provided by women for their own families for free. As labor-market services, they have been performed historically for no wages by women of color during slavery and for very low wages by immigrants and African American women into the present century. As this private uncompensated work has increasingly moved out of the home and into the marketplace, we as a nation must decide the quality of service we want and are willing to pay for. In education I focus on the career ladder from teacher's aide to teacher. Although teachers earn less than people with similar levels of education in other sectors, the pay increase and benefits associated with moving from a paraprofessional position to a teacher is significant. The main question in this career ladder is whether pay raises should be based on completing credits or a college degree. This debate has a parallel in teacher career-ladder programs that a few places are trying. In both cases the debate is about the value of credential- versus performance-based advancement systems.

In principle these three service-sector industries have strong potential for developing career ladders, because they are public-sector services funded largely by government and each faces serious labor-market shortages. As the public grows more aware of these shortages—and of the links between shortages, quality of service, and pay increases—political pressure can be used to increase the funds allocated for training and for wage increases, the two costs of a career ladder.

Manufacturing is also highly instructive, because it illustrates the connection between economic-development objectives and career-ladder strategies. For example, since the biotech industry is so new and production processes are just now being worked out, job categories and qualifications for them are fluid, not lending themselves to particular certifications or even degrees. Community colleges are gearing up to meet the demand for skilled production workers, but, even with significant employer input, establishing the curriculum content is an ongoing process.

In traditional manufacturing, although the total number of jobs is declining, many industries are adopting new and profitable high-performance production methods that can create advancement opportunities for blue-collar workers. Here, too, career-ladder programs can only be understood in the context of broader economic development strategies. If a city or state is not committed to keeping and helping its manufacturers adapt in a highly competitive environment, career ladders will be of little consequence. But even in the most supportive environments, many manufacturing industries are finding it hard to stay competitive. A key research focus is identifying manufacturing sectors in which it makes sense to develop an integrated workforce and economic development strategy.

In terms of people, I focus on those starting with less than a college degree. Although precarious work is affecting people at all educational levels, those without college degrees have more difficulty navigating their way up a career ladder. For people making the transition from welfare to work, advancing out of entry-level jobs is even more difficult, especially for those who do not even have a high school diploma or basic literacy. But career-ladder programs are not just a welfare-to-work strategy. Indeed, if they focus on getting unemployed people into jobs, they will fail at their main mission, which is to create pathways upward from there, pathways into middle-income jobs.

In each chapter I describe current trends in the industry with respect to how they affect employment and career mobility. I then present cases of career-ladder programs operating at different scales. Some are efforts of individual employers in partnership with community organizations. Others are city- or statewide demonstration programs involving multiple partners. All the initiatives can be described as promising, although most are too new to have had long-term evaluations. Much of my emphasis, therefore, is on how the programs were implemented, how they work, how the intermediary is influencing employer practices, and how the program partners are getting legislation and policy initiatives in place. Sometimes I emphasize the story of a program graduate, and at other times the story of a person or group advocating or lobbying for legislative change. A focus of all the chapters is the extent to which codified credential-based career steps are the most effective way to build advancement opportunities. Finally, each chapter raises questions about the impact career-ladder strategies can have in the face of broader economic trends in the industry.

Chapter 2, "Health Care," examines direct care and allied health occupations. Health care is seemingly an ideal sector in which to pursue a career-ladder strategy. There are many entry-level and paraprofessional positions in the industry, and demand will continue to grow with the aging of the population, the growth of community-based care, and the downsizing of hospital care. But the extent to which career ladders exist for, say, dietary aides or certified nursing assistants depends on a number of factors. Three approaches are being tried: helping people move up into progressively better-paying occupations that require more education or training; increasing the pay and professionalism of jobs that currently exist; and creating tiers within occupations that offer pay raises for increased skill and experience. The chapter describes how each of these strategies is being tried in practice. The structure of both direct health care and child care labor markets suggests a need to create additional job categories, and certifications to accompany them, in order to provide workers with clear paths to advancement. Although such a strategy flies in the face of current good management practices, which reduce the number of job categories, doing the very opposite in the areas of direct health care and child care may create opportunities for increasing the skills, pay, and morale of workers and thus reducing costly turnover.

The potential for political action to raise wages, expand training requirements, and improve working conditions of health care workers is high, as it is for child care workers. Both categories of workers have the advantage of being what the paraprofessional advocates Steve Dawson and Rick Surpin refer to as "public employees once removed."[77] Workers in health care also have a middle-class constituency that worries about the care their parents are receiving, which inspires them to advocate for more training and better pay so as to improve the quality of that care. In fact, advocacy organizations have already been effective in lobbying for the investment of more state resources into career-ladder programs for health care workers, but the number of programs still falls short of meeting the demand.

Chapter 3, "Child Care," explores career ladders for child care workers in center- and home-based settings. The situation of child care workers is similar to that of paraprofessional health workers in that the pay is low, workers are often treated disrespectfully, few opportunities exist for advancement, and, ultimately, much of the financing for these jobs is publicly subsidized. In other respects, however, the situation of child care workers is worse. They are even less likely than health care workers to have health benefits, and only a small minority of them are covered by union contracts.

In the field of child care several different approaches to career ladders are being tried at the state, regional, and local levels. As in health care, a middle-class constituency—in this case, parents with children in day care—could be mobilized to advocate for more public resources for career ladders. But with child care, it has taken years of political organizing to obtain funding for training and wages. Convincing employers to participate has also been difficult, since the funds for raising workers' wages has always been temporary and the raises miniscule. Even so, most of the programs seem to be having dramatic effects in job satisfaction, quality of care, and reducing turnover. The key issue overshadowing career-ladder programs for child care workers is whether funding, which has come largely from the states, can be maintained in a time of state fiscal crisis.

Chapter 4, "Education," examines the pathway from paraprofessional to teacher. Paraprofessionals in many schools have years of experience and often work in their neighborhood schools. Since these schools are often urban and difficult to staff, the paraprofessionals are strong candidates to fill teaching vacancies. Foundations, state governments, and school districts have invested in a variety of programs to provide tuition and other supportive measures to help teacher aides earn degrees in education and obtain certification. These programs have been quite successful, but state and local fiscal crises have placed their funding in danger.

Chapter 5, "Biotechnology," focuses on what is currently considered one of the most important emerging industries in the U.S. economy. Many U.S. biotechnology and pharmaceutical companies are just beginning to move from research and testing to the manufacturing of drugs and medical devices. This new manufacturing industry will need highly skilled technicians, but will largely require workers to have only training certificates or associate's degrees for entry-level jobs. Additional in-house training is expected to be provided. Career ladders will be built into the industry. Excellent opportunities will be created for workers without a college education, but the industry will remain small and geographically limited for the foreseeable future. The challenge in biotechnology is not to develop effective training programs—many have already been created—but rather to decide how much and which public funds should be targeted to an extremely volatile industry. Many places are currently chasing after a limited amount of new employment. The three states examined in this chapter—California, Massachusetts, and North Carolina—are using their community colleges to build training programs to attract and retain biotech companies. The approaches differ, but each is hoping to develop this industry and several spin-off industries that could invigorate its economy.

Chapter 6, "Manufacturing," examines career progressions in traditional manufacturing sectors such as metalwork and food. Although manufacturing is often considered an "old economy" job, in fact many of these jobs now require higher-level skills and offer opportunities for advancement. With the dwindling of the American manufacturing sector, career-ladder strategies in these industries must focus on keeping jobs in the United States. To that end, the programs discussed in this chapter all attempt to integrate strategies (and agencies) to expand the workforce and develop the economy.

In the fields of health care, child care, and education, the usefulness of credentials—which package skills and provide portable proof of their acquisition—is fairly well established, and career-ladder programs can make convenient use of them. In manufacturing, however, the question of credentials is not clear: should career-ladder programs rely on nationally recognized credentials and create formal job descriptions at each workplace based on these credentials, or should they work with employers' already established, and often union-negotiated, job categories, which sometimes are specific to each place of business? The chapter examines that debate and focuses on efforts to systematize training in Chicago and Milwaukee. The intermediaries in these two cities have taken entirely different approaches to the issue, and both have advantages and drawbacks.

Chapter 7, "An Agenda for Moving Up in the New Economy," synthesizes the main issues of the book concerning the necessary measures needed for a career-ladder program to succeed in its immediate tasks, particularly what is needed to convince employers to restructure work. This last chapter also outlines policy approaches that would support strategies for career advancement and wage progression. Most of the programs described here are relatively new. They represent promising practices for changing the focus of the nation's workforce development system: instead of concentrating on the provision of jobs, the main goal would be to facilitate career advancement. The ultimate question addressed in the conclusion is whether such programs and policies collectively can have much impact in restoring upward mobility to American workers.

Chapter 2

Health Care

It will not be easy to raise wages and improve advancement opportunities for low-level workers in any American industry. But the way is clearer in the field of health care than in any other because of an unusual confluence of factors. Hospitals, nursing homes, and home health care agencies are increasingly short of staff; as a result, middle-class patients and their families are increasingly dissatisfied with the care that is being provided, and an ever growing number of overstressed workers are represented by unions. All three groups share a strong interest in making caregiving jobs more attractive. And all three know how to bring political pressure to bear on government policy makers, who are a major source of funds in this industry.

Thus it is not surprising to find that far more, and more varied, programs to improve the career trajectories of low-level workers have been started in the health care sector of the economy than in any other. These programs offer important models that may be adaptable to other industries. But they also suggest how far we still have to go, for even in the health care industry workers in the lowest tiers—those providing most of the direct, hands-on, hour-by-hour care of patients—do not yet make a living wage.

The Shortage of Direct Care Workers

As a social scientist, I don't use the word "crisis" lightly, but I do think that over the next 10 years we face a true crisis regarding frontline workers in long-term care.

Dr. KARL PILLEMER, director, Applied Gerontology
Research Institute, Cornell University

The shortage of direct care workers is evident at all skill levels, from home care aides to nursing assistants[1] to licensed practical nurses (LPNs) to registered nurses (RNs). Since 1995 more and more people have been leaving these occupations and fewer and fewer have been entering them. The number of students enrolled in nursing programs increased by 3.7 percent in 2001 and by 8 percent in 2002, but even with these gains there are ten thousand fewer enrolled than in 1995. Nor is the increase enough to meet the replacement demand by 2010 estimated by the Bureau of Labor Statistics.[2] This is primarily because the jobs are stressful and underpaid. Attempts by Medicaid, Medicare, and private insurers to contain health care costs have increased patient caseloads, undermined working conditions, and constrained wages. Moreover, given the industry's traditions and training requirements, the array of unfilled paraprofessional and nursing positions looks less like a career ladder that a low-wage worker might climb than like a series of sealed-off compartments. A glance at the current hierarchy of health care jobs is instructive (table 2.1).

The lowest entry-level occupation is that of personal and home care aide. These workers provide housekeeping services and personal assistance, and are employed mainly by home health care agencies and rarely work full-time. At a slightly higher-skill level are home health aides and nurse assistants. In some states home health aides require more training than nurse assistants, in some the opposite is true, and in others the training requirements are roughly the same. Home health aides make between $8.00 and $10.00 an hour—more in hospitals and doctors' offices than in nursing homes and home health care agencies—but, like home care aides, they seldom work full-time. The majority (65 percent) of nurse assistants work in nursing homes and other long-term care facilities. Although the overall average hourly wage for assistants is $10.12, those working in hospitals earn more than those working in long-term care facilities.

LPNs have high school diplomas or Graduation Equivalency Diplomas (GEDs) and, in addition, have graduated from a year-long certification program. They make considerably more than the aides and assistants, an hourly wage of about $16.00 in most types of facilities. Medical technicians, who have completed other, usually longer certification programs beyond high school earn, on average, slightly more than do LPNs. But in all these jobs, as in the lower-paid jobs, there is little opportunity for advancement without significant further education.

RNs generally have still more schooling. More than half of them are employed in hospitals at an average hourly wage of $25.02. RNs working in nursing homes make lower wages (an average of $22.44 per hour).[3] For RNs, particularly those with a bachelor's degree, there is a further career

TABLE 2.1
Hierarchy of health care jobs, 2003

Occupation	Education/Training	Average Hourly Wage	Number Employed Nationally
Registered Nurse	Two-year associate's degree, three-year diploma school degree, or four-year baccalaureate degree	$24.63	2,246,430
Radiological Technician	One-year certificate, two-year associate's degree, three-year diploma school degree, or four-year baccalaureate degree	$20.03	170,030
Surgical Technician	Programs last nine to twenty-four months and lead to a certificate, diploma, or associate's degree	$15.74	73,250
Occupational Therapy Assistant or Aide	Assistant: One-year certificate or two-year associate's degree from a community college or technical school Aide: On-the-job training	$16.63	25,000
Licensed Practical Nurse	One-year (for a full-time student) community college or private certification program	$15.97	682,590
Pharmacy Technician	Associate's degree	$11.47	211,270
Nurse Assistant	In long-term care facilities the federal government requires seventy-five hours of training for CNA certification and twelve hours of in-service training per year; states may have additional requirements. The training in hospitals varies.	$10.12	1,341,650
Home Health Aide	If Medicare pays for the care, aides must pass a twelve-part competency exam; federal law suggests seventy-five hours of training overseen by an RN	$9.22	583,880
Personal and Home Care Aide[a]	In most states no formal training; in some, forty-plus hours of training with an RN	$8.18	487,220

Source: Bureau of Labor Statistics, May 2003, http://www.bls.gov/oes/home.htm.
[a]Employed by an agency; independent contractors are paid less.

ladder. Nurses can become nurse practitioners, or enter nursing specialties or administration. But lower-tier heath care jobs, given their poor pay and limited possibilities for advancement, are not particularly attractive employment choices, especially in a tight labor market with higher-paying options available. Hence the shortage of direct care workers throughout the industry.

The particulars vary, however, in the different types of health care organizations: nursing homes and other long-term care facilities, hospitals, and home health care agencies.

Long-Term Care

There are currently 12 million people living in long-term care facilities in the United States,[4] and the demand for such care is increasing.[5] The $96.2 billion a year nursing home industry, providing long-term care for people who need medical as well as personal assistance, is expanding particularly rapidly,[6] in part because the population is aging and in part because hospitals increasingly are discharging patients before they can care for themselves at home.[7]

But the ranks of nurse aides—most of them women, often immigrant or minority women, who typically provide some 80 to 90 percent of the direct care in these facilities[8]—are thinning. More than forty states report critical shortages of nurse aides and other paraprofessional nursing-home workers.[9]

One major reason is money. The average *starting* wage for nurse aides in nursing homes is $6.70 per hour, yielding an annual income of $14,000 for full-time workers, most often without benefits. The average wage for *all* nurse aides working in nursing homes is $10.12, suggesting relatively small increases for seniority. A study of job leavers by the National Network for Career Nursing Assistants found that even those who like their work often leave because they cannot support their families on these wages.

Exact rates of staff turnover at nursing homes are difficult to determine because methods of calculation differ, but most sources place the annual rate for certified nurse assistants (CNAs) at between 80 and 100 percent.[10] Such high rates of turnover, combined with cost cutting, mean that most nursing homes are understaffed most of the time. A recently released report of the Centers for Medicare and Medicaid Services found that more than 90 percent of the nation's nursing homes are seriously understaffed.[11] Indeed, the total amount of direct care given per resident per day in nursing homes averages only 3.52 hours,[12] well below the recommendations of professional organizations.[13] And time studies conducted by the National Network of Career Nursing Assistants show that in an eight-hour shift it is impossible for CNAs to perform their five main responsibilities—bathing, feeding, toileting, dressing, and walking patients—for a caseload of twenty patients, not an uncommon assignment. Other studies corroborate the finding.[14]

The result is overworked caretakers and quite often inadequate patient care. A recent report by the Massachusetts Health Policy Forum[15] characterized conditions of work and care in long-term care facilities as lacking in both job and care quality (see table 2.2).

The on-site reviewer of eighty nursing homes for a 1995 *Consumer Reports*[16] investigation found only seven homes that she would consider

TABLE 2.2
Typical job and care quality characteristics in long-term care

Job Quality	Care Quality
Insufficient and declining wages	Rushed or delayed care
Lack of health insurance	Loss of continuity
Insufficient training and career advancement	High risk of injury
Dangerous workloads	Loss of experienced caregivers
Poor management and supervision practices	

Source: Paraprofessional Healthcare Institute.

for her mother. Among nursing homes certified by the Health Care Financing Administration (the managing body for Medicare and Medicaid), over 60 percent do not pass minimum health and safety standards in annual inspections.[17] The late Susan C. Eaton, an expert on the nursing home industry, estimated that 70 percent of nursing homes are low-quality, defined by the quality of care and the treatment of workers.[18]

The need to improve the pay and working conditions of long-term care employees and increase their training (at least eight recent studies have found that both paraprofessional and professional nursing staffs at long-term care facilities receive insufficient training in geriatric nursing specialties) is by now as apparent to patient families and patient advocates as it is to the employees themselves. And it will only grow more pressing over time: the population of people sixty-five years of age and older is expected to double between 2000 and 2030, while the traditional paraprofessional caregiver population, women aged twenty-five to fifty-four, will grow only by 7 percent.[19]

Hospitals

Hospitals, too, are experiencing dire staff shortages. In the case of RNs, this is largely the result of cost-cutting that has degraded their working conditions. Over the past thirty years the federal government has reduced its payments to hospitals under Medicare and Medicaid. The first, in 1974, capped the amounts that hospitals could be reimbursed for care of Medicare and Medicaid patients. This was followed in 1983 by the enactment of a system of predetermined reimbursements for treating a patient with any given diagnosis,[20] a system that provided powerful incentives for hospitals to send patients home quickly. In the 1997 Balanced Budget Act the predetermined amounts were reduced for many diagnoses, adding further incentive to move patients out. Private insurers, too, have been cutting costs by shifting people into managed care to reduce both the number of hospital admissions and the length of hospital stays.[21]

One result is that patients in hospitals are now more acutely ill than they used to be and require more care. Yet to keep costs down, no corresponding shift in staffing has occurred. On the contrary, many hospitals have reduced their RN staff, and all have been hiring low-paid caregivers with limited training and assigning RNs responsibility for overseeing them. The arrangement has not made for the best of relations between them. In a national survey conducted by the American Nurses Association in 2001, 75 percent of nurses reported that the quality of care had declined in their places of employment, largely a result of this change of staffing patterns.[22] Suzanne Gordon, an expert on nursing conditions, points out that, with sicker patients and more supervisory responsibility, nurses are no longer in close enough contact with their patients to fulfill their traditional function as an early-warning and intervention network.[23] And nurse aides, who now spend more time with patients than nurses, simply have neither the training—nor the respect within the hospital—to play such a role.

Another cost-cutting change that has made nursing more stressful for RNs and less reliable for patients is the increased use of "floating" and mandatory overtime to cover understaffed hospital departments. If a nurse in one department is sick or on vacation, a "floating" nurse from another department or a temporary agency may be called in to substitute. Floaters frequently are not specialists in the departments they work in and are unfamiliar with individual patients. If positions cannot be filled with floaters, Gordon reports, nurses are often required to work overtime, even after already putting in a twelve-hour shift.

In response to job stress, large numbers of experienced nurses are leaving the field or choosing part-time or non-hospital work. And nursing schools are not graduating enough new nurses to fill the gap. In fact, nursing school enrollments have declined by 15 percent since 1995.[24] If this pattern continues, the supply of American nurses will likely be 20 percent short of demand by 2020.[25] Hospitals are therefore recruiting nurses from abroad, but vacancy rates remain high and the experts expect them to stay that way.

Hospitals are also experiencing shortages in paraprofessional staff. This is perhaps predictable among nurse aides, whose pay is nearly as low and turnover nearly as high as in nursing homes. Among technicians (e.g., radiology, respiratory, and pharmacy technicians), the shortfall seems to be the result of an educational bottleneck. The nation's technical schools and community colleges are unable to meet existing demand, let alone expand their capacity.

Hospitals, and their patients and employees, are now reaping the consequences of many years of cost cutting. Yet because of their size and the wide variety of jobs and services each encompasses, hospitals have the capacity to increase job satisfaction, reduce stress, and provide advancement opportunities (or, from the hospital's point of view, fill staff vacancies) by offering and encouraging further education and training for their lower-tier workers.

Home Health Care Agencies

Demand for home health care is growing as a result of the demographic trends mentioned above and also because patients who are moved quickly out of hospitals require follow-up care. Further, states are trying to cut costs by moving people with various disabilities out of long-term care facilities and into home and community care programs.[26] The number of agencies providing home health care services, however, rises and falls with the shifting reimbursement policies of Medicare, which pays about 26 percent of the nation's home care bill.[27]

For home health care workers, whether employed by agencies or hired directly by the people they take care of, jobs are unstable, isolated, and dead-end, and the pay is lower than in any other health care occupation. For consumers of these services, the biggest problem seems to be finding competent caregivers. Few studies of the quality of home health care have been attempted, mainly because it is hard to measure outcomes in home settings, but the Institute of Medicine, a nonprofit organization of the National Academy of Sciences that provides information and advice on health and science policy, maintains that training requirements for home health care workers are inadequate to meet the needs of the nation's increasingly sick homebound patients.[28]

Three Career-Ladder Strategies

Unions are the only way for home health care workers to get close to a living wage. Home care workers in the San Francisco area have doubled their wages in the ten years since they organized under SEIU. And the only group of workers who won anything in 2003 in Washington state was the twenty-six thousand newly organized home care workers who got a 10 percent pay increase—to $8.43 an hour.

DAVID ROLF, president, SEIU Local 775

In all three health care settings, raising the skills, pay, and job satisfaction of direct care workers would solve some of the most pressing problems faced by employers and patients, as well as the workers themselves. Creating opportunities for advancement from low-paying, entry-level positions would not only help fill higher-level jobs but would also attract more workers into the entry-level positions. But how do we go about this? In particular, how do we move the impoverished workers who are now stuck in entry-level jobs into better jobs, if they have neither the education nor training for better jobs, nor the time and resources to acquire them?

Three strategies are available for dealing with this constellation of issues: (1) increasing the pay and professionalism of existing direct care jobs; (2) creating tiers within presently undifferentiated occupations, thus recognizing skill increases and making pay increases possible; and (3) advancing people into progressively better-paying occupations that require more education. All three approaches are being tried in the health care industry.

Increasing the Pay and Professionalism of Existing Jobs

The single most effective way to improve both the pay and conditions of work for nurse aides and other paraprofessional health workers is unionization. In 2001 the average hourly wage for union nurse assistants was $10.17, and assistants, on average, earned $8.14.[29] Simply being unionized, with no further advancement opportunities, improves average wages by 25 percent. Both the Service Employees International Union (SEIU)[30] and the American Federation of State, County, and Municipal Employees (AFSCME) are targeting paraprofessional health care workers in organizing drives. But probably the most impressive example of how far this strategy alone can go is found in Los Angeles, where a drive organized by the SEIU led to a change in state policy that is transforming home care workers at the very bottom of the health care hierarchy from poverty-wage freelancers into paraprofessionals who can earn as much as $11.50 an hour.[31]

The situation of home care workers is a far cry from the standard industrial union model. Originally California home care workers, a predominantly female, minority, and immigrant workforce, did not even work for an employer. They were paid with various state and county funds, but no state or county agency was willing to be their employer of record, since such a relationship would entail legal liabilities and responsibility for setting home care standards. Compounding the damage, the state courts ruled that because home care workers had no employer, they were independent contractors with no organizing rights. In the early 1990s a coalition of union organizers, senior citizens, patient activists, consumer groups, and religious organizations finally persuaded the state legislature to authorize counties to act as the employers of record for home care workers, and in 1997 Los Angeles County set up a public authority, the Personal Assistance Services Council, to assume the responsibilities of coordinating training and work assignments for these workers—and entering into collective bargaining with them. This was the necessary first step before home care workers could be organized to demand higher wages and benefits, and, like so many steps toward job improvement in the health care industry, it was won politically.

Once the Los Angeles public authority was in place, SEIU initiated a door-to-door organizing campaign that resulted in seventy-five thousand Los Angeles County home care workers joining the union and reaching an agreement with the county in 1999. To win this victory, the union spent $3.5 million and employed forty full-time organizers. Success also required the continuing support and involvement of the same political coalition that won the right to organize. Indeed, to reassure patient advocates worried about continuity of care, the union accepted a no-strike clause in its contract, and it agreed that the right to hire or fire workers would remain with the client. In exchange, the union won a promise from the Personal Assistance Services Council to upgrade training programs. But essentially it was choosing political alliances and political action, rather than traditional labor tactics (for instance, strikes), as the means it would rely on to win higher wages.

Given where the money for higher pay would have to come from, this was probably wise. Nonetheless, raising wages was and remains a struggle. The Personal Assistance Services Council at first received no funds from the state to pay for wage increases, and the county could not afford to cover the state's share. This in turn meant that the federal contribution would not increase. As John Seeley explained in the *LA Weekly*,

> Most home-care employees serve the elderly and disabled, and so are underwritten by Medicaid, and 51 percent of their cost is reimbursed by the federal government. The state and counties divide the remaining 49 percent on a 2-to-1 basis, so . . . about 32 percent of the money comes out of the state Treasury. While federal policy allows reimbursing labor costs up to twice the minimum wage, the state—under Republican governors—long refused to kick in dollar one for anything beyond the state's $5.50 an hour minimum wage. This reimbursement cap meant counties were free (in theory) to give raises over the minimum, but any such icing would have to come wholly out of county coffers.[32]

In 1999, however, the state allocated funds to increase wages to $6.25 an hour. And in June 2000, in response to continued political pressure from the union-led coalition, the state legislature passed, and Governor Gray Davis signed, the Aging with Dignity Act, which, among other things, committed the state to paying its share for regular increases in the wages of home care workers. Previously the state would not share in wages above the minimum wage. The legislation established that the state would pay its share up to a maximum of $7.50 in FY (fiscal year) 2000, $8.50 in FY 2001, $9.50 in FY 2002, and $11.50 in FY 2003. But the increase is automatic only if state general revenues increase 5 percent over the previous year. In July 2003 the trigger did not happen, and so the state's cost sharing was at the $9.50 rate plus health insurance benefits.[33] Actual wages vary by county.[34] The state's 2000–2001 budget included funding for the first installment, increasing the wages of home care providers to a minimum of $7.50 per hour. This is real progress, but one should keep in mind that a living wage in California for an adult with two children was $13.21 per hour in 2000.[35]

Cooperative Home Care Associates

A rather different version of the same strategy—taking collective action to improve existing jobs—can be seen in the South Bronx, where it is not a union but a workers' cooperative that is changing the jobs of that same bottom tier of home health care workers. Cooperative Home Care Associates (CHCA) was founded in 1985, the brainchild of Rick Surpin, an advocate for the poor who saw home health care as a promising source of employment for people in one of New York's poorest neighborhoods. His idea was to provide better-than-usual training for his students and then convince home health care agencies to pay them higher-than-usual wages. The CHCA's training program for home health aides (approximately equivalent to certified nurse assistants), includes four weeks of classroom learning followed by ninety days of on-the-job training, considerably more preparation than the seventy-five hours the federal government requires of CNAs or the three weeks required by New York state. In addition to technical skills, the program teaches critical thinking, problem solving, and team building. All program graduates are hired by CHCA itself, which is not only a training center but also a home health agency with 750 employees.

The starting wage of CHCA's employees is $6.75 per hour, with benefits. Although the wage is below the national average for home health aides, it includes benefits and approximately 70 percent are employed full-time, which is extraordinary in this industry and, of course, makes an enormous difference in the annual income. The average hourly wage at CHCA is $9.00, with benefits. Moreover, the Cooperative's full-time employees are eligible for health insurance, life insurance, and paid vacation and sick days. (Because CHCA is a cooperative, the share of fees that ordinarily goes to an agency's owners can be used to pay for such things.) In addition, Cooperative members (about 80 percent of CHCA employees) receive annual dividend checks of $200 to $400,[36] their share of the agency's profits.

Employees can advance within CHCA; of the thirty-five current administrative staffers, twelve were former home health aides. And they can earn up to 12 credits at Bronx College for classes taken at CHCA. But, for the most part, the Cooperative is improving its employees' current jobs rather than their prospects for other, better jobs. And it is limited even in this by the current rate being paid for home health care.

But given time and financial backing, the CHCA approach seems to be replicable, which cannot be said for many successful job-improvement strategies. The Paraprofessional Healthcare Institute (PHI), a nonprofit advocacy organization that succeeded in getting the Bronx Cooperative up and running, now has helped to start similar employee-owned health care enterprises in Philadelphia and in Manchester, New Hampshire. Steve Dawson, president of PHI, estimates that it takes about one year of organizing, business planning, and putting together a package of grants, loans, and other financing to create a new co-op. (This is an expensive proposition. The latest co-op, the very small one in New Hampshire, required for its startup a three-year $450,000 grant from the Charles Stewart Mott Foundation, $250,000 in equity capital from a $100,000 long-term loan from the New Hampshire Community Loan Fund, and a five-year, interest-free loan of $50,000 from the U.S. Catholic Campaign for Human Development. It then takes at least a year to train enough people to have an operational agency, and usually several more years to become profitable.)

Creating Tiers within Occupations

If our workers can't feed their children on the wages we pay them, they are hardly going to care if an old woman at work isn't eating.

GAIL KASS, president and CEO of the New Courtland
Network of Nursing Homes

The lowest rungs of the health care hierarchy are relatively easy to reach. Home care aides require no training at all, and training for home health aides and nurse aides is widely available. Unions and community organizations, as discussed above, as well as hospitals and community colleges, offer the short training programs required by federal and state law. But once workers get these entry-level jobs, there are rarely opportunities to progress into jobs that pay a decent wage—for instance, LPN positions—unless one goes back to school for a year or more. For many who are entering the labor force for the first time, just getting used to working full-time is a challenge; qualifying to become an LPN or medical technician can seem out of reach, especially if the additional education required would have to come at the expense of working hours or parenting time. There are also CNAs who do not want to change jobs even for better pay, since they can gain experience and expertise in the jobs they have. Yet few long-term care facilities or hospitals offer pay raises to CNAs as they achieve higher levels of competency, even if they take courses to specialize in areas such as oncology or restorative care. Typically there is no recognition that CNA specialties exist.

However, with CNAs leaving their jobs in droves, a few nursing homes have taken the initiative to create pay and skill tiers within the CNA category as a way to improve the quality of care and reduce staff turnover at their facilities. Generally their approach has been to reward employees who gain expertise with a particular disease. Meanwhile, the National Network of Career Nursing Assistants, in an effort to speed up this slow, facility-by-facility pace of change, is developing national standards for CNA specializations and trying to convince state governments that such career advances merit pay raises.

However, one of the most intriguing attempts at creating career-advancement opportunities for nursing home CNAs who are unable or do not want to become LPNs is a program that does not emphasize expertise in particular diseases; rather, it concentrates on preparing CNAs to be part of a team, to join in developing plans of care for nursing home residents, and to take on leadership roles at the facility. This is the career-ladder program at Apple Health Care, a for-profit chain of twenty-one nursing homes in Connecticut.[37]

Apple Health Care
Susan Misiorski, the former vice president of nursing at Apple who was involved in developing the program, describes it as a move away from a hierarchical model of medical management to one that embraces a philosophy that is more participatory and person-centered, closer to the style of assisted-living residences. Apple's in-house training program for CNAs is based in part on the principles of the Pioneer Network, a national organization trying to change the culture of long-term care facilities and encourage them to gear themselves around the needs of residents rather than staff.

Apple offers CNAs three advanced courses. Each meets two hours a week for eight weeks, and workers are paid for their time in attendance. In the first course CNAs learn how to identify patients' individual needs and adapt their care accordingly. The second class prepares the aides to serve on worker-resident committees whose task is to make their facility a better place to live and work. The third course covers topics like conflict management and peer mentoring.

Apple's CNAs generally start at $9.25 an hour, which approaches the average wage of CNAs in nursing homes nationally,[38] but most Apple employees move into higher pay tiers over time, raising the company's average CNA hourly pay to between $10 and $12. Although the program has not been formally evaluated, Apple managers state that it has paid for itself by reducing turnover and thus the need for temporary staff. According to Misiorski, it has helped to reduce the CNA turnover rate at Apple facilities from 50 to 60 percent per year to 30 percent, which undoubtedly has made a difference in the quality and consistency of care.

The career path opportunity was only one facet of a more comprehensive process to improve the quality of direct care worker jobs. In addition to offering CNAs a career path, Apple also included CNAs in the planning of care, inviting them to have a voice in operations by joining committees; work schedules were made more flexible; and the orientation program was revised to be a minimum of two weeks for new aides. Misiorski emphasizes that "there is no one intervention that improves staff retention when implemented in isolation. The nursing homes that have had the most success in creating a workplace culture that promotes retention are homes that have implemented multiple interventions concurrently."[39]

The Massachusetts Nursing Home Quality Initiative

Although the initiatives of individual nursing homes provide models of how to create in-house advancement opportunities for bottom-rung caregivers, these experiments cannot affect the hundreds of thousands of CNAs in other long-term care facilities across the country. To institute widespread changes in nursing home career ladders requires legislation, and getting legislation passed requires considerable political organizing, as has recently been illustrated in Massachusetts.

In 2000 the Massachusetts legislature passed a two-year, $42 million Nursing Home Quality Initiative. Of that money, $35 million is a pass-through. In other words, the long-term care facilities that receive the money have to use it to increase the wages or benefits or both of paraprofessional caregivers. The pass-through increased the median hourly wage of CNAs in Massachusetts from $9.36 in 2000 to $11.36 in 2002. Another $1.1 million was used to provide financial assistance to students receiving CNA training, with slightly more than half the money earmarked for welfare recipients. The remaining $5 million was allocated to the Extended Care Career Ladder Initiative (ECCLI), which in 2000 funded thirteen nursing homes to try out different ways of developing internal career ladders for direct care workers, and in 2002 made a new round of grants to try to expand the reach of such programs. As of 2004 seventy-two nursing homes and six home health aide facilities/organizations had been funded.[40]

The Nursing Home Quality Initiative is the result of the efforts of the Coalition to Reform Elder Care (CORE), convened in 1998 by Greater Boston Legal Services. CORE is a coalition of labor unions, long-term care providers, and patient advocacy organizations. Barbara Frank, then the director of State Health Policy for the Paraprofessional Healthcare Institute, explains that CORE's hardest task was getting all these groups to recognize their common interests. Consumer advocates such as the Alzheimer's Association were initially focused on the understaffing of nursing homes but came to see the connection between low pay and under-staffing, as well as the link between the quality of care provided to residents and the quality of jobs provided to workers. Frank notes, "Although studies demonstrate that people are more invested in their jobs when they are treated respectfully and receive adequate wages, the average middle class person doesn't feel a personal stake in the circumstances of a low-wage worker. But when that worker is taking care of your parents, low wages and overwork become issues you have to care about."[41] Frank also had to make the issue relevant to long-term care providers. She spent months meeting with nursing home managers to explain how the quality of the work environment affects staff retention, and how spending on higher wages, better training, and the creation of advancement opportunities is a good business investment.

Once the partners were onboard, CORE staff conducted community meetings throughout the state to raise pubic awareness of the shortage of nursing home workers and its relation to wages, on the one hand, and quality of care, on the other. CORE also drummed up media coverage. Coalition members participated in a state task force on the subject and tes-tified at state legislative hearings. In the end, the coalition sold the public and the legislature on the proposition that money earmarked for "workforce development" should be spent to improve and fill jobs in long-term care, thus providing two benefits for each dollar spent—stabilizing the long-term care system while supporting advancement for low-wage workers.

The thirteen nursing homes that received Round I demonstration grants from ECCLI did provide training for CNAs in specialty care areas such as dementia and rehabilitation, as well as training for uncertified aides so they can become CNAs. The legislation required grant recipients to pay at least

50 percent of regular wages to employees while they were taking these classes, to upgrade those who completed the course to a higher job classification, to give them at least a 3 percent pay increase, and to maintain the raise after Round I funding stopped.

In July 2001 Round II grants were awarded to seven consortia representing a total of thirty long-term care providers, thirty workforce development organizations, and ten community colleges. Their mission: to coordinate efforts among these groups, so that all of them support a new system of job classifications (internal career ladders) for CNAs. This has entailed not only training the CNAs but also training nursing home managers and supervisors to treat CNAs differently than they used to.

About six hundred workers in twenty-seven facilities received upgrade training ranging from English as a second language to various courses for improving job performance (e.g., classes on dementia, wound management, and so on). The collective outcomes of the training are mixed. As the Round I experiments were coming to a close, I attended a meeting of participating nursing homes at which administrators reported that their nurse aides were eager for more training. Several managers remarked that CNAs were attracted not just by the admittedly modest pay raises but also by the prospect of personal and professional growth opportunities. Indeed, turnover rates and the use of temporary employment agencies have declined in several of these nursing homes. But the extent to which career ladders have been established is limited. An evaluation of Round II, conducted by independent investigators, suggests that the result so far has been more leadership and self-confidence among CNAs, and better communication with patients and their families.[42] Two facilities offered a 3 percent raise for moving from CNA 1 to 2, and 4 percent for CNA 3. The other five offered trainees a raise of $0.25 to $0.50 per hour for completing a nursing skills course on starting wages ranging from $8.00 to $10.00 per hour. One of the Round II facilities offered a raise of $0.50 per hour for completing courses and advancing to a higher CNA rank. The majority of trainees were satisfied with the courses but reported that the small wage gains did not make much difference in their standard of living. Still, nursing home managers told the investigators that staff recruiting has become easier and retention rates have improved since the experiment began.[43]

Although some wage gains have been made, only two of the seven facilities formalized these tiers with new job descriptions and official promotions, and none has established steps leading beyond the CNA level.[44] Meanwhile, CNA wages remain well below the minimum living wage, as calculated by the Women's Education and Industrial Union, which in

Massachusetts is between $13.50 and $18.50 an hour (depending on region) for a single mother with two children.

Full Career-Ladder Programs

I try to study at work if I can, but sometimes it seems that my coworkers don't want me to succeed. As soon as my boss sees me pick up a book during a quiet time (on the night shift) she finds something for me to do.

JANE DOE, nurse aide, Philadelphia[45]

More ambitious career-ladder programs do exist, however. Hospitals, unions, and government agencies scattered throughout the country are responding to the public's need for more health care providers at all levels. These institutions are also paying attention to the necessity of career ladders for health care workers so that entry-level employees can routinely acquire decently paying jobs, just as entry-level doctors or lawyers or plumbers routinely move up from lower-level, lesser-paying positions. Some of these programs focus on progressions in direct care—from CNA to LPN to RN, for instance. Others concentrate on moving people into technical occupations in hospitals and other health care facilities. The most successful of these programs are adjusted to accommodate the difficult circumstances of their intended students, rather than requiring the students to make all the adjustments.

AFSCME 1199C Training and Upgrading Fund: From CNA to LPN

When ninth grader Ellen Iwer told her guidance counselor that she wanted to be a doctor, she was told that her grades weren't good enough. After Iwer became pregnant before finishing high school, it seemed that any health career was out of reach. Eventually she found a part-time job in a unionized community services program for the profoundly mentally retarded, where she helped residents dress and eat, and earned $9.23 an hour plus benefits. Iwer took a short employer-paid course to become a CNA, which enabled her to take on another part-time job, at $12.88 an hour, in a unionized hospital. The two jobs together did not quite provide a livable wage, but no further job advancement seemed possible while she was supporting and caring for her two children. Then, in March 2000, Iwer's prospects dramatically changed. She entered the first LPN class offered by AFSCME 1199C Training and Upgrading Fund,[46] in a program specifically designed to create second chances and career ladders.

The Training and Upgrading Fund was established in 1974 in negotiations between this Philadelphia union local and about sixty hospitals, nursing homes, and other health care facilities. Management contributes 1.5 percent of gross payroll to the fund, and the union uses the money to provide counseling, placement services, certification testing, a variety of workshops, and, most important, courses that train CNAs and LPNs at a realistic pace. Not only union members but also welfare-to-work clients and community residents can take advantage of these courses and services at the Breslin Center, in a building conveniently located in central Philadelphia.

In 2000 some nine hundred people were enrolled in Breslin Center classes, about three hundred of them in what the center calls "pre-nursing" classes to improve their mathematics, English, or other basic skills before starting a training program. These pre-nursing classes are taught as preparation for future training rather than as remedial classes, and this seems to be important to their success. The lessons relate to health care skills, and they acknowledge the experience the students have already acquired on the job.

About 200 CNAs graduate from the Breslin Center every year.[47] Between March 2000, when the center opened the nation's only union-run School of Practical Nursing,[48] and September 2003, 102 LPNs have also graduated. The LPN course is designed for working students and therefore lasts longer than LPN courses elsewhere, which generally enroll full-time students and run for one year. At the Breslin Center, students attend classes two evenings a week from 4:00 to 10:00 and all day every other Saturday and Sunday for eighteen months. This is a grueling time commitment for working parents but is more financially manageable than the traditional LPN program, since students can continue to work while attending school, and the payoff for completing the course is significant. CNAs in the Philadelphia area start at $10 to $15 an hour in unionized hospitals and $8 to $10 an hour in unionized nursing homes. As LPNs, their pay immediately jumps to $17 to $18 an hour.[49]

Both students and teachers at the Breslin Center say that crucial to the success of the training programs, in addition to technical training, is their emphasis on confidence building. Many of the center's instructors started out as CNAs themselves and worked their way up to an RN or a master's degree in nursing. They understand the obstacles their students face in combining family, work, and education—from sleep deprivation to jealous husbands and colleagues—and they stay focused on overcoming them. Classes also are kept small, which enables teachers to attend to the needs of individual students and promotes a supportive sense of community among students.

When I spoke to students, the effects were apparent. After they described their extraordinary schedules, I asked, "How do you do it?" Their responses: "My teachers won't let me give up on myself." "Some days I really want to quit, but I call one of my classmates and she talks me out of it. I do the same for her." "If I don't, we'll be poor for the rest of our lives."

When I spoke to Tracy Ponton she was two weeks away from finishing a pre-nursing course in preparation for taking the LPN entry test. Ponton had two teenagers, a four-year-old, and a seven-month-old baby. She was attending classes three days a week while working full-time as a CNA in a suburban nursing home, returning home at 2:00 A.M. A classmate, Paulette Jennings, was working as a CNA on the 11:00 P.M. to 7:00 A.M. shift, and working another job from 8:00 to 11:00 A.M. She would go home, prepare meals for her family, take a nap, and then go to class from 4:00 to 11:00 P.M. three days a week. LPN student Stacy King held a full-time job, attended LPN classes, and still found time to tutor pre-nursing students.

"But aren't your kids getting shortchanged?" I asked them. The answer, unanimously, was yes. "Yes, but they know it's for a short time and our lives will be better when I am working as an LPN." "Yes, but my daughter respects me more because I am working and going to school and not just collecting welfare." "Yes, but I have to respect myself if my kids are going to respect me." "Yes, but what are my choices?"

Without the Training and Upgrading Fund, most of these women would have no choices. But the creation of a career ladder that they can climb has not been cheap. The budget of the Philadelphia program in 2003 was $4.8 million. Almost $3 million of this came from employer contributions and the rest from city, state, and federal workforce development grants. Perhaps the greatest difficulty in trying to replicate this successful program elsewhere is simply coming up with that kind of money.

The LPN program is tuition-based for all students. Union members covered under the training fund receive tuition reimbursement. Government funds are used to provide financial aid for other students.

Ladders in Nursing Careers: From LPN to RN
Another possible source of large-scale funding is foundations. The Robert Wood Johnson Foundation, for instance, started a pilot project in New York City in 1988 to help LPNs and other health care workers become RNs. When the project, called Ladders in Nursing Careers or L.I.N.C., was a success—with 93 percent of its first-round participants graduating from an LPN or RN program—the foundation decided to expand it.

Grants averaging $440,000 were given to nine state and metropolitan hospital associations, and each was to advance one hundred low-rung employees into nursing or allied health positions.[50] The foundation subsidized administrative expenses, but the sites had to find other funding for books and education counselors, and participating health care institutions were required to bear the cost of paying employees and replacement workers while the employees were in school.[51] Participants attended school full-time and worked part-time for full-time wages and, in return, signed an agreement to stay on another eighteen months with their employer for every year in school. As in New York, the other sites (except one in Ohio that closed) had high completion rates. Of the 934 participants 402 graduated and another 150 were on track to graduate when the program ended, for a completion rate of almost 60 percent.[52]

Peggy McNally, the national director of Project L.I.N.C., attributes its success to cooperation from local unions, effective counseling, and an approach to remediation similar to that of the Breslin Center programs. McNally tells about a workshop she gave on calculating drug doses, a topic often requested by practicing nurses. When she started the sessions, she noted that many students had trouble with the basic math needed to calculate proportions and percentages, so she included some basic math instruction on the spot and added a remedial math class to those offered by Project L.I.N.C. No one enrolled. Thus McNally learned that adult students do not like being classified as needing remedial work. She then made sure that future workshops on drug dosages would cover the basics of math, and, as a result, enrollment, in fact, increased.

Colleagues in Caring

The Robert Wood Johnson Foundation stopped funding Project L.I.N.C. when the organizations involved filled their personnel needs. A few years later, however, continued interest in the educational mobility of nurses led the foundation to initiate another program that it called Colleagues in Caring: Regional Collaboratives for Nursing Workforce Development. Since 1996 the foundation has funded regional collaboratives in thirty-seven states, which assess future nursing care needs in their regions and adopt workforce-development strategies for meeting the demand.[53] The strategies start with stakeholders in all types of health care and nursing education, and center on reducing barriers to mobility among the various levels of nursing.

A key barrier is the lack of coordination (or as educators call it, "articulation") among the various education institutions that grant diplomas and degrees in nursing. LPNs, as well as nurses who graduated from two-year programs at community colleges or hospital-run diploma schools, are good candidates for further education to fill higher-level nursing positions. Yet, in many cases, the pathway is longer than necessary because course credits earned at technical schools, diploma schools, and sometimes even community colleges typically cannot be applied toward a bachelor's degree. Instead, the nurses have to repeat the very same subjects at the four-year college, which is a serious disincentive to further schooling. Colleagues in Caring encouraged their grantees to design statewide articulation models that give credit for previous learning.[54]

Mary Fry Rapson, the national director of the program, got her start in Maryland, where she helped develop a statewide articulation system in 1984. Her own research reveals that the nursing curriculum at most community colleges is not inferior to university-level curricula. And using that information, Rapson has convinced university administrators to shed several entrenched beliefs: that courses offered by lower-level institutions are not comparable to university courses; that the only way to coordinate curricula is to force all schools to have the same curriculum; and that articulation will lead to the demise of either the feeder or higher-level institutions.[55] Once these issues have been aired and misconceptions dealt with, she works with the educators to use accepted validation methods to measure that the student has mastered the previous learning and to give credit for their learning experiences in the receiving school.

Rapson believes that the nursing profession is becoming more appreciative of the time diploma nurses and LPNs have spent in course work and on the job: "We're recognizing a common core. For a variety of reasons, people come into nursing from different pathways. Many minority nurses have to get education when and where they can get it. It doesn't make sense to punish people because they have chosen a different educational pathway."[56] Indeed, in one study in Cleveland, nurses who had participated in the Colleagues in Caring articulation model showed no difference in their job performance from nurses who been required to retake courses to progress from an associate's degree program to a baccalaureate program.[57] Moreover, Cleveland students are able to upgrade to a bachelor's degree in nursing in 40 percent less time and at considerably less cost than it used to take before the articulation model was designed.

In the Colorado program the state's Council of Nursing Education has eliminated barriers in the career pathway from an LPN to an RN with an associate's degree, and from an RN with a nursing diploma or an associate's degree to one with a baccalaureate degree. The Council discovered that the associate's degree in nursing offered by the state's community colleges was advertised as a two-year program but typically took three years to complete. Several associate's degree nursing programs required 100 or more credits (compared to 60 credits required for most associate's degrees, while 120 credits are required for bachelor's degrees) because courses were added over time in response to employer demands to incorporate new technology and practices. For someone to first earn an LPN certificate (a one-year program) and then an associate's degree in nursing would thus take four years of full-time schooling. To shorten the pathway, the Colorado Community College system placed a maximum 78-credit requirement on all associate's degree RN programs and granted all certified LPNs one year of credit toward the RN associate's degree. Existing courses were combined to eliminate unnecessary duplication. The result is that an LPN can now earn an associate's degree with just one additional year of courses.

That the Colleagues in Caring focus on articulation is important, but it is only one aspect of career mobility. The move from LPN to RN comes with significant salary increases, and many Colorado LPNs are pursuing it now that the articulation agreement is in place. But Colorado's articulation agreement has not motivated significantly more RNs with nursing diplomas or associate's degrees to earn a baccalaureate degree, and the reason seems obvious. Pay for RNs, in Colorado as elsewhere, is typically based on seniority; that is, nurses with diplomas or associate's degrees do the same work for the same pay as baccalaureate nurses. Although the baccalaureate nurses are the ones who are promoted to more senior jobs in nursing specialties and administration, the chance for future advancement apparently is not as compelling as the certainty of immediate acknowledgment. So long as higher degrees do not result in higher pay or other recognition, the desire for them will be limited.

Cape Cod Hospital: Career Ladders to Allied Health Care Professions
The career ladder program at Cape Cod Hospital in Massachusetts is widely admired by people interested in health care policy, but it illustrates another potential difficulty with this strategy. The Cape Cod program is an attempt to build climbable career ladders in one hospital, and tensions between the hospital's union and its management have been a barrier to creating an effective program, while the need for continuing negotiations to improve the program has aggravated labor-management tensions.

In 1981 Bill Pastreich, then president of SEIU Local 767, negotiated a contract that committed Cape Cod Hospital to funding a career-ladders program. A Joint Career Development Committee with three members each from management and the union then created the ladders. The committee identified the qualifications for all jobs in the hospital and found or developed courses to teach the necessary skills. Once this intensive process was completed, the committee began meeting monthly to plan and modify the training and education programs.

The committee identified four paths to career advancement that the hospital would support. The first, on-the-job training, applies to a few entry-level occupations. The position of Nursing Assistant I, for example, advances to Nursing Assistant II—with a pay increase of $0.64 per hour—after successfully completing on-the-job training.

The second pathway, coursework to move workers from nonprofessional to technical positions, requires preparation in basic skills such as math, keyboarding, and medical terminology. The hospital agreed to offer these basic skills classes on-site, bringing in community college teachers to teach them. Courses are offered between shifts, and employees can end their workday one hour early or start one hour late to take a class.

The third pathway is in-house training of higher-skilled workers, such as radiology technicians, to advance to better-paying jobs such as CT scan technician, tumor registrar, or radiation technician. The traineeships mainly teach workers how to do additional procedures within an occupation.

The fourth pathway is outside education, usually at Cape Cod Community College. The hospital agreed to reimburse the tuition costs of employees who pursue this route to advancement.

Neither the union nor the hospital maintains data on how many people have moved upward on these career ladders since the program began. Nor do they release any information on the cost of the program. Both sides agree that about 80 percent of job openings at the hospital are now filled by promoting current employees. As with most internal career ladders, however, there are more openings at the bottom than at the top. The hospital's Employee Relations Manager Arthur LaChance estimates that the most frequent job advancement is from housekeeper to secretarial or clerical support staff. Few CNAs advance at all.

Management has several reservations about the program. A key concern is improving the hospital's return on its investment in career ladders. One problem LaChance points out—and Jane Hewitt, the former acting director of SEIU Local 767, agrees with him—is that workers who take classes to qualify for a higher-paying position often have little idea of the work it involves and whether they would like it. LaChance offers the example of the most frequent job advance, from housekeeper to clerical support staff. Almost all information on a hospital floor is filtered through the unit secretary, who must communicate with doctors, nurses, support staff, patients, and visitors. Many employees who advance into this job leave it quickly because they had not realized the communication and organization skills it required. Likewise, after completing a recent course on how to be a coder abstractor, the person who bills hospital services to insurance companies, no student opted to advance into the position. LaChance and other staff are now working on a new approach, which, among other things, would offer courses based on projections of the hospital's future needs rather than "throwing courses out there because it is mandated." One such effort addresses the shortage of respiratory technicians at the hospital. Recognizing the dire need for these workers, the hospital has approached SEIU about starting a training program and has agreed to pay for it.[58]

Hewitt, on the other hand, believes that more career guidance is needed. Currently an annual job-ladders guide lists all jobs at the hospital and their training requirements. Workers can use the guide to identify the requirements of another job, but the guide does not indicate how often there are openings for the job or whether they are suited for it. LaChance says he agrees that more career guidance would be useful, but he argues that the hospital is an employer, not an educational institution.

Management-union relations deteriorated in 2000 when Cape Cod Hospital became affiliated with Cape Cod Health Care, a holding company that owns twenty-three facilities in the area. Only five are unionized, although they represent about 80 percent of employment, and Richard Kropp, the corporate director of Education and Training Services, maintains that the company needs to develop a career-ladder program independent of the union in order to serve all twenty-three facilities, including those that are not unionized. Union representatives resent management's unwillingness to work with them to improve the current program and suggest that a parallel program will not work without union support. Without cooperation, it is unlikely that either program will thrive.

Bridges to the Future

Labor and management at any one company, may simply have too fraught and complicated a relationship to run a career-ladder program jointly. Independent organizations capable of brokering agreements between unions, companies, and educational institutions appear to have a real advantage in this respect. One of the most innovative of them is Bridges to the Future, a program created by Sarah Griffen, director of Special Initiatives for the Jamaica Plain Neighborhood Development Corporation (JPNDC) in Boston. Griffen had developed a very successful welfare-to-work program, which was training and placing neighborhood residents in housekeeping and food service positions in Boston's world-renowned congregation of teaching hospitals. The jobs, however, paid only $8 to $9 per hour, and, once placed, the new workers had little opportunity to gain new skills and advance. Griffen knew that many of her program's graduates were capable of advancing, and she initiated conversations with human resource directors and managers at the hospitals and the medical schools to find out what the advancement possibilities were. She discovered that all had high rates of turnover and chronic vacancies in middle- and higher-level technical positions. Yet most of the internal training focused on doctors and nurses rather than employees in entry- and middle-level jobs. Griffen saw this gap as her opportunity.

At the same time Fleet Boston Charitable Trust was looking for places to try out the new idea of creating career ladders that low-income workers could climb. Griffen approached the medical centers that participated in her program for entry-level workers—Beth Israel Deaconess Medical Center, Children's Hospital Boston, New England Baptist Hospital, and Harvard Medical School and School of Dental Medicine—to see if she could interest them in career-ladder training. And with their agreement and a grant from Fleet, she began.

In March 2000 JPNDC and the nearby Fenway Community Development Corporation met with human resource managers, department supervisors, and employees at each site to identify the skills and education needed for all positions requiring less than an associate's degree.

They also researched the reasons for current high turnover in these positions. JPNDC then prepared a report for each site that laid out "career maps," or the paths into and out of these positions in each department (housekeeping, food services, administration, patient care, and research). The maps allowed the employers to see the gaps and bottlenecks that prevented workers from advancing. For example, the mapping revealed that one department had one hundred positions at Grade 2 but only three at Grade 3.[59] This step helped hospital staff discover where they needed to change internal structures. The research also guided JPNDC to focus its training efforts on positions with sufficient numbers of openings to justify creating a program (see figure 2.1).

Efforts to create career ladders for nursing and non-nursing positions have been made by an assortment of hospitals, unions, and community colleges. Although all were on a much smaller scale than Griffen envisioned, she and her staff researched their best practices. They then met with a steering committee, composed of supervisors, employees, human resource staff, and a representative from the Harvard Union of Clerical and Technical Workers to develop the specifics of their own career-ladder program. Their focus—good brokers that they were—was as much on the needs of supervisors as employees. Indeed, it is supervisors who hold the key to their employees' internal training and advancement opportunities, and Griffen notes that an inherent problem with career-ladder programs is that they essentially ask supervisors to give up their best workers. "Of course, they're going to ask what's in it for them," she says. "So we worked

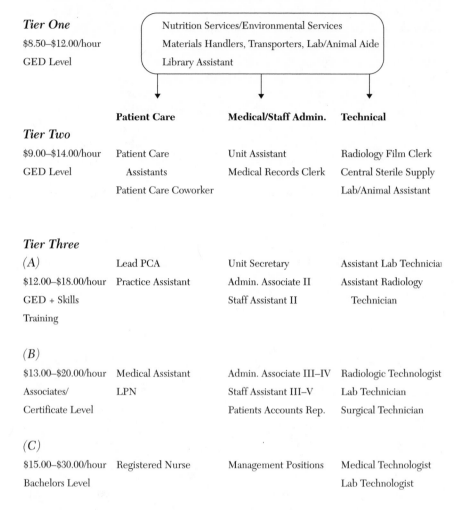

	Patient Care	Medical/Staff Admin.	Technical
Tier One $8.50–$12.00/hour GED Level	Nutrition Services/Environmental Services Materials Handlers, Transporters, Lab/Animal Aide Library Assistant		
Tier Two $9.00–$14.00/hour GED Level	Patient Care Assistants Patient Care Coworker	Unit Assistant Medical Records Clerk	Radiology Film Clerk Central Sterile Supply Lab/Animal Assistant
Tier Three *(A)* $12.00–$18.00/hour GED + Skills Training	Lead PCA Practice Assistant	Unit Secretary Admin. Associate II Staff Assistant II	Assistant Lab Technician Assistant Radiology Technician
(B) $13.00–$20.00/hour Associates/ Certificate Level	Medical Assistant LPN	Admin. Associate III–IV Staff Assistant III–V Patients Accounts Rep.	Radiologic Technologist Lab Technician Surgical Technician
(C) $15.00–$30.00/hour Bachelors Level	Registered Nurse	Management Positions	Medical Technologist Lab Technologist

Figure 2.1. Overview of career pathways at Boston hospitals
Source: Jamaica Plain Neighborhood Development Corporation.

with them to figure out the best strategy for retaining and advancing their existing workforce."

The steering committee and JPNDC staff decided to offer training to supervisors as well as employees. In fact, the first course offered was supervisor training designed to assure understanding of, and support for, the program. This twenty-session course has been offered regularly since

January 2001. It covers time- and stress-management skills, coaching and performance evaluation, workplace communication and diversity issues, retention and advancement strategies, team building, and conflict management.

The first class for employees, called "Foundation Skills," covered similar topics and also problem-solving skills, customer-service skills, medical terminology, diversity issues, and confidence building. It, too, is still offered, meeting one eight-hour workday a week for eight weeks. As with the class for supervisors, students are on fully paid release time. For those not ready for the initial Foundations Skills class, some of the medical institutions involved offer GED and ESL (English as a Second Language) classes. Bridges to the Future also offers child care and referrals to other social service providers—as well as the kind of career coaching that other career-ladder programs showed was necessary.

Prior to Bridges, the Boston hospitals posted vacancies, but people in entry-level jobs did not know what they needed to do to advance into them or what duties the jobs entailed. JPNDC developed job descriptions and charts to help employees map out vertical and lateral moves they might have to make into other departments before advancing into higher-tier jobs (see figure 2.1). Career coaches at workplace and community sites advised employees on how to use these materials to plan their futures. To increase employee knowledge of different occupations, Bridges added mentoring and job shadowing to the program in January 2002.[60] (Job shadowing allows entry-level employees to tag along with someone in a higher-level position to see what it's like.)

According to Joseph Cabral, the manager of Employment and Diversity at Children's Hospital in Boston,[61] the retention rate of employees who participate in the program is 95 percent compared to 78 percent for non-participating employees in the same jobs. He concludes, "The program is too new to have long-term data, but a 95 percent retention rate is huge and tells us it's working." When I asked him whether he worries about investing in training and having the employee leave, Cabral responded, "I'd rather take that chance than have under-trained workers. If we can't offer room for advancement they'll go somewhere else if that's what they want."[62]

A major expansion of the program occurred in the spring of 2002. Under the name the Boston Health Care and Research Training Institute, the program grew to encompass 11 employers, representing about 35 percent of health care and research employment in Boston, two community colleges, one union, four community organizations, and the Boston Private Industry Council. These partners plan to train 550 employees over a two-year period at an institute offering ESL, GED, pre-college, and college courses, as well as skills training in three areas, administration, patient care, and medical technology.

At the end of 2003 the Institute had graduated twenty-four supervisors and sixty-two employees from its Foundation Skills classes. Twenty percent of the first two classes have advanced and 90 percent are still working.[63] The 90 percent retention rate is considerably higher than the overall retention rate in all participating hospitals and health care providers.[64] Although the advancement numbers may seem small, the fact is that it takes a while for most participants to acquire the skills needed for a job at the next level. The intention was to start with a range of courses from GED preparation and ESL to college level, but no one was prepared for college-level work. The first GED class has not finished after nine months. Basic education classes have been directed to participants at fourth- through eighth-grade reading levels. So progress toward advancement will be slow for many, yet over 40 percent have taken multiple steps toward career advancements. At this point, doing well does not necessarily mean obtaining a promotion but rather staying the course to advancement through continuing education.

The ultimate indicator of success is employer satisfaction. In a survey of supervisors, 85 percent indicated that they were seeing improvements in performance, self-confidence, and attendance in employees participating in the training. As part of a national demonstration project of the Aspen Institute, a methodology for identifying measures of return on investment of workforce training is being developed. This tool will enable employers to see the payoffs of their investment in workforce development.

The budget for all this has grown from $200,000 to around $900,000 for 2004, which covers four career coaches, a full-time administrator, administrative and fiscal staff, and teachers. The Institute has developed a diverse funding base. For the first two years, state, city, and foundation funding supported the program. In 2003 the Institute received a $1 million, three-year program grant under the Boston Workforce Development Initiative (discussed in chapter 6 in more detail). And employers are investing $250,000 in the program in 2004, which will pay for 40 percent of the incumbent worker training and one-fourth of the program's budget. Further, permanent space in the Longwood Medical Area will be provided without charge to the Institute in 2006 by a developer.[65]

What Makes Health Career Ladders Work

Public funding for health care creates an inextricable link between public policy and employer practices. We have learned from the ECCLI initiative in Massachusetts that both government and employers need to invest in the caregiving workforce before workers will see improvements in their job quality and real opportunities for advancement.

BARBARA FRANK, former Massachusetts policy director,
Paraprofessional Healthcare Institute

Bridges to the Future, like the 1199C Training and Upgrading Fund, started out relatively small and expanded its offerings once it had developed a track record. Other career-ladder programs—the Extended Care Career Ladder Initiative in Massachusetts, for instance—may start out as demonstration projects, designed to grow steadily. And sometimes a partner in one project starts or joins others, expanding its career ladders almost by annexation. For example, as a result of its successful experience with Bridges to the Future, Children's Hospital in Boston is now participating in another training program for pharmacy technicians, medical technicians, and radiographers. Once workers have exhausted the possibilities of Bridges to the Future, they can enter training for these technical positions, which typically have starting salaries of $40,000 to $50,000. However it is accomplished, effective career-ladder programs almost always grow, because no other approach to the crisis in health care staffing works on so many levels.

What makes a program effective? My observations of the health care projects discussed in this chapter and several others suggest five features that greatly improve a career-ladder program's chances of success:

1. a workplace that minimizes hierarchy and values communication;
2. an educational component designed to be supportive of adult students who may lack confidence;
3. a partnership that benefits all groups involved in creating the program;
4. devoted staff who champion the program; and
5. career pathways that are clearly delineated for workers and clearly recognized by employers.

Each of these features requires further elaboration.

A Less Hierarchical Workplace

Any career-ladder program operates in an organizational context, where established hierarchies and social relationships, often rooted in preconceptions about gender, race, and ethnicity, affect the degree to which job advancement is accepted by management and fellow workers. Many managers have only recently made the connection between the quality of care patients receive and the treatment nurse aides receive from their superiors. As Barbara Frank of PHI, explained to me,

> Historically, managers thought about a nurse aide's job only in terms of patient care tasks, not in terms of the quality of the job for the worker. Similarly RNs are only beginning to understand that their own frustrations over the lack of control over their work environment are also felt by the nurse aides they supervise. Even though RNs are experiencing the same frustrations with understaffing and lack of control over their work environment, they tend to interpret the behavior of the paraprofessionals they supervise as a lack of work ethic. Although attitudes are starting to change, particularly in patient-centered long-term care facilities, we still have a long way to go.

To change such attitudes, a number of career-ladder training projects have made communication skills—for both CNAs and managers—part of their program, helping CNAs to become more articulate in discussing their patients and teaching supervisors to listen to them. According to participants, this pays off impressively. Brian Bedard, executive vice president at Apple Health Care, likes to tell how his company's team-based, problem-solving approach identified a solution when one of the nursing homes in the Apple system received a deficiency notice from the state concerning food service. The food, dished onto plates in the facility's kitchen, was too often cold by the time it reached residents in the dining room or in bedrooms upstairs. Brainstorming among kitchen staff and direct care staff produced the idea of serving the food on steam tables and giving each resident exactly what he or she wanted. Dietary staff now have more interaction with patients, patients are happier with their meals, and costs are lower because of less food waste.

A Supportive Educational Component

The most well-attended and effective programs are those that make class times and places convenient for workers. Successful programs also focus on building students' confidence and acknowledging their successes, both with workplace rewards and with activities such as a school graduation ceremony, which for many of these students is their first ever. The 1199C Training and Upgrading Fund succeeds in preparing students with relatively low literacy rates to pass certification exams, because literacy skills are built into courses and courses build on existing skills students have acquired on the job. As students succeed, they gain confidence in their ability to master more difficult courses. The program completion rate is high because students actively encourage one another and are encouraged by their instructors.

A Mutually Beneficial Partnership

The longest lasting and most effective partnerships are based on considerable trust. When developing Bridges to the Future, Sarah Griffen and her colleagues cultivated individual relationships with each organization involved and made it clear that their communication with each was confidential. Colleagues in Caring built trust among competing colleges, universities, and hospital diploma schools by ensuring them that, by cooperating, they could maintain the quality of their programs as well as tuition revenue. In contrast, at Cape Cod Hospital the lack of trust between management and union is hindering the growth of their career-ladder program.

The most solidly ensconced programs also bring obvious value to the employers involved. Hospitals and nursing homes see real gains for themselves in the increased education and job satisfaction of their employees and in cost savings from reduced turnover.

A Program Champion

There are two kinds of program champions. The first are employers. Without employers committed to overcoming the obstacles that emerge in implementation, the programs would fail quickly. Joseph Cabral at Children's Hospital in Boston was hesitant at first to participate in Bridges to the Future because his hospital had invested in several welfare-to-work programs in the past that did not work. After talking to Griffen, however, Cabral decided that Bridges to the Future had a good chance of actually succeeding. So he took on the task of selling the idea to his hospital's other managers. Without him—and Linda Erk, the director of Human Resources at New England Baptist Hospital, who took on the same task at her hospital, and various other champions—Bridges might never have gotten off the ground.

The second type of champion is committed program staff. The Breslin Center's approach to training was the vision of District 1199C's president, Henry Nicholas, who started the Training and Upgrading Fund in 1974 and remains active in expanding its offerings. James Ryan and Cheryl Feldman of Local 1199C were with the program from its inception and have created new programs, including the LPN school, as the need arose. Rick Surpin and Steve Dawson have shown the same commitment to replicating the CHCA model. Sarah Griffen is a tireless advocate and innovator for the Institute and has expanded its funding base and employer participation significantly in only four years. In each case the programs have continuity as they grow.

Clear Career Pathways

The programs that most successfully advance workers into higher-level jobs specify the precise education and experience needed to qualify for them. Students are also told exactly what they will be doing all day in the more advanced occupation. When Cape Cod Hospital did not provide the latter information, it found itself training people for jobs that they wouldn't take.

On the other hand, credentials probably have to be recognized by more than one employer to create advancement opportunities that are sufficient to entice and serve students. Clearly explaining to a large number of employers what career-ladder students have learned is as important as giving students a clear idea of what they need to learn. One goal of the Extended Care Career Ladder Initiative in Massachusetts is to ensure that all nursing homes in the state recognize ECCLI's three-level career ladder for nurse aides. Likewise Colleagues in Caring seeks to create better articulation among nursing schools.

Even greater success can be expected when employers recognize education with clearly visible promotions and pay increases. In Colorado an articulation agreement among educators has done little to motivate RNs with nursing diplomas or associate's degrees to earn a baccalaureate degree—mainly because nurses do not receive additional compensation for increasing their education if they remain as staff nurses (other career-ladder steps for nurses include nurse practitioner, nurse anesthetist, or certified nurse midwife). The ECCLI sites vary in the extent to which the new CNA levels being created result in permanent wage increases. The problem with this approach, however, is that the ladders are site specific. CNAs who move to different employers are likely to find that their credentials are not recognized. But at least the CNA position is recognized for nursing home workers. Hospitals can define the nurse aide role and its requirements in any way they choose, making it difficult to create a portable credential.

Diverse and Consistent Funding

The two union programs have Taft-Hartley funds as their primary source of funding. These education funds were negotiated by the unions and employers. Unfortunately not many employers who have not already agreed to committing a percentage of payroll to education are likely to take on this financial burden. In fact, a union in one of the large hospitals working with 1199C in Philadelphia lost its tuition reimbursement program in contract negotiations. And, in Massachusetts, Cape Cod Health Care is trying to create an alternative training strategy that would compete with the union program. So the most consistent type of funding available for career-ladder training not only is not increasing but is continually under fire.

Almost all demonstration programs rely on foundations or state demonstration grants for funding. The Boston Institute has diversified its funding base beyond this and has created enough value to convince employers to invest in the program. Ultimately the willingness of employers to invest in education and training because of the value it adds to the organization is the ultimate litmus test of effective programs.

The Public Policy Agenda

Of course, hospitals and nursing homes have limited flexibility when it comes to increasing employee wages and benefits. And those career-ladder programs that do reward CNAs who acquire further training often rely on foundation funding for the purpose. Apple Health Care, which has been able to raise wages without foundation grants, is an exception.

For the most part, government policy is both the key problem and the potential solution to the crisis in nursing care, as Steve Dawson and his colleagues at PHI point out:

> As the single largest funder of health care, the federal government has in essence created an entire labor market of paraprofessional health care workers—a labor market that would not exist without its funding, a labor market that keeps low-income women in the ranks of the working poor. And yet our government has yet to accept responsibility for creating and maintaining literally thousands of poverty-level jobs.[66]

Approximately 70 percent of nursing home revenues come from Medicaid and 8 percent from Medicare, with the remaining 22 percent from private payers. It is unlikely that the federal Medicaid budget will be increased. The federal Balanced Budget Refinement Act of 1999 provided a one-time $15 billion shot in the arm to long-term care providers that lasted through 2004. And there was no requirement that those funds be used to increase staffing, training, or pay levels.[67]

A few special federal training funds have been allocated to improving the quality of nursing home care, but federal policy is contradictory. On the one hand, the "cost-containment" guideline of Medicare and Medicaid is responsible for low wages in the health care industry, which in turn reduces the quality of care and is partly responsible for the shortage of direct care providers. On the other hand, the U.S. Department of Labor creates special pools of funds to improve worker training. These demonstration projects, however, cannot compensate for the overall low levels of funding for training and wages.

Thus far the states have been more responsive to these problems. They have been legislating a hodgepodge of nursing home standards, setting minimum staff-to-patient ratios, training requirements, and wages. Thirty-six states and the District of Columbia have raised required staffing levels. Ten states are considering increasing or improving the training required for CNA certification.[68] Sixteen states already require more than the seventy-five hours of training that the federal government mandates for CNAs. California, Maine, and Oregon require twice as many hours.

Moreover, eighteen states have already adopted what is called a "wage pass through," which requires that a specific amount or percentage of any increase in state Medicaid payments to long-term care providers must be spent on increasing the wages or benefits or both of paraprofessionals.[69] States vary as to whether the pass through is mandatory or voluntary, how compliance is enforced, and whether the increases are designated for workers in some settings (e.g., nursing homes) and not in others (e.g., hospitals). The sixteen states that implemented hourly wage increases ranged from $.50 to $2.14; six states set pass throughs as a percentage of increased reimbursement (e.g., Illinois required that 73 percent of rate increases be used to increase wages and benefits).[70]

In a survey of the states that have enacted pass throughs, the North Carolina Division of Facility Services reports that one-third believed that their pass throughs have had a positive impact on recruitment. Michigan, the only state that maintains data, reports that CNA turnover rates in the state declined from 74.5 percent in 1990 to 67.4 in 1998 as a result of raising wages through a pass through.

In terms of educational policy, states need to invest more in community colleges. Many participants in the Boston Health Care and Research

Training Institute cannot get into community college nursing and hospital technician programs because of long waiting lists. The community colleges cannot pay instructors at the same rate that they are paid in practice, so practitioners have little incentive to teach. The Institute is examining the option of having employers pay nursing staff release time to work as adjunct faculty in community college programs. In fact, the decision to close a community college program prompted 1199C to create the first union-run LPN program. In addition, states need to promote coordination between community colleges and four-year institutions in an effort to reduce course repetition so as to facilitate advancement of LPNs to RNs, and RNs with nursing diplomas and associate's degrees to university programs.

The states alone cannot solve nursing home and home health care problems, and they have even less influence over hospitals. In the North Carolina survey all states identified recruitment and retention of direct care staff as a continuing problem. By now there is fairly wide recognition that the enactment of wage pass throughs and the development of climbable career ladders ought to be part of any public policy to reduce the country's shortage of nurse aides and other health care paraprofessionals. The bottom line, however, is that our investment in upgrading the training of health care workers remains grossly inadequate, and state and federal health care funding is still not enough to create anything approaching self-sufficiency wages.

Chapter 3

Child Care

Child care workers are among the lowest-paid people in America. They are paid on a par with parking lot attendants and earn even less than animal tenders.[1] They are widely presumed to need little education and no particular training. Moreover, the kind of custodial care that untrained, low-wage workers can offer is widely assumed to be all that preschoolers require.

That is not the case in many other Western countries. In France, for example, the presumption is that preschoolers should get more than just babysitting from their day care providers; attention should also be paid to their cognitive and social development. At around age three almost all children in France begin attending *écoles maternelles*, which are part of the public school system and are staffed by professional educators, just as kindergarten is here. Younger children are cared for in creches, whose employees must also attend continuing classes in child development.

But in the United States, where about 65 percent of mothers with children under the age of six are employed[2] and more than 60 percent of children under the age of four are regularly cared for outside their homes,[3] even custodial-type day care is often hard to come by.[4] Educational programs for pre-kindergarteners are rarer still, even though studies have repeatedly shown that such programs (e.g., Head Start) increase cognitive ability and school readiness, and prevent later juvenile delinquency.[5] In fact, early childhood education for poor children arguably offers the best hope for breaking the intergenerational cycle of poverty.[6]

The first interest in child care career ladders in this country has come from groups that want a more educational approach to preschoolers and therefore want to see more child care workers trained to provide it. Their first attempts to establish career ladders have not been particularly successful. They have shown, however, that further development of ladders in this field will depend on how far federal and state governments decide to go toward creating a universally available child care and early-education system. There is simply no one else with the capacity to fund the significant growth or professionalization of these services. Thus the issue is essentially political: for those who want to see improvements in American child care, as well as those who want to raise the wages and advancement opportunities of the impoverished workers who provide it, political action is the primary strategy.

The U.S. Child Care "System"

I have seen a big change in family child care providers. They are more involved in classes and more enthusiastic about the profession. They see it as a profession more than a job.

A CARES stipend recipient, San Mateo County,
California

America's preschool children are cared for in a variety of settings. Child care centers are nonresidential facilities that typically tend large groups of a dozen or more children. Family child care providers take care of a smaller number of children, usually five at most, in the provider's home. Together they account for almost half the child care provided to preschool children of working parents. Almost all the rest are cared for in their own homes or a relative's, by a family member or, in a small number of cases, a hired nanny (figure 3.1).

State and federal governments require little in the way of professional standards in any of these settings. Most states exempt paid care provided by nannies or relatives from any kind of regulation.[7] Some form of licensure for family child care settings is required in forty-seven states, but this varies widely. As the National Child Care Information Center states, "forty-one states allow some number of children to be in family child care that is not covered by licensing."[8] Moreover, only ten states require any preservice training for small family child care licenses and only eleven have orientation or initial licensure training requirements.[9] In all states child care centers must be licensed, but in this setting, too, the requirements mostly concern health and safety, and teacher-child ratios for different age groups.[10] Only six states set standards for the preschool curriculum.[11] Only twenty-one states set educational standards for child care center employees, and, for the most part, they are very low.[12] The National Research Council, a nonprofit institution organized by the National Academy of

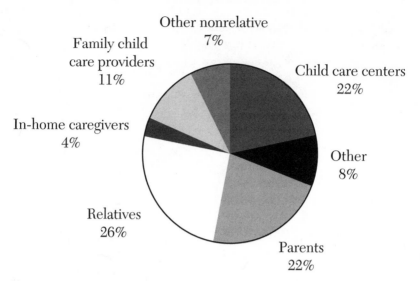

Figure 3.1. Characteristics of child care arrangements of children under 5 with working mothers (1997)

Source: Children's Defense Fund 2001; U.S. Census Bureau, "Who's Minding the Kids? Child Care Arrangements: Spring 1997," Current Population Reports P70–86 (July 2002).

Sciences, recommends that all child care centers be staffed with teachers with bachelor's degrees and specialized training in early childhood education.[13] However, just two states, Rhode Island and New Jersey, require it. Vermont is the only state requiring child care centers to employ at least one person with a master's degree.

The main private accrediting organization for child care centers is the National Association for the Education of Young Children (NAEYC). In 1985 NAEYC established the National Academy of Early Childhood Programs, now the largest and most widely recognized voluntary accreditation system for child care centers and early childhood schools.[14] It sets standards for curriculum, employee education, and other matters.[15] About nine thousand centers, approximately 8 percent of the nation's total, are NAEYC accredited.

In such an environment, the need for career training, much less career ladders, is not pursued very much, and it should come as no surprise that workers suffer as a result. They feel a general lack of respect from other educational professionals and from parents, who often view child care workers essentially as babysitters,[16] and the lack of respect is matched by a lack of pay. Employment in child care centers is generally divided into three tiers: aides, teachers, and directors.[17] At all three levels these employees have had less education and training, on average, than those who work in comparable jobs with older children. And at all three levels center employees, 98 percent of whom are women,[18] earn less than comparable workers in other industries.[19] In 2000, child care center aides earned an average wage of just $7.86 an hour; teachers, $9.66; and directors, $17.47. Only one-third of centers offered health benefits (see table 3.1).

In family child care and home settings, there are no tiers at all and, for the most part, even less connection to notions of professionalism and early childhood education. The average wage in these settings is hard to determine owing to the lack of accurate data. However, evidence of very low wages exists. In North Carolina in 1998, when child care teacher wages were averaging $6.25 an hour, family child care providers were earning $4.00 an hour.[20]

Many studies have concluded that children are ill-served by these arrangements. The National Institute of Child Health and Human Development (NICHD), the branch of the National Institutes of Health that researches the health of children and families, estimates that only about 9 percent of child care centers provide "excellent" care and 30 percent "good" care for children aged two and three, and the majority provide "fair"

TABLE 3.1
Education and pay of employees in child care centers

Position	Educational Level Attained	Average Pay	Number of U.S. Workers Employed in This Position
Child care center director	Bachelor's degree or higher (69%) Some college (27%) High school or less (4%)	Mean hourly wage, $17.47; mean annual wage, $34,940	65,000
Teacher	Bachelor's degree or higher (33%) Some college (47%) High school or less (20%)	Mean hourly wage, $9.66; mean annual wage, $19,320	324,000
Assistant / aide	Bachelor's degree or higher (12%) Some college (45%) High school or less (43%)	Mean hourly wage, $7.86; mean annual wage, $15,720	264,000

Source: Adapted from the Bureau of Labor Statistics, 1999 National Occupational Employment and Wage Estimates and Occupational Outlook Handbook, and National Women's Law Center (Campbell et al. 2000). Wage and workforce size data (2002) are from the Center for the Child Care Workforce (http://www.ccw.org/pubs/workforceestimatereport.pdf).

or "poor" care.[21] Three observational studies conducted in the 1990s found that only between 8 and 14 percent of center and family child care provided in America is of high quality.[22] A key reason, these studies conclude, is the lack of training and the low compensation of child care workers. The problem is circular: low wages deter skilled workers from taking jobs in this field, and as long as the field is dominated by unskilled workers, it is not deemed to require higher wages.

The American disinclination to spend more money "subsidizing" child care has merely shifted the burden elsewhere. This point has been convincingly argued by the women's rights advocates of the National Women's Law Center in their report, *Be All That We Can Be*.[23] "In the absence of a sufficient public investment," they conclude,

> the system is kept afloat, in effect, by a series of hidden sacrifices: by poorly paid caregivers who are subsidizing the system when they forgo decent wages and benefits; by parents who are spending a high proportion of their income on child care and/or making do with poor-quality, inadequate arrangements; by their children, who are incurring the long-term developmental consequences of poor quality care; and by employers who are bearing the costs of an unstable workforce and absent and distracted workers worrying about their children's care.

Public investment is needed to remedy the situation.

The Beginnings of Career Ladders

The hardest part of pursuing my associate and bachelor's degree while working was having to put my family second to my own goals. I missed many a night being able to put my two-year-old daughter to bed. The irony I now find in counseling students in the same situation is that one of the biggest barriers early child care professionals have to going to school is lack of child care.

FLORIANNA THOMPSON, professional development
coordinator, Wake Technical College

To create a better child care system, early childhood education experts say that state governments would have to involve themselves in increasing standards for education and licensure of workers, requiring lower child-to-adult ratios, and improving child care workers' access to training and professional development courses. All but a few states have initiatives in one or more of these areas—forty-one states have programs to improve access to training, but they are mostly small in scale and inadequately funded.

Hardly any of them provide money to permanently or significantly increase wages for child care providers who complete courses or earn certificates or degrees.[24] In most cases people can still earn more working at McDonald's than as child care workers. Even teachers in child care settings earn several thousand dollars less than their counterparts in public kindergartens (an average of $9.66 per hour compared to $26.82 for kindergarten teachers). This does not encourage the best and brightest to continue working with young children.

Nonetheless the embryonic beginnings of career ladders can be found wherever efforts have been made to improve the education of low-level child care workers, and these efforts are worth reviewing. The most common approach has been to provide scholarships to child care workers to attend classes. T.E.A.C.H. [Teacher Education and Compensation Helps] Early Childhood® is the largest such program. It was pioneered in North Carolina in 1990 and now has spread to twenty other states. Taking a different tack, West Virginia tries to improve the skills of child care workers through formal apprenticeship programs, and this approach, too, has been replicated in twenty states. Both are discussed below.

T.E.A.C.H. Early Childhood® North Carolina

In 1990 Sue Russell, the executive director of the Child Care Services Association, a United Way agency working to improve the child care system, raised $23,000 from private foundations for twenty-one scholarships to encourage child care workers to take courses in early child health and development.[25] She was able to convince employers to participate and help fund the scholarships by assuring them that the program would improve the quality of their services and help them retain workers. T.E.A.C.H. has grown enormously since then. In the program's third year, the state allotted $100,000 of its federal child care block grant to expand T.E.A.C.H. to all its counties, and that was just the beginning. By fiscal year 2001–2002, the North Carolina General Assembly was earmarking $2.6 million a year for T.E.A.C.H. in addition to $250,000 from the federal block grant. That year 4,962 North Carolinians received scholarships. Aides, teachers, and directors of regulated child care centers were eligible to participate, as were providers of family child care.

T.E.A.C.H. has four basic components:

- Scholarships. Most participants pay a small percentage of their education expenses and receive scholarships that cover the rest of their costs for tuition, books, and travel. In addition, they are paid for two to six hours per week of

release time from work. In most cases their employers partly fund these
scholarships.

- Education contracts. Participants agree to complete course requirements
  toward a particular credential or degree offered through the state's community college and university system.
- Rewards. Employers agree to give the participant a raise or pay a one-time
  bonus when the education contract is completed. Employers who offer a permanent raise are allowed to contribute less toward the scholarship.
- Employment commitments. Participants agree to stay with the employer
  from six months to a year, depending on the type of scholarship, after completing the contract.

Table 3.2 indicates the scope of training sponsored by T.E.A.C.H.

In addition to the above scholarships for current child care workers,
T.E.A.C.H. in 2000–2001 awarded eight scholarships for $2,000 a year to
college juniors and seniors who committed to working in a North Carolina
child care center for one year after graduation.

According to Russell, over 90 percent of participants complete their education contracts. She also believes that the decline in job turnover among
child care employees statewide—from 42 percent in 1993 to 24 percent in
2003—is attributable to T.E.A.C.H. Remarkable changes in the lives of
individual students must also be counted as a success of the program.

One example is Florianna Thompson, who started out as a T.E.A.C.H.
scholarship recipient and now has a faculty appointment at Wake Technical
College in Raleigh. Thompson had an associate's degree and was working
at Kidworks, a child care facility operated by Wake Medical Center for its
employees, when she applied for one of the first T.E.A.C.H. scholarships
in order to pursue a bachelor's degree in child development and family relations at North Carolina Central University. After two years of attending
classes while working full-time (except for release time) and caring for
her two children, she graduated cum laude. In five years at Kidworks she
went from annual earnings of $8,293 to $30,552 as a result of T.E.A.C.H.
raises and an advance to assistant director. After twelve years Thompson
decided to move on and took a position at a program promoting education
for child care workers. She stayed there for three years before taking
her present position as professional development coordinator and instructor at Wake Technical College, working specifically with T.E.A.C.H.
students.

She was a "nontraditional student" herself, Thompson says, and that
helps her counsel others. Knowing how hard it is to juggle work, family, and
school, she closely tracks student attendance and performance, and she
considers it a major part of her job to keep her students motivated to stay

TABLE 3.2
T.E.A.C.H Early Childhood® North Carolina (FY 2000–2001)

Credential for which Scholarship Is Awarded	Required Course Work	Bonus or Raise upon Completion	Total Participants in 2000–2001
N.C. Early Childhood Credential	4 semester hours in child development at community college	$100 bonus	2,030
N.C. Early Childhood Administration Credential	2–12 semester hours at community college	$150–$300 bonus depending on time commitment	169
Child Development Associate	120 total hours of course work plus 400 hours of work experience with young children	$200 bonus	18
Early Childhood Education Associate's Degree for Child Care Teachers	9–15 semester hours per year in early childhood education, as part of an associate's bonus degree program from a community college	4–5% raise or $550–$700 bonus	1,941
Early Childhood Education Associate's Degree for Family Care Providers	9–15 semester hours per year as part of an associate's degree program from a community college	$300 bonus	359
Early Childhood Associate's Degree for Child Care Center Directors	12–15 semester hours per year in early childhood education as part of a two-year community college degree	$300–$600 bonus	357
Early Childhood Bachelor's Degree	9–15 semester hours per year in early childhood education as part of a bachelor's degree	5% raise or $300–$600 bonus	56
Early Childhood Model/Mentor Teacher	3 semester hours of courses in leadership and mentoring for child care teachers	$900 bonus in first year plus a 3% raise the following year	19

Source: Compiled by the author from published T.E.A.C.H. materials and interviews.

in school. As to her own education, in 2002, when her third child turned two, she enrolled in a master's degree program.

Thompson's story is, of course, extraordinary. T.E.A.C.H. made it possible, but the vast majority of T.E.A.C.H. graduates have seen no such career or wage advances. The average wage for child care workers in North Carolina remains very low—$8.06 an hour in May 2003, according to the most recent data from the Bureau of Labor Statistics (BLS). Even after obtaining a bachelor's degree, teachers in child care centers earn a median hourly wage of only $10.38.[26]

In 1994 North Carolina's child care advocates pushed further and started the Child Care WAGE$ Project to provide salary supplements to child care workers with educational credentials. Typical supplements currently range from $300 per year for a beginning credential to $3,000 per year for a worker with a bachelor's degree. The money is disbursed at six-month intervals to encourage workers to stay on the job. Child Care WAGE$ is funded by a public-private partnership called Smart Start,[27] the same group Florianna Thompson once worked for. Like T.E.A.C.H., the new program started out small and grew quickly. It is now operating in fifty-nine counties. In 2003–2004 the state committed $8.8 million to the WAGE$ initiative. About eighty-six hundred North Carolina child care workers and preschool teachers, about 31 percent of the state's child care labor force, received WAGE$ salary supplements in fiscal year 2000–2001, and T.E.A.C.H. programs in other states are now starting to introduce the WAGE$ supplement or other salary programs.

However, even in North Carolina, where T.E.A.C.H. and WAGE$ have been operating the longest and at the highest level of funding, their impact remains limited. T.E.A.C.H. can be a first step in building a child care career ladder, but absent state regulations requiring better educated child care workers and absent a public investment large enough to support significant increases in wages, the child care labor market is not going to change. And neither will the kind of care that most preschoolers receive.

Apprenticeships in West Virginia

Some states are using apprenticeship programs to educate child care workers. Apprenticeships integrate classroom knowledge with on-the-job training, and because the child care apprenticeships follow an established curriculum approved by the Department of Labor, they could result in the development and spread of a single national credential, if the child care industry were ever required to pay attention to credentials.

In 1989 West Virginia was the first state to create an Apprenticeship for Child Development Specialists (ACDS). Since the program's inception, more than twenty-five hundred West Virginians have completed apprenticeships and achieved journeyman status in early childhood education. The ACDS requires four thousand hours (about two years) of on-the-job training (paid work at a child care center, Head Start, preschool, or family child care facility) and three hundred hours of community college instruction in child care principles and practices over four fifteen-week semesters.

The curriculum is based on the credential Child Development Associate (CDA), a nationally recognized paraprofessional credential.[28] Students also must earn a high school diploma or equivalent before completing the apprenticeship. If they wish to continue their education, their ACDS course work can be counted for up to 33 college credits applicable toward an associate's degree. The program is mostly federally funded, with participants paying only for books and materials. Participating employers are required to give program completers a raise of between $0.10 and $0.25 per hour.

The West Virginia Apprenticeship program does clarify the steps that an entry-level worker must take to move from no credential to journeyman status to college degree. But it does not make them as attractive as they could be. Completing the program does not result in a credential useful elsewhere, and $0.10 to $0.25 is not much money. The state's entry-level child care workers generally start at the minimum wage of $5.15 an hour and progress to, at the most, $6.00 an hour with no further training. In other words, $6.25 is probably the top hourly wage for those who complete the West Virginia apprenticeship, and in the vast majority of cases it comes with no health or retirement benefits. Suzi Brodof, the ACDS Coordinator at River Valley Child Development Services, acknowledges that the program's wage increases are meager. "People go for it because it's the best there is," she says. The state is currently developing a guide for further wage increases along a child care career path, but the guide will only take effect if further funds are allocated.

Although there has been no formal evaluation of the West Virginia ACDS program, the federal government has been satisfied enough to expand it to other states. From 1999 to 2001 Congress appropriated $4 million annually for this purpose, named the Quality Child Care Initiative (QCCI). In three rounds of funding in 1999, 2000, and 2001, thirty-one states and the District of Columbia received between $250,000 and $350,000 each to offer child care apprenticeships.[29] Only a few states, however, have mandated pay raises, and those have been as small as West Virginia's.

Maine is an exception. It has offered two- and three-year child care apprenticeships since 1976, but with its eighteen-month, $350,000 federal QCCI grant, the state decided to completely subsidize tuition for these apprenticeships, and that dramatically increased the number of participants.[30] In addition, Maine requires employers to provide a 5 percent wage increase for every six months that participants are in the program.[31] Over the course of a three-year apprenticeship, that adds up to a compounded 34 percent wage hike. Nonetheless the average hourly wage for non-professional child care workers in Maine was only $7.90 in 2001. According to BLS data, it was better than West Virginia to be sure, but still $10.46 less than the median hourly wage of U.S. workers whose highest level of education is high school.[32] It is still far from a living wage, which would be $16.64 per hour in Maine for a mother and two children.

Like T.E.A.C.H., the various apprenticeship programs are tinkering at the margins of systems that need major overhauls. T.E.A.C.H. programs have distinguished several tiers of child care and early-education skills, and the Department of Labor–approved apprenticeship has the advantage of creating a standardized curriculum for child care workers. But minimum credentials for child care workers are not required in any state, and higher tiers are not widely recognized. Nor are credentials linked anywhere with significant, permanent wage increases. A plus of both programs is that they can be "articulated" to community college and university degree programs, meaning that all course work can build toward a higher degree. This could help the most dedicated students advance out of direct care work, as Florianna Thompson has. But without opportunities to earn a decent living within the occupation, child care itself is not going to change. T.E.A.C.H. and the Apprenticeship for Child Development Specialists have the potential to be the core of defined career-ladder systems, but they have not yet reached that goal.

Fully Defined Career-Ladder Programs

Programs like CARES and WAGES Plus fill in plugs in normal life that were just gaping. Participants were able to fill in some of the holes that people who earn higher wages take for granted. I saw people go back into a classroom who hadn't been in a classroom in years. I saw people starting to be valued and recognized for the work that they do.

SHEILA NORMAN, director, Candlelight Child
Development Center, San Francisco, California

Low pay seems to produce the same effects on labor supply and turnover in child care as in other industries. Turnover rates of child care workers vary from about 59 percent for assistants, 51 percent for teachers, 34 percent for teacher-directors, and 36 percent for directors.[33] In accredited child care centers that pay higher than average wages, turnover is considerably lower than in nonaccredited centers, suggesting that pay is a major factor.[34] One study conducted by the Center for the Child Care Workforce,[35] a project of the American Federation of Teachers Educational Forum, which works on improving the quality of children's early care and education, revealed that NAEYC-accredited centers pay wages between 9.5 percent and 33.7 percent higher than do nonaccredited centers, depending on job category, and have retention rates twice as high.[36] Not only low-level workers are affected. Another study indicates that turnover at the lower levels also affects the job satisfaction and, ultimately, retention of center directors.[37] Several other studies have found that high turnover among child care workers creates inconsistent and inadequate care.[38]

In turn, the unattractiveness of child care jobs is already creating shortages. A recent report by the National Council of Jewish Women chronicles cases in Colorado, Maryland, Kansas City, Los Angeles, and Washington, D.C., where child care centers have closed because of their inability to find workers, leaving nearby centers filled to capacity. Families have had to put themselves on waiting lists before their children are even born.[39] And such problems can only multiply as the demand for child care continues to grow. (According to BLS projections, the demand for child care workers will continue to expand at almost triple the growth rate of the economy as a whole for some time.)[40]

These are not negligible problems. But the issue that seems most likely to arouse the American public and lawmakers—as it has in North Carolina, West Virginia, and Maine—is the shabbiness of child care services here, services that other countries provide universally and with a high degree of professionalism. In turn, the desire for child care and preschool workers who have an understanding of the principles of child development or early education should lead directly to career ladders. When the majority of current child care workers do not even have high school diplomas (about 22–34 percent in regulated settings and 33–46 percent in unregulated settings),[41] the only way to upgrade the field is to create career ladders that untrained, entry-level workers are able and motivated to climb. What is needed, as the health care industry is finding, is a skill-based hierarchy of occupations, clear requirements for advancing from one occupation to the next, and real wage increases for the skill increases acquired.

Those who think it cannot be done should look at the U.S. military. The Military Child Care Act of 1989 created a new system of child care for all branches of the American armed forces. The results demonstrate that a large, poorly operating system can be turned around in short order.

The Military Child Development Program

In the late 1980s the state of child care in the military was so bad that it endangered the recruitment, retention, and motivation of soldiers. Child care workers, who were often military wives, were not happy with it either. Annual employee turnover rates reached as high as 300 percent in many child care centers, although to some extent that reflected transfers of military spouses. The 1989 legislation created the Military Child Development Program (MCDP), which addressed the problems head-on.

The MCDP increased the number of military child care centers, building 208 new centers in twelve years.[42] It provided significant pay increases for child care employees tied to their continuing education. It hired a training and curriculum specialist for each of its child care centers. It established standards covering staffing ratios, qualifications for different child care jobs, child abuse prevention, fire protection, facility conditions, developmental programming, and health and safety,[43] and it instituted quarterly unannounced inspections (something no state currently has)[44] to ensure that centers meet those standards. Finally, the MCDP created a sliding scale of fees, in all cases heavily subsidized, so that its child care would be affordable to all military families.

Beyond those actions designed to deliver high-quality child care, the MCDP also wants to provide some degree of preschool education. It thus made a further commitment to strive to meet or exceed the standards set by early-childhood education experts for quality of curriculum, environment, and personal interactions. As a result, approximately 95 percent of military child care centers are accredited by NAEYC compared to 7 percent of centers nationwide.[45]

For employees, the requirements and rewards for moving from one rung of the MCDP career ladder to the next are now clearly defined, manageably incremental, and used throughout the system (see table 3.3). New hires take an eight-hour orientation course and spend an additional four hours observing the center's activities. In their first six months of employment, they must complete thirty-six hours of additional training in child development and first aid. Within eighteen months, they must complete fifteen competency-based training modules. All employees, regardless of their educational level, have to master this material so that everyone understands the regulations and the child care philosophy of the MCDP centers. For completing these training requirements, all employees are rewarded with pay increases. For the MCDP career ladder for paraprofessionals, see table 3.3.

The annual cost of the military's new child care program averaged out to about $7,600 per child in the 2000–2001 school year, which is about 7 percent more than it costs to operate civilian child care centers, according to the federal government's General Accounting Office. The military's higher costs are the result of higher staff-to-child ratios, a greater percentage of spaces dedicated to serving children under age three, higher education and training costs, and better pay for caregivers (MCDP centers pay an average of $1.04 per hour more than civilian centers do).[46]

Families were able to afford this higher-cost care because the Defense Department paid about half the total bill. In 2000–2001 parent fees

TABLE 3.3
Military Child Development Program qualifications for program assistant positions

Grade	Requirements to Enter at This Level	Experience and Education or Training			Hourly Pay without Benefits	Hourly Pay with Benefits
		Experience	Experience	Education or Training		
1 GS-02 Child Development Program Assistant Entry Level	• 18 years old • high school graduate • speak, read, write English • pass physical exam • immunizations • food handlers' certificate • favorable background check • satisfactory completion of mandatory training and demonstrated competency within required time	None	None	N/A	$8.32–$11.80	$10.15–$14.40
2 GS-03 Child Development Program Assistant Intermediate Level	All Grade 1 Requirements	• 6 mos. working in a group program for young children	• completion of 3 child development modules or related	• 15 semester hours in high school (HS) in child care field or completion of secondary vocational program in child care	$8.32–$11.80	$10.15–$14.40

TABLE 3.3—cont.

Grade	Requirements to Enter at This Level	Experience	Experience and Education or Training	Hourly Pay without Benefits	Hourly Pay with Benefits
3 GS-04 Child Development Program Assistant Target Level	Same as 1	• 6 mos. equivalent to 2 level working in a group program for young children	• completion of child development modules • 30 semester hours above HS that included at least 15 semester hours in child development or directly related field	$10.19–$14.82	$12.43–$18.08
4 GS-05 Child Development Program Assistant Leader Level	Same as 1	• 12 mos. experience to 3 level working in a group program for young children	• an AA degree in ECE or a current CDA	$10.19–$14.82	$12.43–$18.08
5 GS-05 Child Development Program Technician	Same as 1		• 12 mos. equivalent to 4 level and either an AA or CDA	$10.19–$14.82	$12.43–$18.08

Source: Provided by Barbara Thompson, Office of Children and Youth, U.S. Department of Defense (wages based on OPM 2003 General Schedule Locality Pay Tables).

at MCDP centers ranged from $40.00 to $116.00 per week. The average fee parents paid was $77 per week per child for up to fifty hours of care.[47]

All in all, the Department of Defense spent $352 million on child care in 2000–2001,[48] about 73 percent of that on MCDP child care development centers, which provide care primarily for children of preschool age, and the rest on family child care for children of military personnel and Department of Defense civilians, and programs for school-age children.[49] The total expenditure can be expected to rise further in the future; indeed, the Department of Defense 2004 budget for MCDP is $394 million, a 12.2 percent increase over what was spent in 2000. Because forty thousand more spaces for children from infancy to age twelve are needed just to meet current demand, all branches of the military have strategies in place for increasing their available child care spaces over the next five years.[50]

There is no question that the MCDP has improved the availability of child care and the earnings and working conditions of child care employees. Annual turnover among child care workers is down to 30 percent, which may be as low as it can get given military transfers.[51] In addition, the MCDP seems to have significantly improved the quality of care. An evaluation completed by RAND, one of the nation's most respected private think tanks, found that bringing military child care centers up to accreditation standards increased the number of child-initiated activities as well as the number of age-appropriate activities and disciplinary techniques, and improved staff morale. Surveys of center directors and parents reveal high levels of satisfaction with the curriculum and the quality of care.[52]

The speed of these changes was also remarkable. According to the RAND study, the wage increases and parent fee structure were implemented by 75 percent of centers within a year of the enactment of the Military Child Care Act in 1989. The inspection and accreditation systems took only a few more years to put in place.[53] Given the size of the military child care system, this is quite remarkable.

The reform of the military's child care system is a model to follow. But first the public has to be convinced of the value in putting this kind of money and professionalism into child care.

Seattle Worthy Wages

We knew we couldn't advocate for raising wages on the backs of parents who were already struggling to pay for child care.

KIM COOK, president, SEIU Local 925

Washington state has come closer than any other to replicating the military model. In 1999 Governor Gary Locke allocated $4 million of the state's discretionary funds under the federal welfare program to launch what he called the Early Childhood Education Career and Wage Ladder.

It took a great deal of political work for him to arrive at that point. The first to call for public funding of a child care career ladder like the military's was John Burbank, the founder of the Economic Opportunity Institute (EOI), a public policy group that focuses on issues of concern to middle-class families and low-income workers. Another community organization calling itself Seattle Worthy Wages for Child Care Teachers had been agitating for years to get the public and legislators interested in increasing state funding for child care. But little progress was made until 1997, when Worthy Wages joined forces with Local 925 of the Service Employees International Union (SEIU) and succeeded in unionizing twelve child care centers in Seattle.

Kim Cook, then the regional director of District 925 and currently the president of the local, says that political action was always the heart of their strategy, since raising wages ultimately would require higher levels of government funding. So they focused on the idea of a career ladder, which the public and politicians could see as a way to obtain higher-quality child care. The directors of the twelve unionized centers were supportive largely because they hoped that a publicly supported career ladder might result in wages high enough to reduce their troubling turnover rates. All these groups worked together to fine-tune Burbank's original career-ladder proposal into a workable program to present to the legislature, and then they started lobbying. The union created the political opening and the workers created the advocacy "noise" that enabled Burbank to influence his many political contacts.

The result was the Early Childhood Education Career Development Ladder, a three-year pilot program that required participating child care centers to pay a specific base wage and additional wage increments reflecting an employee's experience, job responsibility, and education. The state covered the cost of the education increments and part of the cost of the experience increments (see table 3.4). In the program's first year, 120 (about 7 percent) of the state's child care centers were selected by lottery to participate. In 2001 Washington allocated $8.2 million of its Temporary Assistance to Needy Families (TANF) savings (from reduced enrollments) to continue the program for another two years in the same centers.

To be eligible to participate a child care center had to be state licensed or certified, and at least 10 percent of its enrollment had to be low-income children. In addition, besides agreeing to the state-mandated wage ladder, participating centers were required to provide a minimum of twelve days of paid leave (including holidays), pay $25 per month toward each worker's health benefits, help employees apply for the state's "no frills" health plan, and form a quality-care committee to provide a forum for teachers, child care assistants, and directors to discuss issues and problems.[54]

The career ladder that participants adopted was similar to the military's, although entry-level teacher aides did not require a high school diploma. Upon completing a GED, they received a $0.50 hourly raise. Completion of the state's continuing education requirements resulted in another $0.50 increase. The next steps up, in consecutive order, were attainment of the Child Development Associate (CDA) credential, an early-childhood education certificate called STARS (a state-designed, one-year program offered by most community colleges in the Washington state area),[55] and then associate, baccalaureate, and master's degrees in early-childhood education. There were additional pay raises for every year of work experience at any of these levels (see table 3.4.)

The Washington program did not cover an employee's tuition and other educational expenses, nor did it require employers to do so, but the state has other programs in place through which most child care workers can receive tuition aid. And workers not eligible for state programs can apply for T.E.A.C.H. scholarships. Information about available aid is provided at the participating child care centers.

An external evaluation conducted for the state by researchers at Washington State University in 2004 compared the pilot centers (all the original centers selected to participate in the Early Childhood Education Career Development Ladder) and an equal number of comparison groups, and found that the program had positive effects on quality of care, employee morale, and wages. The care received by children in pilot centers ranked higher than that received in the comparison centers on scales of both structural and process quality; compared to employers in the comparison centers, employers in pilot centers reported that their employees had higher morale; and the average hourly wage for pilot participants was $9.68 compared to $8.94 for comparison group employees.[56] Moreover, the pilot group's median wage of $9.00 was 8 percent higher than the state median of $8.27.[57] The Washington wage increments were not only larger than those connected to T.E.A.C.H. and other scholarship programs around the country; they also applied to a much larger group of workers—all the employees at more than one hundred participating centers, not just the one or two who might win scholarships at each center.

But a program that reaches only 7 percent of child care centers and has no guarantee of continuing from one year to the next still leaves much to

TABLE 3.4
Early childhood education career development ladder wage scale for participating child care centers in all counties (except King County, where wages are higher)

Position	Years at center	No HS	HS/GED	STARS	15 credits	CDA or 45 credits	AA or 90 credits	135 credits	BA or 180 credits	MA
Assistant	0	$6.92	$7.20	$7.70	$7.95	$8.70	$9.20	$9.70	$10.20	$11.20
	1	7.17	7.45	7.95	8.20	8.95	9.45	9.95	10.45	11.45
	2	7.42	7.70	8.20	8.45	9.20	9.70	10.20	10.70	11.70
	3	7.67	7.95	8.45	8.70	9.45	9.95	10.45	10.95	11.95
	4	7.89	8.20	8.70	8.95	9.70	10.20	10.70	11.20	12.20
	5	8.14	8.45	8.95	9.20	9.95	10.45	10.95	11.45	12.45
Lead Teacher	0			$8.20	$8.45	$9.20	$9.70	$10.20	$10.70	$11.70
	1			8.45	8.70	9.45	9.95	10.45	10.95	11.95
	2			8.70	8.95	9.70	10.20	10.70	11.20	12.20
	3			8.95	9.20	9.95	10.45	10.95	11.45	12.45
	4			9.20	9.45	10.20	10.70	11.20	11.70	12.70
	5			9.45	9.70	10.45	10.95	11.45	11.95	12.95
Site Coordinator	0				$9.20	$9.70	$10.20	$10.70	$11.20	$12.20
	1				9.45	9.95	10.45	10.95	11.45	12.45
	2				9.70	10.20	10.70	11.20	11.70	12.70
	3				9.95	10.45	10.95	11.45	11.95	12.95
	4				10.20	10.70	11.20	11.70	12.20	13.20
	5				10.45	10.95	11.45	11.95	12.45	13.45

Program Supervisor					
0	$10.20	$10.70	$11.20	$11.70	$12.70
1	10.45	10.95	11.45	11.95	12.95
2	10.70	11.20	11.70	12.20	13.20
3		11.45	11.95	12.45	13.45
4		11.70	12.20	12.70	13.70
5		11.95	12.45	12.75	13.95

Source: Economic Opportunity Institute, Seattle, Washington.

Funding of the 25¢ Wage Increments for Each Year of Job Experience

Subsidized Low-Income Children at Center	Center Pays	State Pays
Under 25%	25¢	-0-
25–50%	15¢	10¢
50–75%	5¢	20¢
75–100%	-0-	25¢

be desired. So, in 2002, the same coalition that got the career ladder started campaigned for a Seattle ballot measure that would have expanded it to include 40 percent of the city's child care centers and would have provided a permanent source of funding for the program: a tax of $0.10 per order on Seattle's favorite beverage, espresso.[58] The initiative failed by a wide margin (68 percent voted against it) probably because the tax seemed arbitrary. Also the initiative might have been more ambitious than the public was ready for. Besides increasing the number of centers participating in the original career-ladder program, it would have increased child care subsidies for low-income children and funded a pilot preschool program meant to be the first step toward creating a universally available pre-kindergarten in the public schools.

With the failure of this initiative, the career-ladder program also remained hampered by the state's low level of spending on regular child care. Consider, for instance, Interlake Child Care and Learning Center in an upper-middle-class neighborhood of Seattle. With its five state-subsidized, low-income students, Interlake just made the cutoff to qualify for participation in the Early Childhood Education Career Development Ladder. But the subsidies the state paid were so low that Interlake barely came out even. State payments for the care of low-income children varied by the age of the child but were typically about $785 per month for full-time care, or less if the center charged less. That rate is well below that charged by King County (Seattle area) child care centers. For Interlake, the state reimbursement amounted to only 65 percent of its regular fees. In budgeting, the center had to determine how much to charge paying families based on the number of subsidized children in the program. For child care centers like Interlake, the career-ladder program compensated for the inadequate funding coming from other state child care initiatives rather than adding funds for staff advancement.

Interlake's executive director, Mike Kasprzak, like the heads of most participating child care centers, can name several staff members who were thinking of leaving the field because of the lack of advancement opportunities and, as a result of the career-ladder program, stayed. Yet he says that he would rather see the state paying the real market rates for subsidized child care, because that would allow for better pay for all child care workers.

On the other hand, one of the successes of the career-development ladder was that it created a vocal constituency that continues to lobby for caregiver education and wages. The failure of the Seattle ballot initiative and the ending of the three-year state program owing to lack of funding have not stopped the lobbyists' activism. Some progress, although on a much smaller scale, has been seen. In 2004 the Families and Education

Levy, a property tax measure supporting Seattle-area health and education initiatives, was passed. An annual $220,000 of this $161 million, seven-year levy, was allocated to the career-ladder program, meaning that ten of the original twenty-two Seattle centers could be funded. The Economic Opportunity Institute continues to seek longer-term legislative solutions, and it is John Burbank's belief that the program will maintain enthusiastic support precisely because it benefits all families rather than being exclusively a welfare-to-work benefit for poor families.

California CARES

Efforts to establish something similar in California took off in the late 1990s in San Francisco and across the bay in Alameda County. At the time new state legislation limiting kindergarten through second-grade classes to twenty or fewer children was creating a huge demand for additional public school teachers and pulling many of them out of child care. In the public schools they could earn $6,000 to $7,000 more per year in addition to benefits seldom offered by child care centers.[59] Meanwhile, welfare-to-work programs were promoting child care as a career for women coming off welfare. The result was an influx of minimally trained workers into the child care field just as the most highly educated workers were leaving. In 1997, needing to move quickly to retain educated child care workers and convince others to acquire more education, the two counties stopped waiting for the state to act and put their own money into a program called CARES (Compensation and Retention Encourage Stability), which the state legislature had twice tried to fund but California governors Pete Wilson and, after him, Gray Davis had vetoed. After several local programs were up and running the legislature finally allocated the program $15 million in 2000. Since this legislation (AB 212) was signed, forty-seven of California's fifty-eight counties have implemented CARES programs; the AB 212 funds were distributed in varying amounts to supplement these county programs.[60]

CARES is not a full-fledged career-ladder program because it does not designate specific job categories. But it does provide incentives for workers to pursue additional education and stay on the job, mainly by providing taxable annual stipends. Workers who have been with their employer for at least one year and commit to completing a minimum of twenty-one hours per year in continuing education receive an amount based on the number of hours they work and the occupational level.

The first stipend, $500, comes with just a commitment to the program. However, recipients must complete three or more college units in early-childhood education or child development in order to receive another $500 the following year. In the second year of participating, they must complete three additional units. To receive a third stipend, participants must complete a three-unit field placement or practicum and must qualify as an associate teacher. There are additional stipends for child care center employees who are fluent in a language used in their center other than English, as well as for teachers, master teachers, site supervisors, and program directors who engage in state-approved professional growth activities.

CARES does not *require* California child care workers to meet minimum educational standards, but, says Caroline Vance, the director of CARES San Francisco (SF CARES), "We're hoping that as participants see that their stipends increase if they move to higher positions on the matrix, they will be motivated to enroll in continuing education."

San Francisco, however, was already moving further ahead. A Living Wage Campaign there resulted in the passage of a local ordinance in 2001.[61] And even before that, with the issue of low-wage workers at the forefront of local politics, Mayor Willie Brown decided to redirect the city's budget surplus[62] to provide better wages for workers in targeted sectors. Brown saw child care workers as a good first target, because better wages and more training would benefit both low-paid workers and families with children. Michele Rutherford, the child care program manager for the city's Department of Human Services, received a call from the Mayor's Office of Budget in May 2000 and was asked to develop a living-wage program for child care workers with a starting budget of $1 million for FY 1999. Rutherford wasted little time and had the program up and running a month before the living-wage ordinance was passed.

The first step was to establish standardized pay rates for all child care occupations. Based on discussions with John Burbank in Seattle, Marcy Whitebook, founder of the Center for the Child Care Workforce, and other child care advocates, Rutherford decidesd to adopt wage floors. She started with the occupational matrix that the state had developed for CARES, a matrix that identifies the minimum qualifications for all child care positions in centers participating in CARES. And to that Rutherford added wage floors for each position. The new San Francisco program was called WAGES Plus (Wage Augmentation Funding for Entry-level Staff Plus).

This is how the program works: participating child care centers have to bring employee wages up to a minimum rate ($7.50 an hour for aides and assistants), and WAGES Plus pays the difference between that and the new floor wage ($9.00 an hour for aides and assistants). The centers also receive $200 a month for administering the program. To participate, they have to be licensed and serve a minimum of 10 percent subsidy-eligible children or, alternatively, 25 percent children from families with incomes lower than the metropolitan median[63] (see table 3.5).

In the second year of WAGES Plus, participating centers were encouraged to join Quality Plus, a program that requires them to undertake a self-assessment or a university-conducted assessment. Almost all the WAGES Plus centers complied, including those in San Francisco. Any shortcomings found in a center's assessment are to be addressed in its training programs.

WAGES Plus is currently serving thirty organizations operating child care programs at sixty-six sites, serving approximately three thousand children.[64] It reaches about one-quarter of San Francisco's 233 child care centers, which is almost all those that are eligible. At the participating centers it has raised the wages of over 80 percent of staff in most occupational categories (see table 3.6). With virtually all eligible centers participating, and with Head Start programs and those operated by school districts or local colleges already paying at the $9.00 per hour level or higher, WAGES Plus is now starting to work with family child care providers to raise their wages and improve their training.[65] Although funding has increased over time, so have expenses. For the second year the city provided $1.35 million through California's State Children and Families Commission (which was created in 1998 through Proposition 10 and adds a cigarette tax of $0.50 per pack), bumping up the total to $2.975 million, although interim SF CARES director Anna Smeby comments that a cut in FY 2006 is likely. In 2001 state funds kicked in for a total of $3.8 million. Data on the child care workforce and program participation are not maintained in any of the counties. Smeby estimates that SF CARES grants stipends to about thirteen hundred of the city's child care assistants and teachers, with about 70 percent of participants returning for a second round of classes. The problem this creates from a funding perspective is that, as workers move up the matrix, their stipends increase. The average stipend has increased from $1,886 in 2000 to about $2,500 in 2003, which means that fewer participants can be funded each year.[66]

A survey of directors at the end of the first year of WAGES Plus revealed that 69 percent felt that the program increased both employee retention and advancement; 80 percent noted an improvement in morale among their staff. A more formal evaluation of both CARES and WAGES Plus is currently under way. While WAGES Plus receives continuous support from the community, providers, Department of Human Services (DHS), and the Mayor's Office, its funding is not secure and it is unlikely to become a statewide program like CARES anytime in the near future.

Like the scholarship and apprenticeship programs discussed earlier, the efforts in Washington and California are focused mainly on upgrading child

TABLE 3.5
WAGES Plus staff categories and wage floors

Category	Educational Requirement	Wage Floor	Authorization/Responsibility	Alternative Qualifications	Experience Required
Aides and Assistants	0 Early Childhood Education (ECE) units	$9.00	Assist in the instruction of children under the supervision of Associate Teacher or above	Accredited Home Economics Related Occupations (HERO) program (including Regional Occupation Programs [ROP])[a] or Commission on Teacher Credentialing (CTC) approved training	None
Teacher Assistants	6 units of ECE or Child Development (CD)	$9.50	Assist in the instruction of children under the supervision of Associate Teacher or above	Accredited HERO program (including ROP) or CTC-approved training	None
Associate Teachers	12 units ECE/CD including core courses	$11.15	May provide instruction and supervise an assistant	Child Development Association credential or CTC-approved training	50 days of 3+ hours per day within 4 years
Teachers without General Education (GE) Units	24 units ECE/CD including core courses	$11.65	May provide instruction and supervise an assistant	Child Development Association credential or CTC-approved training	50 days of 3+ hours per day within 4 years

	Units	Wage	Duties	Permit Requirements	Experience
Teachers with 16 General Education (GE) Units	24 units ECE/CD including core courses + 16 GE units	$12.15	May provide instruction and supervise all the above (including aides)	AA or higher in ECE or a related field with 3 semester units supervised field experience in ECE setting or CTC-approved training	175 days of 3+ hours per day within 4 years
Master Teachers	24 units ECE/CD including core courses + 16 GE units + 6 specialization units + 2 adult supervision units	$13.85	May provide instruction and supervise all the above (including aides); may also serve as coordinator of curriculum and staff development	BA or higher with 12 units of ECE with 3 units supervised field experience in ECE setting or CTC-approved training	350 days of 3+ hours per day within 4 years
Site Supervisors	AA (or 60 units) with 24 ECE/CD units (including core) + 6 units administration + 2 units adult supervision	$17.05	May supervise a single site program and provide instruction; may also serve as coordinator of curriculum and staff development	BA or higher with 12 units ECE with 3 units supervised field experience in ECE setting, Teaching or Admin. Credential with 12 units of ECE with 3 units supervised field experience in ECE setting or CTC-approved training	350 days of 3+ hours per day within 4 years, including at least 100 days of supervising adults

Source: Los Angeles Unified School District's Early Childhood Education Division website: http://www.lausd.k12.ca.us/lausd/offices/cdd/per_03-1.html.
ªHERO and ROP help prepare high school students and adults for jobs as assistants and aides in child development settings; the training involved qualifies participants to acquire a Child Development Permit at the assistant level.

TABLE 3.6
Wage changes in first twelve months of WAGES Plus

Category	All Participating Centers before WAGES Plus				All Participating Centers after WAGES Plus		
	Number of staff	Average hourly wage (pre-WAGES Plus)	Range: lowest hourly wage	Range: highest hourly wage	New wage floors	Number of staff to receive an increase	% of staff to receive an increase
Aides/Assistants	156	$7.74	$5.50	$20.00	$9.00	138	88%
Teacher Assistants	153	$8.12	$6.04	$11.28	$9.50	130	85%
Associate Teachers	148	$9.70	$6.50	$17.77	$11.15	125	84%
Teachers without 16 GE Units	51	$11.11	$7.50	$15.57	$11.65	39	76%
Teachers with GE Units	98	$10.94	$7.45	$17.77	$12.15	79	81%
Master Teacher	43	$13.24	$7.86	$21.06	$13.85	36	84%
Site Supervisor Teachers	43	$15.10	$10.43	$23.36	$17.05	35	81%
All Other Staff	208	$15.16	$5.00	$50.00	$9.00	51	25%
TOTAL	900					633	
Average		$11.39	$7.04	$22.10			76%
Number of participating organizations	33						
Number of participating programs	59						

Source: WAGES Plus.

care, not on creating the kind of pre-kindergarten schooling that is now a staple of European education. In the United States pre-kindergarten is not as widely appreciated. However, it does exist. Illinois in 2000 spent $200 million providing pre-kindergarten to 15 percent of the state's three- and four-year-olds. South Carolina spent $23.6 million providing preschool to 30 percent of its four-year-olds. Texas spent $9 million to reach 22 percent of its four-year-olds. (Annual per child spending ranged from $3,600 in Illinois to $1,210 in Texas.) And Georgia, since 1993, has provided universal pre-kindergarten for all four-year-olds in the state whose parents want it for their children. In the 2002–2003 school year 56 percent of the state's four-year-olds participated at a cost of $261 million ($3,831 per child).[67]

Georgia's Voluntary Pre-kindergarten[68]

Georgia's pre-kindergarten is one part of then governor Zell Miller's Georgia P-16 Initiative, created to reduce the state's high school drop-out and teen pregnancy rates. The model program received a National Innovation in American Government Award from the Ford Foundation and Harvard University in 1997, and now senator Zell Miller continues to be a zealous proponent. The pre-kindergarten is funded by state lottery money, a large and relatively secure source, which shields it from budget competition with other programs. And it is housed not in the state's Department of Education, an outsized bureaucracy in which it was at first getting lost, but in a new agency, the Office of School Readiness (OSR), which reports directly to the governor. To deliver the program, OSR contracts with public and private schools, Head Start programs, community centers, universities, and private child care centers. Researchers have identified all these factors as explanations for the program's extraordinary growth and longevity.

The pre-kindergarten classes operate on the regular school calendar: six hours a day, five days a week, 180 days a year. The maximum child-to-staff ratio is 10:1, with no more than twenty children in a classroom. Each class has a lead teacher and an assistant. About 64 percent of the classrooms use the High/Scope curriculum (a nationally recognized early childhood model focusing on active, hands-on learning), and the remainder opt for proprietary curricula such as Kindercare or Montessori.[69]

Since 2001 lead teachers have been required to have, minimally, a postsecondary technical institute diploma in early-childhood care and education. Also acceptable is an associate's degree in early-childhood education or a Montessori diploma. To reach the highest salary levels, a teacher must also hold a Georgia or out-of-state teaching certification. OSR offers a variety of training to upgrade the teaching skills and certification levels of lead teachers and assistants.[70]

As in child care programs, this career ladder by itself is not enough to guarantee a good supply of high-quality pre-kindergarten staff. In 2001 Georgia State University concluded an eight-year longitudinal study of the program. It identified a 45 percent teacher turnover rate as a problem and pointed to low pay as the major culprit. Some 84 percent of the state's pre-kindergarten teachers have at least a four-year college degree, but their pay does not reflect it. The minimum annual salary for certified teachers is $24,912; for those with a four-year college degree and no certification, it is $18,969.[71] Georgia's regular kindergarten teachers start at $27,650.[72]

Making Career Ladders Work

Three features define a full-fledged career ladder. First, the program establishes clear educational qualifications for each rung of a widely recognized ladder of occupations. Second, the distance from one rung to the next is manageable, and the credits required at each level build toward higher credentials or degrees. Third, sufficient funding is allocated to allow permanent wage increases upon the completion of the training specified for each level. In the field of child care and early education, few programs have all three features in place.

The development of consistent national and statewide definitions of child care occupations and their training requirements would be of help to existing and new career-ladder programs. What would this look like? Logically the CDA credential should be the minimum requirement for all child care workers, but that would disqualify many now in the field. Thus states with career-ladder programs have added rungs before the CDA. Washington state has added, as pre-CDA steps, completion of a high school diploma or GED and completion of the more basic STARS program. WAGES Plus does much the same but requires a set number of education units rather than the CDA certificate. In both programs the associate's degree is the next step, and it, too, should be recognized as a next-rung requirement nationwide. Although community-college programs in early-childhood education vary throughout the country, they are sufficiently consistent to include this degree in a common career ladder. The more manageable the educational increments and the more widely recognized the course work, the more workers will be encouraged to continue their education and advance.

Of course, reliable wage increases with each step would be even more encouraging. But here is where the issue becomes most politically fraught.

With parents and child care providers already paying all they can, the question for those trying to raise the quality of American child care and the wages of child care workers is how much government will pay and what kind of system it will pay for.

The annual cost of full-time care for a toddler typically ranges between $4,000 and $10,000, a stretch for many American families.[73] Government (federal, state, and local) funds pay for approximately 39 percent of child care and early-childhood education through full and partial subsidies or through tax credits. The private sector, including businesses and philanthropists, pays for 1 percent. That leaves 60 percent of the nation's child care costs to be borne by families; in contrast, families pay about 35 percent of the cost of a college education (public and private).[74]

This is still true even though government funds for child care have increased substantially since 1990. As a result of welfare reform, federal and state spending on child care doubled between 1997 and 2000. In 2000 the federal government alone spent $6.1 billion on civilian child care, with another $4 billion spent by the states.[75] Nonetheless, as documented above, child care workers remain low paid and untrained, with many centers providing low-quality care. And many families that need affordable child care are not getting it. The U.S. Department of Health and Human Services reports that nationally only 12 percent of eligible children are receiving assistance and attributes this low coverage to lack of federal funding.[76]

To be eligible for a federal subsidy, a family must have income no higher than 85 percent of the state median, adjusted for family size. But most states have set lower caps to stretch limited funds. Seven states cut off eligibility at 40 to 49 percent of median income, thus limiting aid to only the poorest families. To stretch funds further, most states also require co-payments from families, which can make child care unaffordable even with subsidies. At the same time, as we saw in the case of Seattle, states reimburse providers at less than the actual cost of care. Most states pay child care centers at 75 percent of the market rate for paying families, leaving the centers to absorb the remaining 25 percent. As a result, many of the best centers do not accept subsidized children because they cannot maintain quality at the rates the government pays.

The need for more funding is critical, and, expecting nothing further from the federal government, the advocates are looking to the states for funds. That is where the campaign for increased child care spending and fully funded career ladders is now being fought. And its most significant challenge is the ongoing fiscal crisis in most states.

But there is also strong political resistance to using public money to pay for what many people believe is a private good. Former governor

Pete Wilson's justification for vetoing the CARES program in California is illustrative:

> I do not believe it is appropriate for the State of California to provide wage subsidies or otherwise interfere in the private child care market. This bill would introduce state regulation of wages into a field that is currently controlled by the market, and allow direct wage supplements to private sector employees. This may constitute a gift of public funds.[77]

Wilson's sentiment is shared by some childless people who insist that a person's decision to become a parent is a choice that the rest of society should not have to subsidize. The growing "child-free movement" actively opposes what its members see as a redistribution of the nation's wealth through government programs that benefit parents.[78] In this group's view, working parents, particularly mothers, are the consumers of child care and should bear the responsibility of paying for it.

Yet a good case can be made that all of society benefits when children are well cared for.[79] They are, after all, our future. Even in the present, it appears that the benefits of child care spending outweigh the costs. Child care tax credits, for example, more than pay for themselves through the tax revenue (federal, state, and local) generated by working mothers. There is also solid evidence that poor children are disadvantaged in physical, cognitive, and emotional development, that they begin to accrue considerable deficits before they reach school age, and that these disadvantages can be ameliorated or even prevented with enrollment in a high-quality early childhood education program.[80] Several cost-benefit studies of long-term preschool projects around the country have calculated that the reduced need for public expenditure on remedial education and crime produces a return of $7 for every dollar invested in high-quality early education.[81]

A review of seven programs (including some discussed in this chapter) linking wages to increased education and training for child care staff by the Institute for Women's Policy Research (IWPR) found that they had positive outcomes on worker wages, educational levels, and reduction in turnover. To develop, improve, and sustain successful programs, the IWPR recommends higher *starting* salaries; adequate supports for participants (e.g., transportation and child care); ongoing mentoring services; articulation of credits earned toward college degrees; provision of a variety of training and education options; and, of course, sufficient funding to adequately sustain programs.[82]

It is true that to establish even the modest career-ladder initiatives discussed in this chapter required sustained political organizing and advocacy.

It took three years of effort by the Economic Opportunity Institute, SEIU Local 925, and Seattle Worthy Wages to persuade the governor of Washington to fund that state's career ladder. California CARES is the result of twenty years of advocacy by the Center for the Child Care Workforce in collaboration with several child care advocacy organizations and service providers.[83]

But it is also true that these political initiatives eventually did succeed—as did the push to upgrade military child care and the Georgia effort to make public preschools universally available. The staff of the Center for the Child Care Workforce concludes that each such success is "helping to build more effective coalitions of people committed to change."[84] The next chance to judge the public mood on this question may come soon. At the end of 2002 a ballot measure was filed in Massachusetts called Early Education for All. It had the support of a broad coalition of leaders from business, labor, religion, health care, child care, education, and philanthropy, and received $2 million in private donations. In July 2004 a few parts of this original bill were adopted, creating a board and consolidated Department of Early Education and Care. In December 2004 "An Act for Establishing Early Education for All" was filed for the 2005–2006 session. While the campaign faces fiscal challenges, supporters are encouraged by the results of a recent poll indicating that almost 75 percent of Massachusetts voters support the public funding of high-quality early education for all children, and by the co-sponsorship of the bill by 132 Massachusetts senators and representatives, equaling 66 percent of the state legislature.[85]

The economist Barbara Bergmann, an expert in child care financing, argues that child care should be wholly de-privatized and that child care work should be a civil service job with benefits, just like teaching. Bergmann estimates that providing such care for all lower-income families would cost an additional $15 billion a year nationally, beyond the $2 million the public currently provides in the form of income tax breaks to middle-class parents and the $10 billion the government spends on child care for low-income families. Another option, in which parents would pay for child care according to a sliding scale based on income—as is now done in the military—Bergmann estimates would cost the nation about $50 billion.[86]

Although these price tags are high, they are not out of line with what other well-off nations spend. Many European countries have universal systems that link child care and education, a link that our own National Research Council and most child care advocates agree is needed.[87] Sweden and France, among countries with the most comprehensive child care systems, spend about 1.8 and 1 percent of the GDP, respectively, on child care, averaging about $2,000 and $1,000, respectively, per child through age fifteen.[88] Bergmann's $50 billion estimate for a U.S. program would amount to about 0.5 percent of America's GDP.[89] Currently, however, only 0.2 percent of the GDP is spent on child care in the United States.[90]

The United States can afford high-quality, universally accessible day care provided by a fairly paid staff. All that is needed is for voters and elected officials to view it as a priority.

Chapter 4

Education

The nation faces a shortage of experienced teachers in urban and rural schools, and, at the same time, a new wave of concern about the competence of America's teachers.[1] Career-ladder programs have struck many as an answer to both problems. Career ladders that help teacher assistants to further their education can not only upgrade the skills of these paraprofessionals, they can also turn some of them into credentialed teachers.

Thus, while there used to be virtually no possibility of advancement for education paraprofessionals,[2] that is now changing. Since the late 1980s, when teacher shortages emerged as a national problem, career-ladder programs have helped thousands of education paraprofessionals to earn college degrees and teaching certificates. These programs are preparing new teachers who know what they are getting into and, as a result, seem to stay in the field longer than traditionally trained teachers. They also stay longer in hard-to-staff, inner-city schools. Moreover, because so many teacher assistants are members of racial and ethnic minority groups, the career-ladder programs are increasing the diversity of the teacher labor force.

In an effort to improve the quality of teaching, there has also been a recent surge of experimentation with career-ladder and pay-for-performance programs for teachers already certified. These programs offer rewards to teachers who continue their education or demonstrate exemplary skills, rewards such as higher pay or new roles as mentor teachers or both. In this way the programs are meant to ensure that the best teachers do not have to move out of teaching into administration in order to advance. There is still not a consensus about how to design these career ladders for teachers. The experiments are beset with controversies over how to evaluate teaching skills fairly and how to make a system of skill-based advancement compatible with the seniority-based pay that is the mainstay of teacher unions. But given the widespread and long-standing belief in the usefulness of continuing-education and career-advancement programs for education professionals, these experiments are certain to persist and to attract considerable attention. For that reason they are not the focus here.

This chapter, like this book, is concerned instead with career ladders for low-skilled workers, which is a much newer and less examined phenomenon. Neither school officialdom nor the public is entirely convinced that significant skill upgrades are even possible among school paraprofessionals—or worth the money that would have to be spent on education and training. Thus, as the following cases illustrate, one of the major issues facing those who have tried to put paraprofessional career ladders in place is whom they should try to move upward, given limited funds and increasingly higher standards for teachers.

The Need for Training

Paraprofessional-to-Teacher programs provide an environment in which the experience of paraprofessionals is valued and their commitment to students celebrated. In our Transition to Teaching program, paraprofessionals become licensed special education teachers in a context that encourages collaboration. Participants say that this is one of the most rewarding learning opportunities they have ever had.

> CAROL DOHERTY, director, Professional Development
> Program, Northeastern University School of Education

The first teacher-assistant jobs were introduced after World War II, but the number of paraprofessionals began increasing dramatically in the late 1960s as the federal government began requiring and paying for extra attention to certain groups of students. The creation of Head Start in 1965 generated the first big call for teacher aides. The Elementary and Secondary Education Act (ESEA) of 1965 with its Title I funding for schools in poor neighborhoods,[3] the Bilingual Education Act of 1968, and the Individuals with Disabilities Education Act of 1997 each ushered in a new increase in teacher assistants. Today there are 1.3 million of them nationwide.[4] About half of them work in special education programs for the disabled, and it has been estimated that around 18 percent work in Title I programs and 15 percent in bilingual programs. Most of the others work in regular classrooms, the vast majority in elementary schools.[5]

These paraprofessionals perform a variety of support services under the supervision of a teacher. Tasks range from supervising playgrounds and lunchrooms and performing clerical work to providing instructional support such as tutoring, working with students in computer labs, administering tests, and grading tests and homework. On average, paraprofessionals who provide instructional support spend about 60 percent of their time working with small groups and 30 percent with individual children.[6] The remaining 10 percent is spent on non-instructional tasks.

By and large these workers are not impoverished, as are so many health care and child care employees. Figures are hard to come by, in part because paraprofessional jobs in education are called by different names in different school districts, but the best available data indicate that, in 2000, the mean annual salary in this occupation was $18,680,[7] which includes the 43 percent who worked part-time.[8] Moreover, about 40 percent of education paraprofessionals belong to unions. The American Federation of Teachers (AFT) and its New York City affiliate (the United Federation of Teachers [UFT]), the National Education Association (NEA), the Service Employees International Union (SEIU), and many state school employee associations all have paraprofessional units.[9]

Many of these paraprofessionals, however, now find their jobs at risk. The federal No Child Left Behind Act of 2001 requires any school district receiving Title I funds to increase its education qualifications for paraprofessionals. The law gives current teacher assistants until January 2006 to meet the new requirements. Their options are to obtain an associate's (or higher) degree, complete two years of college-level study, or pass a state or local test of their knowledge of reading, writing, or mathematics instruction techniques. This national mandate replaces a hodgepodge of state-level requirements, most of which were minimal,[10] and it has increased these school employees' interest in programs that will further their education.

Educators have other reasons as well to favor ongoing education for paraprofessionals. Most believe that today's teacher assistants need further training in instructional strategies, behavior management, and child development just in order to perform their jobs.[11] Current teacher shortages, combined with an increase in students with special needs, has led to an increased dependence on paraprofessionals, many of whom are now working with little or no supervision.[12] Most do not have the educational background and expertise to assume these responsibilities; currently only 13 percent have bachelor's degrees.[13]

In addition, many educators see teacher assistants as an excellent pool of potential teachers.[14] Paraprofessionals, they say, have classroom experience and know what they are getting into in inner-city schools; many are bilingual; and since most of them are minorities, they could help create a teacher workforce that looks like the students they teach.[15] (About one-third of public school students are nonwhite, but, at present, only 10 percent of teachers are.)[16]

With paraprofessionals, teachers, and school administrators largely in agreement on this, more than half the states and a number of individual school districts have developed programs to encourage teacher assistants to obtain further education, up to and including certification to become full-fledged teachers.[17] Some of these programs merely reimburse tuition costs for paraprofessionals who take college-level courses of any type. However, Recruiting New Teachers, Inc., an organization that promotes strategies for increasing and improving the pool of teachers, estimates that there are currently 149 programs nationally that are focused specifically on preparing paraprofessionals to become teachers. These programs enrolled about nine thousand people—about one-third of them Latino and 29 percent African American.[18] Overall these programs have lower rates of attrition than traditional pathways to teaching. And at a median cost of $3,400 per participant per year, they seem to be achieving their goals efficiently and effectively.[19]

Foundations fund some of these programs, states fund others—most extensively in California, Connecticut, and North Carolina[20]—and several are sponsored by urban school districts, often in cooperation with teachers' unions.[21] Four examples are discussed in the following sections.

Pathways to Teaching Careers: A Foundation-Funded Career Ladder

I'll never forget the words of one principal of a hard-to-staff urban school commenting on the effect of Pathways: "I still can't believe that all it took to transform a good paraprofessional into an excellent teacher was some funding and a little bit of support! Why don't more districts do this?"

BEATRICE CHU CLEWELL, Urban Institute,
Pathways evaluator

The DeWitt Wallace–Reader's Digest Funds launched Pathways to Teaching Careers in 1989 to facilitate entry into the teaching profession along nontraditional routes. The program focused on turning paraprofessionals, career changers, and former Peace Corps volunteers into teachers. Participants agreed to teach in an urban school for two years after receiving their degrees. Before it ended in 2002 the program had provided $50.1 million to forty-two partnerships of colleges and universities and urban school districts. The foundation money was used to pay for program faculty, administrative support, and counseling services. It also was used to pay students at least 80 percent of their tuition costs and to provide other student supports, such as stipends for child care, transportation, and books.

In Pathways programs, 633 paraprofessionals and 1,300 other participants earned teacher certification, at a cost ranging from $14,814 to $22,855 per participant.[22] Because the foundation made participation contingent upon cooperating with the evaluators, Pathways was more rigorously evaluated than most career-ladder programs. And it was found to be an unequivocal success. Pathways increased the national teacher pool by 4.4 percent and increased the number of minority teachers by 14.7 percent. Moreover, Pathways had a 15 percent higher completion rate than traditional college or university teacher-preparation programs. Traditional teacher-credential programs graduate about 60 percent of enrollees, and Pathways graduated 75 percent. Among paraprofessionals, the Pathways completion rate was 67 percent, still well above the traditional rate.

Furthermore, 81 percent of Pathways graduates stayed in teaching for at least three years compared to 71 percent of teachers entering the field straight from college. At the time that the Pathways evaluation was published in 2001, 88 percent of the program's paraprofessional graduates were still teaching in urban districts. Based on PRAXIS,[23] a performance-based tool used to assess teachers' knowledge and performance, those who became teachers through a Pathways program were also, on average, performing better than teachers hired through traditional channels. Principal ratings of teaching effectiveness of paraprofessionals who became teachers through Pathways are significantly higher than those of other novice teachers in their schools.[24]

The evaluators point to several factors in explaining this success. Each program was planned and implemented by a partnership between a college and a local school district, and each college followed its own curriculum to meet state licensure requirements, but the programs did have common elements. All the programs placed a high value on diversity and made sure that their curricula reflected this. All participants worked in the classroom while attending classes, and thus theory and practice were more closely linked than in traditional education programs. The programs also taught innovative instructional practices, which are proving effective in urban schools.

What the evaluators found to be most important for program participants, however, was the high level of support that participants received. The universities and colleges involved in Pathways partnerships developed special services for participants and their families. Introductory sessions explained the program to family members and prepared children and husbands for the reality that their moms and wives would have less time for them (almost all participants were women) and offered suggestions for coping. Family social events created a sense of community and allowed family members to feel that they were part of the process. Counseling was also available for the participants themselves, which was especially critical when their husbands were not supportive and the women participating needed to increase their confidence in their ability to complete the program.

Beatriz Chu Clewell, one of the two lead evaluators of the Pathways programs, cites the willingness of universities to accommodate employed adult students as another important factor. The colleges held classes during the evening or on Saturdays, and kept learning centers and other facilities open during those hours. Some offered longer Friday classes in coordination with school districts that gave paraprofessionals paid release time to take them. In some cases the universities arranged for advanced students from their traditional education programs to replace the paraprofessionals at work on Fridays. This arrangement allowed the university students to fulfill fieldwork requirements and relieved the school districts of the need to find and pay replacements.

One lesson that took about two years to learn was that paraprofessionals with little college experience were unlikely to finish the program. Foundation officers and local program administrators wanted Pathways to be more inclusive, but they found that people with little or no college experience could not complete the course work in a timely fashion while also working. Thus they decided only to accept participants who already had earned 60 college credits. In addition, they instituted a two-stage screening process to ensure that these applicants met university admission criteria and that their academic skills and commitment were adequate to complete college-level work.[25] This change allowed the foundation to achieve its goal of helping as many participants as possible to earn bachelor's degrees during the ten-year grant period.

Another important lesson was that the local partnerships required considerable nurturing. Edward Pauly, director of evaluation at the Wallace–Reader's Digest Funds, points out that while many state universities have working relationships with suburban schools, few had strong relations with urban schools when Pathways began, so it usually took a few years for partnerships to get off the ground. And the partnerships then had to cope with the high levels of turnover that are typical among teachers and administrators in urban schools. This often left programs in the hands of partners with no shared history.

The foundation hoped that when its funding for Pathways ended the program would be institutionalized by the schools involved and replicated elsewhere. The Urban Institute, the think tank that evaluated the program, developed a handbook for states and school districts to use for the purpose.[26] Further, in the program's last year, Wallace–Reader's Digest Funds helped local administrators to write funding proposals to other foundations and government agencies so that they could continue their programs. Clewell estimates that about one-third of the sites obtained the funding to continue. Although many districts requested the manual for developing a Pathways program, there is no information on how many new programs have been started.

In 1997 the federal Department of Education expressed an interest in funding Pathways sites as part of the reauthorization of Title II of the Higher Education Act of 1965. Clewell provided advice on tailoring the program to meet the needs of target populations, including tuition funding, academic advising, mentoring, tutoring, child care, and transportation expenses. In the fall of 1998 Congress reauthorized the Higher Education Act, which appropriated funding under Title II for two types of teacher-quality enhancement grants: $33.4 million for state grants and $9.6 million for teacher-recruitment grants. These recruitment programs replicated the Pathways model. In the fall of 1999 twenty-four state grants and twenty-eight teacher-recruitment grants were funded—the first of several cohorts of programs to be funded under this legislation.[27]

Clewell argues that the federal government should invest more in recruiting and educating paraprofessionals, given the clear evidence that they can become effective teachers. She says that there may be an unconscious bias favoring programs for midlife career changers over those for paraprofessionals, even though there is little data available about the effectiveness of the former.

New York City's Career Training Program: A Career Ladder Designed by School District and Union

New York City's Career Training Program for education paraprofessionals was created in 1970 in contract negotiations between the school district and the United Federation of Teachers. Under this program the district pays the tuition of any teacher assistant who is taking up to 6 college credits per semester and also provides release time for attending classes.[28] In addition, the district pays a stipend of $240 to those who enroll in summer courses worth 6 credits.

The New York City program includes more steps in its career ladder than the Pathways model. Participants receive pay raises and new job titles as they complete education credits and gain experience (see table 4.1). Taking courses, for that reason, is very popular. In a school district with 17,000 paraprofessionals, between 2,500 and 5,000 participate in the Career Training Program in any given semester, according to the Department of Education, and 400 to 600 become teachers every year.

Neither the union nor the school district maintains data on the rate of degree completion in the Career Training Program. But it is possible to arrive at a ballpark picture. The union's Division of Paraprofessionals counts more than 7,000 paraprofessionals who have become teachers through the program since 1970, and union figures suggest that the program has paid for about 250,000 student-semesters over that period. Assuming an average participation rate halfway between the district's figures of 2,500 and 5,000 students per semester, and counting 33 semesters since the program's inception, the total would be 247,500 student-semesters paid for. If every participant started with no previous college credits and took 6 credits per semester, as the program requires, it would take each one 20 semesters, or 10 years, to earn a BA degree (or 7 years if attending 3 semesters per year). Thus training 7,000 teachers would take, at most, 140,000 student-semesters, leaving more than 100,000 student-semesters either in the BA pipeline or unaccounted for. The data suggest, therefore, far more course-taking than degree-earning. It would be worthwhile for the district and

TABLE 4.1
New York City paraprofessional career ladder, 2001

Job Title	Required College Credits and Experience	Base Pay	Number Employed
Teacher	BA	$39,000	
Educational Associate A	90 credits, enrollment in a degree program and 2 years experience as an educational paraprofessional	$26,458	5,409
Educational Associate	HS diploma, 60 credits +2 years of experience as an educational paraprofessional; or 90 credits +1 year experience as an educational paraprofessional	$24,461	3,517
Educational Assistant B	45 credits	$21,389	1,894
Educational Assistant A-II	30 credits	$20,605	1,348
Educational Assistant A-I	15 credits	$20,329	1,176
Educational Assistant	6 credits	$20,048	2,671
Teacher Aide	0 credits	$18,203	639

Source: New York City Department of Education.

union to find out which students are able to obtain degrees—not so they can exclude the others, like Pathways does, but so they can at least see where they need to focus remedial efforts.

Indeed, participants receive the same benefits and pay raises whether they choose to enter a degree-granting program or simply take courses. In terms of inclusiveness, the New York City career ladder is thus the opposite of the Pathways model. Not surprisingly it has rather the opposite set of problems. District officials are concerned, for example, that many program participants may be following a non-degree path not by choice but because they lack career counseling and have little understanding of their other options. In 1994 the Department of Education created the Paraprofessional Academy to remedy this problem. The Academy originally offered a two-course sequence to acquaint paraprofessionals with the basics of the job, each of which counted as the equivalent of 3 credits on the school district's pay scale, but these courses have been cut owing to budget constraints. The Academy provides counselors at a central location in Manhattan who help paraprofessionals and teachers assess their credits and develop personal education plans.[29] The emphasis is on finding degree programs that fulfill individual career goals. To date, there are no data on whether more people are enrolled in degree programs than before the Academy started advising them. The Academy plans to undertake research to determine the impact it has had.

Meanwhile, the debate over the New York City school district's career ladder continues. On one side are those who believe that the program should be about earning credentials. Thalia Moshoyannis, the director of the Paraprofessional Academy, for instance, concedes that the flexibility of the Career Training Program has advantages, but she argues that basing the school district's pay scale on credits earned rather than progress toward a degree emphasizes quantity over quality. And she suggests that not many paraprofessionals can earn degrees because of their life circumstances: "The typical paraprofessional is forty [years old], with two kids and about 30 college credits. To assume that the majority can maintain the B average required to get into most education programs and complete a bachelor's degree at the rate of 6 credits per semester while working and caring for their families is unrealistic." She says that it is not uncommon for paraprofessionals to have earned more than 100 credits without completing any degree requirements. (In general, a BA requires 120 credits, but they have to be in specified courses and departments, and students must maintain a specified grade point average (GPA). For their part, school district officials suspect that many paraprofessionals keep taking lower-level classes in order to avoid having to meet a college's GPA and other requirements. The district sees this as a waste of its funds.

On the other side are those, such as Maria Portalatin, the vice president of the union's Division of Paraprofessionals, who think that all sides benefit if employees take courses of any kind, even in disciplines other than education. Portalatin, moreover, estimates that, although many paraprofessionals do not want to become teachers, they do want to take courses to meet the new requirements of the No Child Left Behind legislation. People in this group, she says, should not be discouraged from taking individual courses. Nor should they be denied opportunities for career advancement short of becoming teachers.

Under the current contract, the DOE pays Career Training benefits (tuition assistance) until the paraprofessional receives a baccalaureate. Participants must matriculate into a degree-granting program after completing 90 credits in order to be placed at maximum pay. New York City's Department of Education is trying to get the union to agree to scale that back and require participants to matriculate into a degree program after completing 60 credits. The union, however, is resisting. Both arguments have merit, but in a time of constrained budgets, it is hard to justify the public's paying for courses that do not have a direct link to classroom practice.

Better integration of the city's four-year and community colleges is needed for those who do want to earn bachelor's degrees. Several CUNY community colleges offer associate's degrees in education or early-childhood education. Both Kingsborough and Queensborough Community Colleges offer 45-credit education degrees, for example, but the credits that transfer to CUNY colleges only transfer as liberal arts electives. Many paraprofessionals take the courses because they think they are working toward a bachelor's degree, when, in fact, only one or two of their education courses will count toward a degree.

But Moyshoyannis questions the assumption that the goal should be for all education paraprofessionals to become teachers. For many, an associate's degree is a sufficient credential. Requiring the associate's degree for some would establish a degree of professionalism and respect that does not currently exist in this occupation. The problem, of course, is that the district could not afford to start the majority of education paraprofessionals with the salary a degree would command, given that $18,200 is the current starting pay for someone with no college credits. About 70 percent of the district's paraprofessionals are above the Ed Associate A level, so it would be quite costly to raise salaries even more than the program offers.

California's Paraprofessional Teacher Training Program:
A State-Funded Career Ladder

Most of the people who start as paraprofessionals fell in love and got married or had children rather than going to school. The career ladder gives them a second chance to build a career.

YETIVE LOWERY, paraprofessional turned teacher,
Los Angeles

California's School Paraprofessional Teacher Training Program (PTTP) was created by the state legislature in 1990 in order to address a shortage of bilingual and special education teachers, increase the diversity of the teacher labor force, and improve the quality of instruction offered in the state's schools. The program is open to all paraprofessionals, from those with no previous college credits to those who already have a bachelor's degree in a discipline other than education. The program helps participants pay for tuition, certification fees, books, and child care, and also offers tutoring for state examinations. Regardless of the participant's previous education, PTTP supports all his or her training until full teacher certification is achieved. In California, certification requires completion of a bachelor's degree, a local district's one-year Professional Preparation program, and a period of supervised teaching. Teachers also have to pass a test of skills.[30]

The PTTP is a collaborative effort between the state, local school districts, and the various union locals representing paraprofessionals. The state provides the funding. School districts can contribute additional money of their own, but to make it possible for the poorest districts to participate, the state does not require local matching funds.[31] The school districts are responsible for developing programs to meet their specific needs, but they must follow state guidelines. All local programs must, for instance, require participants to complete a minimum number of credits each quarter or semester and to continue working as paraprofessionals while going to school. After becoming fully credentialed, participants must teach one year in the school district for each year of financial aid received. Those who do not fulfill this part of their contract must repay their grants. Each local PTTP is also required by law to establish a career ladder, defined as a developmentally sequenced series of jobs—most including salary increases—which lead from an entry-level paraprofessional position to an entry-level teaching position. The specifics of each district's ladder are negotiated with the union.

Although the PTTP legislation passed in 1990, the state did not fund it until 1994, when a meager $1.478 million a year was allocated to serve no more than a total of 600 participants in thirteen districts. However, the program proved a success at the thirteen initial sites, and the California legislature voted in 1999 to add another $10 million to the annual budget, which increased the number of programs to forty-two and brought the number of participants up to 2,266 by 2002.[32] This reauthorization measure also capped the state's per-participant expenditure at $3,000 per year, which in California is almost enough to cover tuition, the cost of books, and fees at a community college or at one of the twenty-two campuses of the state university. This funding is available to students until they finish, provided they are making satisfactory progress. Participants who choose to attend private colleges or the University of California must pay the difference themselves, or with other grants or tuition assistance.

This per-participant limit does not seem to have harmed the program. By the summer of 2003 the number of fully credentialed program completers stood at 829.[33] Unfortunately statewide completion rates for the program are not available, making it difficult to assess California's success in making all paraprofessionals eligible to become teachers. Those who do complete the program seem to stay in the field. An October 2002 report by the state PTTP director Marilynn Fairgood found that the retention rate after five years was 97 percent.[34] Fairgood, who is also a consultant with the California Commission on Teacher Credentialing, attributes this extraordinary retention rate to the fact that paraprofessionals have been in the classroom for years prior to becoming teachers and know exactly what the job entails. The program is also achieving its goal of increasing diversity in the field. Some 85 percent of the new teachers belong to racial or ethnic minorities, and 65 percent are bilingual.[35]

The largest of the local PTTPs is the one in the Los Angeles Unified School District (LAUSD). Yet even prior to the establishment of PTTPs and the availability of state funds, LAUSD had begun on its own to address the training of paraprofessionals, setting up the LAUSD Paraeducator Career Ladder Program. The district's paraprofessionals' union, SEIU Local 99, approached the L.A. Board of Education in 1993 and asked that a labor-management committee be formed to investigate implementing a career-ladder program locally, instead of waiting for the state to start funding the PTTP initiative. The board agreed, and within three months the committee had developed a training matrix that described the education that needed to be completed and the skills that had to be mastered at each step along a ladder from entry-level paraprofessional to certified teacher (see table 4.2). The school board allocated $1 million to the program for the next fiscal year (1993–1994); funding has decreased over the years and currently stands at about $600,000. (This LAUSD

TABLE 4.2
Los Angeles Unified School District's teacher-training matrix

Level	Educational Benchmarks	Performance Area	California Standard for the Teaching Profession
5	Completion of BA or BS Enrollment in a teacher education program	5a Student teaching	Comprehensive review of all of the standards
4	90 semester units or 135 quarter units	4a Delivery of lesson plan prepared by teacher and participant	Planning and organizing learning experiences
3	60 semester units or 90 quarter units University enrollment Declaration of major, specialty, and grade level	3b Introduction to lesson planning 3a Instructional assistance	Understanding and organizing subject matter
2	12 semester units or 18 quarter units	2b Behavior management 2a Student supervision	Creating and maintaining effective environments
1	High school diploma	1c Knowledge of programs and policies 1b Communication skills 1a Basic classroom organization	Developing as a professional educator

Source: Los Angeles Unified School District.

Paraeducator Career Ladder Program is run alongside, but separately from, the local PTTP.)

The money is used to partially reimburse participants for their tuition and other education costs, as well as to provide advisement services. Unlike a full-fledged career ladder, the program offers participants no pay raises for moving through the levels, only the substantial raise when they become teachers. The director of the L.A. program, Steve Brandick, explains that it would be difficult to connect pay raises to the district's more than one hundred job classifications for paraprofessionals. LAUSD paraprofessionals earn between $9 and $18 an hour—or an annual $14,040 to $28,080 if they work full-time[36]—depending on job class and seniority. As teachers, they start at about $40,000 plus benefits.

There is no way to know if the failure to connect interim pay raises to educational progress has discouraged participation in the L.A. program. The program supports everyone who applies.[37] Currently, of the district's fifteen thousand paraprofessionals, about four hundred are receiving full scholarships and another fifteen hundred are partially supported. The scale of this program is second only to Pathways in New York City.

Participants and staff say that the program's specialized support services are essential to its success. LAUSD pays for advisement services at four California State University campuses.[38] These services were added because it was found that students lacked access to advisers at both community colleges and universities, as well as access to adequate information on courses at community colleges.[39] For example, some participants had even completed an associate's degree in child development before finding out that only two of their courses would transfer toward a BA in education. One of the goals of the career-ladder advisers is to ensure that participants' community college credits transfer to degree programs.

But part of the explanation for the success of the L.A. program may also be the decision to concentrate the program's resources on its more advanced students. In the early years, career-ladder staff noticed a trend that had also been evident in the Pathways program: students who entered the program with no previous college credits rarely finished. As several staffers told me, people with no college experience had to figure out how to "do" college at the same time that they were trying to balance work, family, and school, and for a period of many years. Apparently it was too difficult for most. The staff concluded that paraprofessionals entering at Level 3 or 4 of the Los Angeles district matrix who had had the equivalent of two or more years of college classes were more likely to complete the program. Thus, while the LAUSD Career Ladder Program awards scholarships to both community college and university students, more funding is provided to those who reach or begin the program at Level 3, as college juniors. The per-unit reimbursements increase with the number of credits already earned and the number of credits taken per quarter or semester (see table 4.3). The district claims that this reimbursement schedule motivates students to complete their degrees more quickly.

In 2003 the cost of tuition at a California community college for state residents was $11 per unit (students typically take thirty units per year, making the annual total $330). The cost at a California State University campus is approximately $2,500 per year.[40] The L.A. program's stipends, therefore, cover a significant portion of community college tuition (particularly for students taking seven or more units per semester). University tuition is more expensive, and the reimbursement (although more for students in levels 3 through 5) does not cover a sizable portion of it.

Tight funding is one reason why the L.A. school district has taken this approach. The district allocated $1 million for its paraprofessional career-ladder program in FY1994, but the amount dropped to $900,000 in FY1995,

TABLE 4.3
Los Angeles Unified School District's tuition reimbursement schedule: Per-unit stipend each term

Training Matrix Level	Total Units Taken in a Semester		Total Units Taken in a Quarter	
	1–6	7 or more	1–8	9 or more
5	$30.00	$60.00	$20.00	$40.00
4	$25.00	$50.00	$17.00	$33.00
3	$20.00	$40.00	$13.50	$26.50
2	$8.00	$10.00	$5.50	$7.00
1	$5.00	$7.00	$3.50	$4.75

Source: Los Angeles Unified School District's Career Ladder Program.

when state money became available, and it stayed at that level through FY2001. In 2002, owing in part to local effects of the state's fiscal crisis, the school district reduced its contribution to $600,000, where it currently stands. Thus constancy is not an attribute of this program.

On the other hand, the tuition reimbursement schedule does seem to be a reasonable middle ground between the exclusivity of the Pathways model and the inclusivity of the New York City career ladder. By the end of the 2002–2003 school year, 2,503 participants in the L.A. program had become teachers.[41] The five-year retention rate for teachers hired through the program was 87 percent, and the eight-year retention rate was 83 percent (see table 4.4). By comparison, it has been estimated that 30 percent of *all* new teachers in L.A. quit within three years.[42] Brandick reports that some of the earlier graduates are now moving into administrative positions.

Participants in the Los Angeles PTTP have come to teaching on a variety of paths. One program graduate whom I interviewed, Raquel Shepard, had been working as an administrative assistant in private industry and had been laid off three times in six years because of corporate mergers. She started taking classes at a community college and was searching for a new occupation that would provide a decent salary, benefits, and more time with her two young children, when she discovered the L.A. school district's paraprofessional career ladder on the Internet. She got a job as a special education trainee, working with students who have moderate to severe disabilities, and immediately enrolled in the career-ladder program.

Although Shepard's pay as a trainee, at $13.78 an hour with no benefits, was less than she had earned at her previous job, she signed up because the trainee position was the first rung on the education career ladder. The

TABLE 4.4
Los Angeles Unified School District's career ladder program retention rate for paraprofessionals
who become teachers, 1994–2002

Years since Certification	First Year of Teaching	Program Completers Hired		Program Completers Who Left the District		Retention Rate (%)
		No.	%	No.	%	
8	1994–95	12	100.0	2	16.7	83.3
7	1995–96	115	100.0	15	13.0	87.0
6	1996–97	260	100.0	37	14.2	85.8
5	1997–98	357	100.0	46	12.9	87.1
4	1998–99	421	100.0	56	13.3	86.7
3	1999–2000	404	100.0	34	8.4	91.6
2	2000–1	334	100.0	29	8.7	91.3
1	2001–2	339	100.0	9	2.7	97.3
Total		2242	100.0	228	10.2	0.0

Source: Los Angeles Unified School District's Career Ladder Program.

job also allowed her to experience several different special education settings and arrive at a sense of the type of classroom she wanted to teach in.
She chose a four-year college that accepted most of her community college
credits. She was able to finance her education completely by combining the
career-ladder stipend with a federal Pell grant for low-income students, a
Cal State University grant, and a grant from an education foundation that
pays back $2,000 per year for up to four years to teachers who commit to
teaching in an economically deprived school.

Shepard started the career-ladder program in 1999 and received her
bachelor's degree in 2001. She passed the California Basic Education Skills
Test, took a job as a teacher, and entered the school district's Intern Program
for teachers who are not yet fully certified.[43] The beginning intern salary
was $34,853 with full benefits. Interns teach full-time and attend evening
training sessions and weekend discussion groups. It takes three years in the
Intern Program to become certified, compared to two to three semesters
as a traditional, full-time student.[44] Shepard has almost reached that point;
she is teaching in special education and says that she never would have
known that working with high-needs kids was so rewarding if she had not
experienced it as a trainee.

José Rodríguez completed his degree in less than two years and, like
many program participants, took a teaching job at the school where he was
working as a paraprofessional. As a new teacher, he enrolled in the LA

Unified District Intern Program, an alternative pathway to certification. Teachers of the same grade work together in cohorts for the three-year program. They teach full-time, attend a four-hour weekly evening session, and meet on some Saturdays to discuss their practice. Rodríguez comments that placing teachers in cohorts creates a sense of comradery. "Everyone becomes disillusioned at some point in the first two years," he notes, "and having people to talk to who are going through the same thing helped most of us get through it." The internship qualified Rodríguez for the Bilingual Cross-cultural Language and Academic Development certificate. He has gone from earning $8 per hour without benefits to an annual salary of $41,000 with benefits.[45] After five years of teaching, Rodríguez was appointed the Bilingual Coordinator at his school.

Different elements of the L.A. program seem to appeal to different participants. Child care was essential to Shepard. Her children attended the campus day care facility while she attended classes. Other students I talked to cited the specialized advising and the exam-preparation course paid for by the career-ladder program. Yetive Lowery spoke of the support group arranged by the program. "As soon as we started meeting we felt like family," she recalled. "Most of our husbands didn't understand our going to school. It made them feel insecure." Group members studied together, helped one another with child care, and provided encouragement.

In this respect Lowery was fortunate. L.A.'s large program, with students enrolled in many different colleges, often does not have enough students at any given campus to maintain a support group. Program staff tried to overcome this problem by organizing support groups geographically by where participants live, but because participants who lived in the same area were teaching in different schools and attending different colleges, they did not achieve the same sense of community that cohort- or school-based support groups have, according to Brandick. Nowadays, instead of support groups, the school district offers mini conferences four times a year to advise program participants on curricular and other issues associated with managing family, work, and school.

Mentoring is another way to create a supportive learning environment, and in L.A. some former students who are now teaching have become mentors, or "career-ladder facilitators," to current participants. Mentors are paid an annual stipend to encourage paraprofessionals to enter the program and to support them when they do.[46] Lowery is now a career-ladder leader in her school. Shepard volunteers at quarterly career-ladder recruitment forums. Perhaps it is the sheer variety of supports tried in L.A. that has made this program so successful.

Project PET and Project Nobel: Career Ladders for Teachers of Bilingual Students

In many cases immigrants working as paraprofessionals are more experienced than the teachers they work under. They are an untapped resource in addressing shortages in bilingual education.

ELLEN RINTELL, professor of education,
Salem State College

The Los Angeles program tries to be everything to everyone. In Massachusetts, Project PET (ParaEducator to Teacher) takes the opposite tack, tailoring a career ladder to a narrow group. PET was started in 1999 by Ellen Rintell, an education professor at Salem State College in Massachusetts, who discovered that many paraprofessionals in the area's public schools had been teachers in Latin American countries before moving to the United States. Knowing of the shortage of bilingual teachers in cities served by the college, Rintell decided to match supply to demand. She applied for and received a five-year $1.3 million grant from the U.S. Department of Education, which at the time was funding such efforts. And she set out to prepare twenty-five Latina paraprofessionals to become certified bilingual and ESL teachers, and another twenty-five to obtain master's degrees in fields such as reading and special education. With a second grant obtained in 2000, she was able to start Project Nobel, adding a new cohort of twenty-four undergraduate paraprofessionals and twenty-six graduate in-service teachers.[47] While participants in this second program were trained as teachers of bilingual students, they themselves were no longer required to be bilingual—therefore a portion of this new population was U.S.-born.

Applicants for Project PET were recruited through the school system. School principals and partners of the school system were contacted in order to reach out to paraeducators who were bilingual in Spanish and English. Preference was then given to applicants who had had some college.

Both programs pay tuition and a small stipend for six courses per year per student; most students take two courses each semester and another two during the summer. Undergraduate courses cost about $500 per three-credit course and graduate courses are about $650. In addition, students receive $150 per semester toward books. ESL courses are offered, if needed, before enrolling in college-level classes. Twelve of the original twenty-five paraprofessionals took ESL courses twice a week for two semesters before enrolling in regular undergraduate courses. Students take undergraduate and graduate classes in the evening education program offered through the Division of Continuing Education.[48]

An important aspect of the programs is the sense of community they create among students. Each class is invited to a banquet at which all students are given a gift with the college logo and program name. Whether a briefcase, a sweatshirt, or a portfolio, the item builds a feeling of kinship among students. A seminar that meets every other Saturday orients students to the campus and support services. Students in the seminar hold study sessions and help one another get through the program. Several students related the ways in which the group became like family: they helped one another by sharing books and materials and provided child care or transportation.

Although mentoring was intended to be a key program component, few paraprofessionals have worked with mentors because many of them change schools almost yearly, sometimes in the middle of the school year, making it difficult to establish a relationship with a teacher. Rintell is changing the focus by matching students from the first cohort as mentors to students in the second cohort. (The PET program at Salem State College in Massachusetts started out by using teachers as mentors. When this did not work out because paraprofessionals moved from schools too frequently to establish long-term relationships with teachers, advanced students in the program were asked to become mentors.)

Participants often have difficulty with the literacy and communication section of the Massachusetts Test for Educational Licensure (MTEL), which became a requirement for certification after the Salem State College PET program started. The exam, particularly the literacy and communication section, is rigorous and especially difficult for non-native English speakers. In response, Rintell added an MTEL preparatory course geared to non-native speakers. Without grant funds for these classes, fewer paraprofessionals would achieve certification. Even with the extra preparation, several paraprofessionals did not pass the exam. Thus, for Project Nobel, which was funded with the second grant, Rintell only accepted students with 45 college credits (which could have been earned in their native countries) who are recommended by administrators in their school.[49] Moreover, because of the institution of this exam, Project Nobel, in contrast to Project PET, did not require participants to be bilingual. According to Rintell, the MTEL "is really excluding anyone who speaks English as a second language" from becoming a teacher.[50]

The goal of both programs, according to Rintell, was to accept as many people as possible who had had some college so that they could come closer to graduating. After the five-year grant term, a no-cost extension will be available to cover tuition only.

To date, five paraprofessionals have completed degrees and become teachers. Only two students have left the program, and the rest are still working on their bachelor's degrees. Nine students have finished master's programs, and the rest remain in the program. In the first three years of the program for which data are available, the average grade point average among PET participants was 3.27.[51]

What Makes Education Career Ladders Work

If success is measured by the percentage of participants who complete a course of education and stay on in their districts as teachers, then all four of the programs discussed in this chapter are successful. If measured by the percentage of district paraprofessionals who further their education, the success of these programs is more mixed. The New York City Paraprofessional Career Ladder is the only program among the four discussed here—and one of only a few in the country—that is available to all paraprofessionals and provides substantial raises for completing college credits regardless of whether they lead to a teaching degree. The California career ladder is supposed to be open to all paraprofessionals, but because of limited funding there are waiting lists in most districts to join the program.[52] And in Los Angeles the program concentrates its resources and attention on those who will become teachers. Course work to improve the practice of paraprofessionals plainly *can* be part of a career ladder, but to this day few districts seem to be pursuing this.

For paraprofessionals, successful advancement programs have characteristics quite similar to those in health care and child care: flexibility, learning communities, screening of applicants, and stable funding.

Flexibility

Paraprofessionals in career-ladder programs who are balancing work, family, and school need scheduling flexibility. In almost all the programs, colleges offered evening and weekend classes to accommodate work schedules. Even more important are learning centers, open during nontraditional hours, where students receive guidance counseling, tutoring, financial aid counseling, and other support services. Another strategy that has been effective is alternating semesters so that paraprofessionals can work full-time one semester and go to school full-time the next. This schedule allows them to incorporate what they are learning into their practice, and also relieves the pressure of trying to manage work, home, and school simultaneously.

Creating a Learning Community

It has become apparent in many community-college programs targeted to low-income workers that students who are part of a cohort or community are more likely to finish.[53] Learning communities can be formal support groups with regular meetings organized by the college or informal networks. Although many women have to drop out at various points, members of support groups help their friends determine when they are just temporarily overwhelmed and need encouragement versus truly needing to take time off. And having a learning community member stay in touch increases the chances that a participant who has left the program temporarily will return. Further, as reported by students in the Salem State College program in Massachusetts, members of the groups help one another with child care and transportation—two of the biggest problems students confront when trying to continue their education.

Salem State and other colleges provide outreach to family members as well as students. In these orientation sessions, family members are told that they may not be getting the kind of attention they are used to and are advised on how to be supportive rather than resentful. Participants often report that pride in being a role model for their children helps them to persevere in the program.

Mentoring is another way to create a supportive learning environment. As noted above, when the use of teachers as mentors in the PET program at Salem State College did not work out because paraprofessionals moved from schools too frequently to establish long-term relationships with the teachers, advanced students in the program were asked to become mentors. Similarly participants in the Los Angeles career-ladder program are mentored by former students who have become teachers. Whether through a support group or by means of a teacher or student mentor, having a dependable source of advice, counseling, and inspiration available to participants is what makes career-ladder programs work.

Screening Applicants

Career ladders for paraprofessionals have two objectives: to create better-trained paraprofessionals and to encourage paraprofessionals to become teachers. Of course, it may be unrealistic for those with little college experience to finish college. Many program directors admit that they were most successful when they did more intensive screening to ensure that participants would complete their programs. Although they would like to include every motivated applicant, the pathway is simply too long for those with few or no college credits. Without any knowledge of what college course work is like, these students have a more difficult time managing work and school. Most of the forty-two sites in the Wallace–Reader's Digest Funds Pathways to Teaching program found that paraprofessionals who had fewer than 60 college credits when they started the program were unlikely to complete their degree requirements. Likewise, at Salem State College, Ellen Rintell had to establish more stringent selection criteria because paraprofessionals starting with few college credits were having difficulty completing the program and passing the MTEL. Now students are required to have 45 college credits and to be recommended by administrators in their school. The many paraprofessionals in her program who are from Latin America can include college credits from their home countries by having their transcripts evaluated through an international education documentation center.

Screening does not necessarily rule out the possibility of advancement. Not all paraprofessionals want to be teachers, but most would welcome opportunities to increase their skills and pay. The New York City Paraprofessional Career Ladder is one of few that is available to all paraprofessionals and provides substantial raises for completing college credits regardless of whether this leads to a teaching degree. Although the United Federation of Teachers and the Department of Education debate as to whether more rigid criteria should be placed on course taking, the point is that course work to improve practice can be part of a career ladder.

Preparation for Licensing Exams

Students in all the programs cited assistance in taking licensing exams as essential to their passing. While the Massachusetts Test of Educational Licensure is appropriately rigorous, the literacy and communication sections are especially difficult for non-native English speakers. In response, as mentioned above, Rintell added an MTEL preparation course geared to non-native speakers to the Salem State University paraprofessional program. In Los Angeles, paraprofessionals noted that courses in test-taking skills were most important in enabling them to pass certification exams. Many colleges and universities offer test-preparation courses for traditional graduates; these are even more essential to paraprofessionals.

Stable Funding

The funding needed to run these programs is still unclear. The cost of the Wallace–Reader's Digest initiative ranged from $14,814 to $22,855 per participant. The California PTTP is capped at only $3,000, which is considerably less, yet both programs have comparable retention rates. Having a private foundation behind an initiative is clearly an advantage, but a district must think ahead about what to do when funding expires since only about one-third of the Wallace–Reader's Digest sites were able to obtain funding after the foundation project ended. Advancement for paraprofessionals who either are unlikely or do not want to become professionals appears to be the first thing sacrificed when funds are limited.

The Future of Paraprofessional Career Ladders

Almost every paraprofessional-to-teacher program seems to produce a higher percentage of teachers, and a higher percentage who stay in the field, than traditional teacher-training programs do. Therefore if states and school districts experiencing shortages are serious about creating the teacher labor force they need—in terms of size, quality, and racial and ethnic diversity—funding for such programs ought to be found. Exactly what the programs aim to achieve remains to be worked out.

The key question is under what circumstances should paraprofessionals be given pay raises: for taking courses that improve their performance, for earning an associate's degree, or only for completing a bachelor's degree and becoming a certified teacher. The New York City UFT views paraprofessional education differently than does SEIU Local 99 in Los Angeles. The New York program is an education benefit that may be used for pursuing education credits in any field, although most paraprofessionals use it to complete degrees in education. SEIU Local 99 only supports the state and L.A. programs that offer support for pursuing a teaching career. The key difference is that the New York UFT offers an education benefit as part of its collective bargaining agreement, whereas SEIU supports an explicit career ladder. Given the fiscal crisis facing most districts, it seems unlikely that they will be able to continue supporting education benefits that do not explicitly ease teacher shortages.

At some level this question has already been answered by the No Child Left Behind legislation, which requires paraprofessionals to have associate's degrees or the equivalent by 2006. But for those who are between associate's and bachelor's degrees, the debate on whether to base pay on performance or on seniority and achieving the next credential will be ongoing, as it is for teachers.

Chapter 5

Biotechnology

If any industry epitomizes the new economy it is the biotechnology industry. Biotechnology involves the manipulation of cellular and genetic structures for applications in medicine, animal health, agriculture, marine life management, and environmental management.[1] In 2003 the biotechnology industry employed only 191,000 people in 1,457 companies nationally. But it is expanding, and it is important. Indeed, biotechnology is expected eventually to have as great an impact on society as the advent of electric power or computers. No wonder virtually every state in the union includes this industry among those it wants to encourage.

And another attraction is that the manufacturing side of the industry is likely to take off over the next decade, as more and more research and development operations reach the stage of winning product approval from the U.S. Food and Drug Administration (FDA).[2] With manufacturing should come a wave of new, high-paying jobs with good advancement potential not only for highly educated research workers but also for workers without a college degree. In North Carolina, one of the few places that keeps statistics on this issue, about 75 percent of the production-floor workforce in biomanufacturing has only a high school diploma.[3]

Biotechnology is also part of a broad industrial cluster that includes manufacturers of pharmaceuticals and medical devices,[4] and medical device manufacturers, in turn, are linked to manufacturers of electronic goods, precision metal components, and plastics.[5] Firms in these businesses seek—and create markets for—many of the same support services and amenities, so they benefit from being near one another. A region with a strong biotechnology industry is thus likely to attract and keep a range of well-paying jobs.

But if this is the jackpot, only a few regions are likely to win it, for very few regions have significant concentrations of biotech R&D activity, and

logic suggests that these are also best positioned to capture the manufacturing end of the business since proximity to R&D is essential for refining
the production process, especially in its early years. Moreover, even if most
companies would prefer to diversify their locations, those states that win
the first biomanufacturing plants will have a real advantage in keeping them
and winning the next. That is because permitting by the FDA is site-
specific, so firms are unlikely to close or relocate a plant once it has passed
the lengthy FDA-approval process. And once regulators grant such a
permit, they are more likely to grant a second in the same place.[6]

There are other factors, too, that ought to temper many states' enthusiasm for biotechnology. My interviews with employers and workers suggest
that biomanufacturing companies are more open than most to hire nontraditional job candidates, such as displaced workers from other industries.
(Particularly prized are displaced workers from other government-
regulated manufacturing businesses.) This could present unusual opportunities in whatever states are lucky enough to snag these companies. But
there is also a floor here. Even entry-level workers in biomanufacturing
need to understand basic science and mathematics related to the industry,
and even the bottom rungs of biomanufacturing work are likely to require
specialized skills, often ones that are company-specific. As a result, any state
trying to train workers for this new industry will find that the undertaking
is very costly. Specialized training facilities are required, and they are expensive to build, to operate, and to staff.

Meanwhile, although the payoff may be grand when a biotech company
succeeds, not all of them will. According to one expert in the field, it takes
about fifteen years, on average, to bring a drug to market, at a typical cost
of about $304 million (in 1996 dollars).[7] About 80 percent of drugs in early
trials never get that far,[8] and only about 30 percent of drugs that do make
it to market produce profits higher than their R&D costs.[9] The state of the
economy will further aggravate this already volatile situation, as we saw in
the 1999 recession, when the biotech industry was hit hard and its projected
job growth was stalled by at least several years.

In brief, states that court the biotech industry with the usual entice-
ments—job-training programs, tax abatements, venture capital, and other
incentives to reduce a new company's start-up costs—are taking a big risk.
And, in most cases, it probably is not a smart one. Three-fourths of the
largest biotechnology firms are concentrated in just nine metropolitan
areas,[10] and most of the growth in the industry is happening in just four.[11]
The Boston area has the largest concentration of biotechnology activity in
the country, followed by San Francisco and San Diego. North Carolina
is quickly developing its own concentration, mostly centered in the Raleigh-

Durham–Chapel Hill area, known as the Research Triangle. In most other places, the chances of luring biotech jobs on a scale sufficient to justify the cost of competing for them seem to be slim.

But even where biomanufacturing has a very good chance of taking off, what (if anything) should states and localities be doing to encourage it? And, in particular, what should they be doing to ensure that biomanufacturing jobs offer the good advancement prospects that everyone expects of this industry—and also to ensure that these good jobs are available to those in greatest need of them? In other words, how much money and effort should the states and localities invest in creating accessible career ladders in biomanufacturing?

These are difficult questions to answer at this time. Biomanufacturing is such a new industry that our knowledge of how it will be organized is slim. The Mass Biotechnology Council has put together a chart (table 5.1) describing what seem to be the four basic types of production workers in a biomanufacturing plant—facilities technicians, aseptic fill technicians, instrumentation and calibration technicians, and manufacturing techni- cians—and the education generally required to obtain these jobs.

Within these technician occupations, workers can usually advance from Level 1 to 2 to 3 as they gain education (usually in-house training) and expe- rience with a specific manufacturing process. But if North Carolina's sta- tistics about educational levels in biotechnology jobs are any indication, there is little room for further advancement without a bachelor's degree.[12] In theory, technicians can become team leaders or shift supervisors; and with an associate's degree, they should be able to move from blue-collar to "white-coat" jobs in the laboratory or make lateral moves into a company's quality control, quality assurance, and validation divisions. But it is not at all clear whether, in reality, certificate programs or even associate's degrees would offer significant opportunities for advancement.

Biomanufacturing plants generally have a category of less-skilled employees one rung below the basic technician positions. These are mate- rials handlers, who take care of inventory-type jobs. These workers receive, collect, and distribute materials to the various departments; wrap materials for safe transportation and storage; stacks items for inventory; and maintain inventory records. Theoretically they, too, can advance with experience and training—for instance, into technician positions. But perhaps because so many facilities are so new, such advances seem to be even less common than advances for technicians.

In fact, our hopes for biomanufacturing are largely based on what we know about advancement and employment stability on the R&D side of this industry, where employee commitment to companies is relatively high and

TABLE 5.1
Biotechnology technician job descriptions

Position	Responsibilities	Entry-Level Education
Facilities Technician	Monitors, repairs, and performs preventive maintenance on systems and equipment; documents repairs and may suggest changes to Standard Operating Procedures	AA/AS degree in mechanical/electrical field or high school diploma and 5 years of experience
Aseptic Fill Technician	Assists in operating and maintaining production systems; sets up and operates labeling and packaging equipment	AS (preferred) or Biomanufacturing Certificate; 1–2 years of experience; knowledge of regulations
Instrumentation/ Calibration Technician	Maintains, tests, troubleshoots, and repairs circuits, components, analytical equipment, and instrumentation; calibrates instrumentation and performs validation studies; requires continuous monitoring of equipment	AS in electronics technology or related field; 2–4 years of experience; GMP experience
Manufacturing Technician	Assists in specific production-related operations in cell culture/fermentation; operates and maintains production equipment (e.g., fermenters, bioreactors, cell harvest and separation operations); weighs, measures, and checks raw materials	High school diploma; Biomanufacturing Certificate

Source: Mass Biotechnology Council, http://www.bio-link.org/pdf/JobDes.pdf.

advancement common,[13] even though employees do not expect or want to stay with the same company for their entire career. An intensive study of biotech R&D companies by the late Susan C. Eaton found that "careers in biotechnology are not linear, but they do as a rule appear to provide opportunity for growth and movement up a shifting hierarchy of job titles and responsibilities."[14] But we simply do not know if the same culture of opportunity will or can exist on the manufacturing side.

This chapter looks at the three states with the greatest employment in biotechnology—California, Massachusetts, and North Carolina—each one committed to luring biomanufacturing firms, in part by providing them the trained workforce they need. California and Massachusetts got their start as biotech centers because of the strength of their research universities and not through the efforts of state economic development agencies. North Carolina, on the other hand, although its universities have also been a magnet of sorts, has won its spot among the top three more by dint of aggressive state and local economic-development strategies. But all three are now competing to land the manufacturing side of the industry as it develops. And each of the three, although in quite different ways, is emphasizing career ladders in its strategy. Common to all three is that the community college is at the core of their education and training efforts.

Because definitions of biotechnology have not been refined, it is difficult to draw an accurate picture of how many people the industry employs (see table 5.2). Numbers reported by one source can be quite different from those reported by another. As one California report stated,

> Determining the number of Californians employed in non-farm bioindustry is difficult. Industry classifications overlap in areas such as medical device, pharmaceutical, agricultural, process development, and health care. The definitions of a biotechnology employee also vary widely. Further, not all companies have converted from the Standard Industrial Classification (SIC) Codes to the new North American Industry Classification System (NAICS). Some entities that count biotechnology and bioindustry employees have not yet made use of NAICS codes.[15]

What is clear is that employment is concentrated in the three states and in one or two cities in each state.

This chapter examines career-ladder efforts, although it is too early to say much about their results. So far California is in the lead in biotech employment, and the other two states are neck and neck for second place. (Over the past five years the number of biomanufacturing jobs has grown faster in North Carolina than in Massachusetts—with 15 percent growth in North Carolina and 10 percent in Massachusetts—while Massachusetts started from a larger base and continues to have many more employees in the industry.)[16] More instructive at this juncture is to examine the approaches the three states are trying out and the additional questions their efforts are raising.

North Carolina

Some biopharmaceutical industry observers project that manufacturing capacity will need to increase significantly just to take care of new biopharmaceuticals now waiting for approval. North Carolina is poised to attract as much of this new manufacturing capacity as possible. The key to doing so is equipping our community colleges and universities to train this workforce.

Window on the Workplace 2003, report by the North Carolina Biotechnology Center

TABLE 5.2
Biotechnology, medical device, and pharmaceutical industry employment

	United States	Massachusetts	California	North Carolina	Boston	San Diego	San Francisco	Raleigh-Durham
Biotechnology								
companies	1,473[a]	275[b]	2,500[c]	180[d]	141	94	800[e]	72
employees	198,300[f]	26,329[g]	61,120[h]	18,500[i]	25,000[j]	11,697	13,000[k]	5,371[l]
Medical Devices								
companies	12,000[m]	264[n]				160[o]	100[p]	
employees	335,800[q]	20,756[r]	77,526[s]	17,360	12,180	4,910[t]	30,982[u]	
Pharmaceuticals								
companies	710[v]	57[w]	120[x]	25[y]	67	77	74[z]	19
employees	115,781[aa]	5,612[bb]	78,400[cc]	5,960	10,070[dd]	11,302	27,687[ee]	3,679

Note: Data are for different years, based on data availability, as indicated in the notes to the table.

[a] http://www.bio.org
[b] http://www.massbio.org
[c] http://www.bio.org/events/2004/media/cabio.asp
[d] http://www.ncbiotech.org/ncindustry/quickfacts/quickfacts.cfm
[e] http://www.bio.org/events/2004/media/sfbirth.asp
[f] http://www.bio.org/speeches/pubs/er/statistics.asp
[g] http://www.tbf.org/indicators/technology/indicators.asp?id=296
[h] Mary Pat Huxley, "Operational Review Document," Applied Biological Technologies Initiative, California Community Colleges Economic and Workforce Development Program (uses Ernst & Young 2002 data to calculate figure).
[i] http://www.ncbiotech.org/ncindustry/quickfacts/quickfacts.cfm
[j] http://www.nycp.org/Web_News/General_Partnership/Gotham%20Gazatte%20-%20Rebuilding%20NYC%20%20Biotech%20A%20Boon%20for%20Lower%20Manhattan.htm
[k] http://www.ci.berkeley.ca.us/news/1999/99aug/0801g9bbb.html
[l] http://www.forwardwi.com/industries/BIOTECH1.pdf
[m] Thomson Dialog, Medical Device Register, file 167, http://library.dialog.com/bluesheets/pdf/b10167.pdf.
[n] http://www.massbenchmarks.org/issues/02winter/02winter_feature.html
[o] http://www.tradeandindustrydev.com/issues/article.asp?ID=42
[p] http://www.bayareabioscience.org/indprof.html
[q] http://www.massbenchmarks.org/issues/02winter/02winter_feature.html
[r] http://www.massbenchmarks.org/issues/02winter/02winter_feature.html

TABLE 5.2—cont.

[s] http://www.chi.org/brandomatic/othermedia/chi/CHIstatewidereport_ppt.pdf
[t] http://www.new-econ.com/National%20Biocluster%20Report.pdf
[u] http://www.chi.org/brandomatic/othermedia/chi/PDF_IDPC_RPT_CHI_Bayarea_2002.pdf
[v] http://www.brookings.edu/es/urban/publications/biotech2.pdf
[w] http://www.massbenchmarks.org/issues/o2winter/o2winter_feature.html
[x] 1997 Economic Census data, NAICS code 325412.
[y] 1997 Economic Census data, NAICS code 325412.
[z] NAICS Category #3254 for San Francisco-Oakland-San Jose CMSA, http://www.census.gov/prod/ec97/97m31-ca.pdf
[aa] http://www.brookings.edu/es/urban/publications/biotech2.pdf
[bb] http://www.massbenchmarks.org/issues/o2winter/o2winter_feature.html
[cc] http://www.chi.org/brandomatic/othermedia/chi/biomed/pdf
[dd] http://www.new-econ.com/pdf/o4-NationalBioclusterReport.pdf
[ee] http://www.chi.org/brandomatic/othermedia/chi/PDF_IDPC_RPT_CHI_Bayarea_2002.pdf

North Carolina is highly regarded for effectively linking its activities toward developing the workforce with those directed toward economic development. The state's community college system, the third largest in the country, supports the state's agenda for economic development by providing high-quality, customized worker-training programs at no cost to firms locating or expanding in the state. The community college system was created in 1957 to deliver job training, adult literacy instruction, and adult education. More recently it has been given the added responsibility of helping the state make the transition from an economy based on the failing tobacco, textile, and furniture industries to an economy of the twenty-first century. In this the community colleges have been very effective. In the 1990s residents who completed community college programs significantly improved their employment opportunities and wages.[17] Moreover, the state is famed (and, no doubt, feared in places such as Massachusetts, which have lost businesses to North Carolina) for its success in luring new-economy industries—largely with the promise of trained workers.

The community colleges are now at the heart of the state's bid to attract and retain biotech manufacturing companies. North Carolina development experts predict that, between 2003 and 2006, the state's biotechnology industry will add some six thousand jobs that will not require bachelor's degrees.[18] The community colleges have geared up to train new workers, and to retrain workers displaced from declining industries, to fill these new jobs.

BioWork and Beyond

Seven of North Carolina's fifty-eight community colleges offer biotechnology-related degree programs, mostly for pharmaceutical and chemical lab technicians. But in the mid-1990s employers who had to fill manufacturing positions could not find enough graduates from these programs. What was needed was a shorter-term course of study to provide displaced workers and career changers with sufficient background in basic science, math, lab, and manufacturing methods to do the new jobs. The solution was a statewide certificate program called BioWork.

BioWork got its start when the human resource representative from Novozymes, a producer of industrial enzymes, contacted Vance-Granville Community College in 1995 about starting a certificate program for entry-level workers. Novozymes was expanding its manufacturing operations and planned to hire about one hundred operators and technicians. Because the company had had difficulty finding qualified workers for these positions in the past, Joanne Steiner, the director of business services for Novozymes, was ready to invest in developing a training program. The company's goal was to shorten people's on-the-job learning curve by providing preemployment training. Steiner also hoped to reduce turnover by providing potential workers with a preview of what the specific jobs would entail.

Steiner met with production managers to identify the skills an ideal candidate would have, and she worked with the college to develop a course that would cover these areas. The result was an introductory overview course that teaches basic scientific principles and familiarizes students with manufacturing technology.

The initial run of the program was a success. Fifteen students completed it and were hired by various companies, including Novozymes. Both Steiner and Garland Elliot, the director of economic development services at Vance-Granville Community College, attribute the high placement rate of graduates to careful screening of applicants to make sure that they had basic math and reading skills. They add that the class allowed them to observe how well students worked cooperatively on projects—a key need in the industry—and to hire accordingly. Steiner reports that turnover among workers recruited through the program has been lower than among other hires. And managers report that employees hired through the program are performing better than others who were not in the program.

Realizing that much of the state's job growth in biotechnology would be in manufacturing, the North Carolina Biotechnology Center (NCBC), a biotech economic development agency, already had been looking for ways to help educational institutions meet those workforce needs. And with many employers complaining of skills deficiencies among new workers—even workers with AAS (Associate in Applied Science) and bachelor's degrees—the association's vice president for education and training programs, Kathleen Kennedy, was eager to adopt the model pioneered by Joanne Steiner and Vance-Granville. She organized a team made up of staff members of the Biotechnology Center, administrators from the community college, and business experts to develop BioWork, a curriculum that was made available to all community colleges.

The 128-hour BioWork course is presented in nine segments over a three-month period. Since many students are working, the course is offered part-time. Students attend classes for eight hours a week over sixteen weeks. Specific skills covered include reading process diagrams and gauges; using the metric system; making chemical solutions; preparing growth media; and following standard operating procedures and good manufacturing practices established by the Food and Drug Administration (see table 5.3). The more than fifteen companies involved in developing this curriculum also have donated funds, equipment, and instructors. Novozymes, for example,

TABLE 5.3
BioWork units of study

Unit 1. Your New Job. Orientation to the process manufacturing industries (4 hours plus two field trips)	**Unit 4. Measuring Process Variables.** The metric system and variables critical to controlling processes (20 hours)	**Unit 7. Controlling the Process.** Basic principles of feedback control systems (8 hours)
Unit 2. Working Safely. Basic safety attitudes and approaches (4 hours)	**Unit 5. Transforming Matter.** Basic chemistry for process technicians (20 hours)	**Unit 8. Maintaining Sterile Processes.** Working in aseptic manufacturing environments (12 hours)
Unit 3. Building Quality into the Product. Say what you do and do what you say (12 hours)	**Unit 6. Learning the Nuts and Bolts.** Process manufacturing equipment, systems, and plant utilities (20 hours)	**Unit 9. Growing Living Cells.** Bioprocess manufacturing principles and operations (12 hours)

Source: North Carolina Biotechnology Center, http://www.ncbiotech.org/ouractivities/education/bioworkcourse.cfm.

donated $250,000 to Vance-Granville Community College to create and equip a training lab.

Company and college officials decided that, to enroll, students must have a high school diploma and score at the eighth-grade level in reading and math. Kennedy notes that successful students have mechanical ability, have good trouble-shooting and problem-solving skills, and can pay attention to detail. After completing the curriculum, graduates are ready for entry-level positions as process technicians.

Between 2000, the year the first BioWork course began, and 2003, 378 students enrolled in the course at Vance-Granville, and 234 (62 percent) successfully completed it and found jobs. By 2003 as many as 1,218 students had completed the course at seven other community colleges. The colleges do not track student outcomes, so employer and employee feedback is the only mechanism for evaluating longer-term success. My conversations with graduates revealed a surprising variety of experiences.

Warren Branch had been employed in a warehouse, which he describes as easy but boring work with little chance for advancement. He always had an interest in biology and chemistry, he says, so when he saw an ad in the newspaper for the BioWork program, he applied. Branch passed the entry exam and enrolled in Vance-Granville Community College in April 2001. Novozymes hired him as a chemical operator as soon as he completed the three-month program. Although he did not take additional classes after that, he advanced to lead operator, and then to shift supervisor in three years. Branch credits BioWork for giving him the opportunity that enabled him to advance so quickly. His starting salary at Novozymes was $5,000 more a year than his previous job, and he now makes about $40,000 with full benefits. Branch has looked into associate's degree programs at Central Carolina Community College (the one he wants is not offered at Vance-Granville). He says he cannot manage it presently because he works a swing shift, but he hopes to go back to school some day, using the company's tuition benefit to pay for it.

Tracy Crudup completed two years of college as a biology major but left school to earn money to continue and never made it back. Once he married and had a child, he found himself stuck in a job that paid well enough but was not very fulfilling. Like Branch, he read about BioWork and enrolled. Immediately upon completing the program in 2002, he was hired by Novozymes as a chemical operator. Although he has not yet advanced, he plans to. The easiest path to advancement, he says, is to move into a supervisory position, but Crudup would rather become a senior operator, which requires three years of experience and completion of his bachelor's degree. The company has offered him unpaid time off to complete the degree, but for now he is content and fears that school would cut into his family life too much. Eventually, though, his goal is to obtain a BA. At $35,000 a year with full benefits, he is making more than he did in his previous job. Having his entire family covered under his medical-benefits package also made this job a big step up.

As these stories suggest, the payoff for completing BioWork is considerable. Students pay $65 in tuition and $60 for texts to prepare for entry-level process-technician positions that start at around $15 per hour, with benefits. But North Carolina's community colleges recognize that finding entry-level jobs for people with entry-level skills does not amount to a complete workforce-development program. Thus Vance-Granville is taking the lead in building a biotech career ladder with upward and downward links to the BioWork program. The college put together a sixty-hour PreBioWork course in 2003 that builds employability, mathematics, and reading skills and provides an overview of BioWork so that students can decide if they are interested in this line of work. By the fall of 2004 four sessions with about fifteen students in each have completed the program. Elliot reports that almost all have enrolled in BioWork. The greatest barrier for these students is math. For those who have completed BioWork or have equivalent skills, Vance-Granville has submitted an application to the State Board of Community Colleges to establish an associate degree in Bioprocess Manufacturing Technology. When the new degree program is approved, BioWork graduates will receive 3 college credits toward this credential. This may turn out to be particularly important if North Carolina biotech manufacturers start requiring entry-level workers to hold AAS degrees. Already two companies, Wyeth and Biogen Idec, have said that they will be doing just that.

Several community colleges also provide customized training for workers in biotechnology and related firms as part of the North Carolina Community College System's Economic and Workforce Development Division. As mentioned above, North Carolina offers free employee training to companies that locate or expand in the state. Currently customized training does not earn college credit, but Larry Keen, the college system's vice president of economic and workforce development, is trying to change that. A committee is examining how to divide customized curricula into modules that can accumulate toward an AAS degree, and from there toward a bachelor's degree. Modularization should also make it easier for students to accumulate credits, since the shortened courses would provide flexibility for people trying to combine work and school.

The North Carolina community colleges provide a model of involvement in economic development that others envy. Nonetheless there is more that needs to be done. For example, North Carolina community college salaries are fourth from the bottom nationally and second from the bottom in the Southeast, which makes it hard to hang on to instructors in high-tech fields. In one case I encountered, a biotechnology company lured away a community college instructor by offering to pay him $70,000 a year, nearly double his teaching salary. Yet, at the same time, the colleges are supposed to be expanding their training programs to meet the growing needs of the industry. The demand for more degree-level biotechnology training is particularly pressing. The quality and size of programs must be improved to meet the need in biotechnology. In 2001, the last year for which statistics are available, only twenty-three people in North Carolina graduated with AAS degrees in chemical, bioprocessing, or biotechnology programs, and few community college graduates continued on to pursue bachelor's degrees.[19]

Money for making improvements was granted in August 2003. A year before that, a statewide economic-stimulus initiative was financed by the Golden LEAF Foundation, North Carolina's tobacco settlement fund. Golden LEAF put up $85.4 million to help the state's economy make the transition from tobacco to growth industries. Part of this is earmarked for helping local agencies to certify industrial sites. The centerpiece of the initiative ($42 million of the total) is a venture debt and venture capital fund for bioscience and biotechnology companies in the state. More remarkable is the integration of workforce development in a follow-up initiative. To help the state university and community college systems develop a Biotech

Training Consortium, the foundation gave them a $60 million grant. Funds are being used to improve biotechnology programs at both the community-college and the university levels, and for creating better articulation agreements so students can transfer from one to the other without losing credits. This should help build career pathways in the industry. The Golden LEAF Foundation invested almost $200,000 into community colleges in 2003. Few other states have made a comparable commitment to workforce training. Yet, as community college officials pointed out during the state's 2003 budget hearings, to bring the salaries of biotechnology faculty and other community college instructors up to the national average would require almost $100 million over a two-year period; and with growing enrollment in biotech programs, another $223 million is needed for equipment alone.[20]

The new emphasis on the manufacturing (rather than the theoretical) aspect of biotechnology will be centered at two universities, North Carolina State University (NCSU) and North Carolina Central University (NCCU), a historically black school in Durham. Both are part of the University of North Carolina system.

With the Golden LEAF funding, NCSU is building a state-of-the-art bio-manufacturing plant at its Raleigh campus, which will also be accessible to the sixteen other campuses of the University of North Carolina. The facility will be completed in 2007. Further, the university is adjusting its degree programs to make them more responsive to the needs of biomanufacturers. Peter Kilpatrick, the chair of the chemical and biomolecular engineering department at NCSU, explains how his department is doing this. As one of the nation's top ten producers of chemical engineering graduates, Kilpatrick was frustrated that few of his graduates were able to find jobs in the state. When he began talking to employers, he discovered that they seldom hire biochemical engineers who have less than two to four years of workplace experience. The employers told him that the university's curriculum needed more practical instruction in industry operating procedures to complement the students' theoretical understanding of biological processes. In response, the department created a minor in biotechnology, which requires hands-on instruction in lab skills and aseptic (clean-room) procedures, as well as familiarity with Current Good Manufacturing Practices (CGMP), the regulations issued by the U.S. Food and Drug Administration for pharmaceutical, medical device, and food manufacturers making products for human use. About 35 percent of chemical engineering students (about thirty-five students a year) now complete the minor, with about fifteen graduates a year landing a job in one of the state's bio-manufacturing companies. The plan is to increase this number to thirty to forty students per year.

NCCU's role in the initiative is to establish a new Biomanufacturing Research Institute and Training Enterprise (BRITE) Center for Excellence. The Golden LEAF Foundation has allocated $17.8 million for this state-of-the-art research facility, and industry has kicked in another $1.3 million. When fully operational the BRITE Center will train approximately two hundred students per year, offering them both theoretical and hands-on experience at the bachelor's, master's, and doctoral degree levels. Advancing science has been a long-standing priority at NCCU, and the campus is now home to a number of programs like BRITE, which can benefit from one another's presence. Among them is the Julius L. Chambers Biomedical/Biotechnology Research Institute (BBRI), named for the NCCU chancellor who conceived it, which was built with $12.2 million in funds allocated by the State of North Carolina General Assembly and opened in September 1999. Another is the new $36 million science complex for basic and applied research in biomanufacturing, which will house six science departments when it is completed and eight training areas that simulate small biotechnology companies.[21]

With a $400,000 grant from the Southeast Consortium for Minority Engineers and the Bill and Melinda Gates Foundation, NCCU is also developing a program to prepare minority high school students for college-level work in the sciences. This program, Early College High School, will expose junior high school students to jobs in the field and will let high school students take their junior and senior years on the college campus.

The Impact on Employment

Because of the Golden LEAF Foundation, North Carolina is blessed with more money to invest in workforce development than most states have, and one way it is planning to use these funds is to press forward with the development of a job-training system that supports career advancement in biomanufacturing. BioWork laid the groundwork for this, and now, to meet the needs of the biotechnology industry generally and biomanufacturers specifically, the state's community colleges and universities are strengthening higher-level programs as well. The programs are not just centered at a few schools but are being built statewide so that all residents have access to them. This human-capital approach to attracting biotechnology companies should have other payoffs as well. Even if workers do not get jobs in biotechnology, they are building skills that can be used in other high-tech industries.

But even BioWork, the oldest of the training programs, is relatively new.

And so is biomanufacturing itself. It will take time to see how graduates of the North Carolina programs advance and to discern the education credentials that are needed for them to do so.

Massachusetts

Harvard, MIT, and Boston's world-class hospitals have been strong magnets for biotech research firms—without much help from state or local economic development agencies. Massachusetts is fortunate in this way, but the state has lately awakened to the fact that capturing the manufacturing side of the industry as it develops will take some effort. North Carolina's success in luring Biogen Idec, a Massachusetts firm, to build most of its manufacturing there, including a $300 million plant in Research Triangle Park in 2003,[22] has made the need for a Massachusetts strategy even more urgent, and a plan is just starting to gel.

In 2003 Governor Mitt Romney launched a $2 million marketing campaign called "Massachusetts, It's All Here" to attract biomanufacturing and medical device producers. Another Romney economic development initiative set aside $125 million in subsidies to attract biopharmaceutical and medical device companies that create manufacturing jobs.[23] In addition, the legislature approved a $25 million program to help companies commercialize new technologies. The Massachusetts Alliance for Economic Development, a public-private consortium created a decade ago to provide industry with information on sites,[24] expects to launch a web-based tool in late 2004 for the use of biotechnology businesses. The website, MassConnect, will contain an inventory of locations that are pre-approved—having met all regulatory, zoning, and other requirements—for particular types of biotech activity (pre-approved, for instance, for all phases of biotechnology research and production, or for plastics manufacturing).

But community colleges in Massachusetts have never had a strong link to the state's economic development agenda. And they have long been under-funded. Indeed, *New Skills for a New Economy*, a report released in 2000 by the nonprofit policy organization Mass Inc., concluded that the state's workforce development system was insufficient in scale and focus to serve the state's key growth industries, including biotechnology.[25] The report sent shock waves through the state, and the then governor Jane Swift responded in April 2001 by creating the interagency Task Force to Reform Adult Education and Worker Training. Within three months, the task force produced its own report, *Climbing the Ladder*, which proposed developing job-training programs in biotechnology and other growth sectors, which could be offered in community colleges statewide. The task force further recommended that an initiative to that end be funded with $30 million and run by the governor's office and by state agencies focusing on economic development, workforce development, and education. The proposals made by the task force won wide support, but then the state's economy soured, and the initiative, called Building Essential Skills Training (BEST), ended up with only $3.5 million in state and federal funds. Biotechnology companies put in another $1 million worth of equipment, employee wages (paid during training), and assistance in curriculum development and delivery. This helped, but hardly enough, given that an estimated sixty biotechnology research companies in Massachusetts were close to expanding into commercial production. A workforce development system that could meet their hiring needs was essential, if biomanufacturing was to be kept in the state.[26]

BEST and Beyond

Genzyme took a chance on me because I only had a high school diploma and the BEST program. I've learned a lot on the job and will advance once I complete my associate degree.

GREG JOHNSON, lab technician, Genzyme

In 2001 a multi-agency consortium led by the Commonwealth Corsporation, the state's primary workforce development agency, formed the BEST Biotechnology partnership, which included two workforce investment boards, two One-Stop Career Centers, two community colleges (Roxbury in Boston, and Middlesex in Lowell), the Massachusetts Biotechnology Council (an industry association), and four biotech firms (Genzyme, Wyeth BioPharma Genetics Institute, Biogen Idec, and ImmunoGen, Inc.). The partnership was charged with creating a biomanufacturing curriculum to be administered through the community colleges.

The project partners originally wanted BEST training to reach low-income groups as well as displaced and incumbent workers. But since the largest share ($2 million) of BEST's final funding came from the state's Division of Employment and Training, which provides workforce training for incumbent workers, the training program's primary target had to be incumbent workers. In addition, many companies wanted the community colleges to focus on providing entry-level training, after which the firms would provide the specific additional training that their workers needed. The BEST certificate program was designed accordingly.

Roxbury Community College and Middlesex Community College piloted the BEST certificate. Working with BEST's industry partners, teachers at the two colleges created a four-week training program that presents an introduction to all aspects of biomanufacturing. Classes are held eight hours per day for four days each week, and a fifth day is spent doing on-site training at the employee's company. The curriculum covers laboratory skills, basic science, and basic operating procedures. The curriculum is presented in lectures, hands-on exercises, and videos. Employees from the partner firms teach segments on the importance to the industry of accountability, integrity, team building, precision, documentation, and the reporting of problems.

By the end of 2003, three groups—comprised, respectively, of eleven, thirteen, and fourteen employees of the partner firms—had completed the BEST program at Middlesex and one group of twelve had finished at Roxbury. About 85 percent of the students were incumbent employees of the four partner companies. The rest entered the program by passing a screening test for math and reading levels given at one of the participating community centers and were then hired while they completed the BEST course. This was as close as the program has gotten to including people the companies might not have hired on their own, but all managers reported that those hired through the BEST screening were working out as well as incumbent employees.[27] Moreover, they said, by encouraging the companies to consider candidates they otherwise would not have considered, BEST helped them to achieve their diversity hiring goals.

As for the trainees, they earned a minimum of $13 an hour plus full benefits while attending the course and, after completing the training, advanced to wages of $15 to $20 per hour. BEST program evaluators interviewed all those who were new hires, and all said that they could identify clear career-advancement opportunities and thought their employers were supportive of their goals. Several reported being disappointed by the repetitive nature of the work; they had thought that jobs in this high-tech industry would be different from jobs in traditional manufacturing industries. But despite this drawback, all but one of the new hires planned to stay with their employer, and all want to stay in biotechnology.[28]

BEST graduate Edwin Grant, for example, had lost his job of thirty-two years when Polaroid closed in 2001. After a year of unemployment, he took the qualifying test for the BEST program, performed well, and was hired by Genzyme. He started the BEST course immediately and is grateful for the opportunity the program provided. Grant comments that between the skills he already had as a technical specialist at Polaroid and the specific new skills and information he learned in the BEST course, he felt fully prepared for his first position in a therapeutic protein lab.[29] He has now moved to a job in the manufacturing division and is earning about $18 per hour—only a little more than half his wages at Polaroid—plus benefits. At age fifty-three, Grant sees only limited opportunities for advancement, even though he has an associate's degree in engineering technology. However, Grant is pleased to have found a job that utilizes his skills and is also rewarding. The importance of the work, he notes, permeates the organizational culture: "We're all working for a reason, and we don't take that lightly."

For others the career change into biotech is more of an advance, and BEST has played a role in that. Greg Johnson, for instance, was a truck driver for eight years before starting at Genzyme in 2000. After working a year as a material handler in Genzyme's warehouse, he applied for a lab-technician opening. Although the job description called for a bachelor's degree and Johnson had only a high school diploma, the company decided to take a chance on him. He started the new job in 2001 at $14.50 an hour plus benefits, and within a year he had advanced to a technician position in cell culture, based on the skills he had learned on the job. Shortly after that he was promoted to an associate position at $18.40 an hour. In September 2003 he enrolled in the BEST certificate program at Middlesex. Even though he had two years of experience, Johnson says, he learned a lot through the course and realized that without continuing his education he could not advance much beyond where he was. So he planned to enroll at Middlesex in an associate's degree program in biotechnology in September 2004. Johnson could not be happier with his job and its possibilities for advancement: "I love it," he says, "because there is a lot of room for growth and opportunity, and I know that what I'm doing helps a lot of people."

BEST is only the first step. Middlesex Community College offers an AAS degree in biotechnology. Middlesex and Bunker Hill Community College, which is now developing a biotechnology program of its own, are also members of the Northeast Regional Biomanufacturing Collaborative,[30] which is currently working to identify the necessary competencies for ten biomanufacturing occupations, information that will then be used to develop new job-training curricula.[31] The Collaborative is based at New Hampshire Community Technical College, just over the Massachusetts state line.

None of these programs is yet part of an articulated career ladder. The BEST certificate, for instance, does not provide credit toward higher-level certificates or an associate's degree in biotechnology, and, as of 2003, no students had moved from BEST to further their education. But promising career paths are likely to develop in this industry. Biotech employers expect to use high-road manufacturing methods that place a premium on additional skill training and career advancement, and BEST instructors say that they encourage graduates to return to school after they have gained experience on the job. Paul Patev, the director of the BEST program at Middlesex, points out that the first year of working at a biomanufacturing firm requires a lot of on-the-job learning that would make it difficult to go back to school. He expects to see more program graduates returning after they have completed their first year of employment.

Of more concern to anyone interested in getting low-income people onto career ladders is that neither the BEST partnership nor community college–based training programs (except in San Francisco) has found a way to bring biomanufacturing opportunities to this population. The problem is in meeting basic mathematics and reading levels, and having some science background. Getting these skill levels to an acceptable level prior to biotech training would take years.

Other groups are trying to address the issue, but the problem may be essentially unsolvable. For example, the Commonwealth Corporation and the biotech industry association have started a biotech pipeline for low-income groups. The two have joined with five community-based organizations to form the Biotechnology Workforce Project (BWP). In October 2002 the project received a $65,000 grant from Social Venture Partners Boston,[32] and in the summer of 2003 each of the community organizations recommended three candidates for BWP training. The goal is to prepare students for BEST training. The first class of twelve students ran from September through December 2003.

Finding even this small number of students qualified to start the course was a struggle. Few clients of the community organizations met the threshold levels of eighth-grade math skills and tenth-grade reading skills needed for the BWP course. Further, as Tom Siegel, the lead partner from Social Venture Partners, explains, personnel departments at biotech firms are looking for workers with a stable employment history (ideally having held the same job for a minimum of two years). Even fewer of the clientele of the community organizations could meet that threshold. BWP recently offered a fourteen-week pre-training course to help clients qualify for its regular training course. To date, only four of the six clients who completed it have reached the threshold requirements for further training. The program is now on hold.

The Impact on Employment

Although we didn't get beyond the first offering of the Biotechnology Workforce Project, bringing together community-based training providers for this project enabled them to work together more effectively. As a result, they have successfully retooled to train low-income residents in another industry.

MISHY LESSER, vice president for strategic
collaborations, Commonwealth Corporation

As it happens, biotech hiring slowed just as BEST got started, so the program has not expanded beyond the first two community colleges. In fact, at the time of this writing, it was on hiatus even at the two. Lydia Harris, the project manager for BEST at the Massachusetts Biotechnology Council, predicts that hiring will pick up in late 2004, at which point another round of the program will be offered at Middlesex Community College.

The BEST partnership seems to have forged effective collaboration among the state's education and workforce development agencies and biotech businesses to create a point of entry into jobs with good advancement potential in an industry which itself has high growth potential. But, thus far, BEST has taken only a first and limited step, and, even so, the program remains to be tested when the industry starts hiring again.

California

Whole new segments of Life Sciences activity are already beginning to appear, as breakthroughs occur and as new technologies emerge from the convergence of the Life Sciences with areas such as Information Technology and nanotechnology.

*Taking Action for Tomorrow: Bay Area Life Sciences
Strategic Action Plan*

About 30 percent of the nation's biotechnology firms are located in California, employing between eighty-five thousand and one hundred thousand people.[33] The San Francisco area is considered the birthplace of the industry, which grew out of research being conducted at Stanford, the University of California (UC) Berkeley, UC San Francisco, UC Davis, and UC Santa Cruz in the 1960s and 1970s. The world's first biotechnology company, Genentech, Inc., opened there in 1976.[34]

Practically from the beginning, the state government made at least a modest effort to support the industry. In 1985 Governor George Deukemejian organized the Interagency Taskforce on Biotechnology to coordinate the actions of state and federal agencies, streamline regulatory policies, and educate the public about the new industry. In 1994 Governor Pete Wilson created the Council on Biotechnology, an organization of biotech CEOs, to recommend how to expand the state's efforts. In 2000 the state created four Institutes for Science and Innovation—partnerships of the University of California, state government, and high-technology firms— and committed a total of $100 million to each one to support basic research in fields with industrial promise.[35] One of these, the California Institute for Quantitative Biomedical Research, focuses on bioengineering, bioinformatics, computational biology, genomics, and related areas.[36]

None of these initiatives included a workforce development component; that was left to the state's community colleges, whose efforts to help in the development of the biotechnology industry began in the late 1980s. The mission was formalized in 1996 in legislation that created the Applied Biological Technologies Initiative—as well as initiatives aimed at nine other targeted industries—under the colleges' Economic and Workforce Development Program. Geographically, and in every other way, California is much larger than Massachusetts or North Carolina, and the community college system chose to divide these statewide initiatives into more manageably sized projects. The college system designated a handful of regional centers and assigned each of them responsibility for responding to the economic and educational needs of businesses in the targeted industries. In 2000 alone these centers leveraged $17 million in state grants to raise a total of $67 million for job training and related activities. Industry contributed heavily to this total—$23 million in matching funds contributed to the broader initiative and $37 million in fees paid for job-training services.[37] The Applied Biotech Initiative in 2000 had a budget of $1,225,750 to run six regional centers, and the budget remains the same in 2004.[38]

The funding has not met the need, however. Currently 32 of the state's 109 community colleges offer biotech courses or programs, and 20 others are planning to start programs. Community college leaders say that the colleges in both groups need more resources than they are presently getting. The regional centers are meant to provide the community colleges with the necessary equipment, faculty training, and curriculum development to offer biotech courses and programs. They are also meant to help the colleges develop partnerships with high schools, universities, and industry, and to keep them connected to the appropriate government agencies.[39] But only some of that is happening at the first two regional centers to open, one based in San Diego in the southern part of the state and the other in San Francisco in the north.

San Diego

Biogen Idec was the first biotech company in the area to go into large-scale manufacturing. We wanted to hire locally and realized that if we didn't work with the community colleges to create workforce education programs and facilities, programs wouldn't
exist in time to meet our hiring needs.

MARY SCHWALEN, manager of manufacturing education
and training, Biogen Idec, San Diego

San Diego area business groups and economic development organizations have been active in promoting the biotechnology industry. When
the defense downsizing of the 1990s struck a blow to the regional economy,
the San Diego Association of Governments (SANDAG) adopted a regional
economic development strategy that centered on helping defense-related
companies convert to other products and services.[40] Unveiled in 1998,
the strategy called for preserving existing manufacturing employment
and expanding the region's high-tech industries, including biotechnology
and pharmaceuticals. This was to be achieved by a mix of traditional
economic development assistance and workforce development activities.
In 2001 the County of San Diego developed a Biotechnology Action
Plan to simplify site permitting, develop procedures for waste management,
identify sources of venture capital, and strengthen high school and
adult training curricula[41] (see table 5.4). With seven community colleges in
the San Diego area already offering biotechnology programs, the community colleges were to be the main source of training for new workers, incumbent employees, and displaced workers.

Augustine Gallego, the chancellor of the San Diego Community College
District from 1990 through 2003, is active on the board of BIOCOM, the
region's biotechnology industry association, and has worked for a long time
to keep biotech degree and job-training programs up to date at the district's
three campuses.[42] San Diego City College has a Technology Incubator that
is home to ten start-up companies. The focus in the San Diego district has
been on the R&D side of the industry. In 1997, as part of the Applied
Biotech Initiative, San Diego's Miramar Community College was designated the statewide BioScience Workforce Development Center, and it
began developing and testing new educational programs to train technicians
for positions in biomanufacturing and biomedical device firms. Between
1997 and 2003 the center was awarded close to $2 million in grants for this
work from the state and federal government (including from the National
Science Foundation).

Miramar is creating curriculum to be used statewide. Just north of San

TABLE 5.4
Partners in promoting San Diego's biomedical and biotechnology sectors

Organization	Role in Promoting Biotechnology
BIOCOM, the local industry association	Promotes the industry's needs in state and local policy; coordinates with economic and workforce development organizations; assists educational institutions in curriculum development
San Diego Workforce Partnership, the organization that manages the area's Workforce Investment Board	Develops overall workforce development strategies for targeted clusters; works with employers and community colleges to develop training programs that meet industry needs
San Diego Community College District and other community colleges in the region	Develop curriculum in cooperation with employers to meet the needs of key regional industries; the BioScience Workforce Development Center and Technology Business Incubator develops biotechnology education and enterprise programs, and is responsible for running several regional community college–based training programs, including one for biotechnicians
University of California, San Diego	Has the Connect Program, which assists faculty in obtaining patents or licensing agreements to encourage new business start-ups
San Diego State University	Participates in the California State University Program for Education and Research in Biotechnology (CSUPERB), which keeps channels of communication open between CSU, industry, government agencies, the Congressional Biotechnology Caucus, and the public

Source: Compiled by the author from program documents and interviews.

Diego, in the city of Oceanside, MiraCosta Community College became the first regional center under the Applied Biotech Initiative from 1996 to 2000 (it is now located at San Diego City College). Its focus was on research and development, which built the groundwork for programs for the manufacturing side of the industry. After the Applied Biotech Initiative moved to San Diego City College, MiraCosta College began working with Biogen Idec (then IDEC Pharmaceuticals), which is building a $400-million production facility in Oceanside.[43]

The collaboration began well in advance of the plant opening, says Mary Schwalen, the Manufacturing Education and Training Manager at Biogen Idec, to make sure that there are enough skilled workers for the seven hundred jobs that will exist when the plant reaches full capacity.[44] (Full production is expected to start in 2006.) Schwalen explains that the company has had difficulty finding qualified employees for its existing San Diego plant. It had to recruit from outside the area to find the one hundred employees it hired between 2001 and 2003, and it has had trouble keeping some of them—largely, Schwalen suggests, because highly qualified workers can command higher wages outside San Diego, one of the costliest real-estate markets in the country and a city of "sun-based" compensation packages. To avoid running into the same problem at the Oceanside plant, the company is planning to find potential employees who are rooted in the area and train them at MiraCosta.

Schwalen says that the highly automated Oceanside plant will require workers who pay attention to detail, have knowledge of the biotech production process, and have troubleshooting skills as well as the ability to communicate with engineers to solve problems. She anticipates that approximately 7 percent of employees at the new plant will have a high school diploma, 55 percent a certificate or associate degree, and 38 percent a bachelor's degree. Biogen Idec worked with MiraCosta to add a manufacturing certificate to their existing lab assistant and R&D certificate programs. The company has contributed more than $450,000 to the college in equipment, technical assistance, faculty, and facility funding. A new faculty member was hired for the start-up of the manufacturing program in the fall of 2004. The first group will have between fifteen and twenty students and Ric Matthews, the dean of Arts and Sciences, expects class enrollments to increase each round.

Two of the certificate programs prepare workers for different production occupations (see figure 5.1). The curricula are based on the internal career paths identified at Biogen Idec and Intvitrogen, another biomanufacturing firm in North Coastal San Diego County. In each case these certificates take longer to earn than the entry-level certificates in biotechnology at most community colleges. The MiraCosta programs have high entry requirements. Students lacking the necessary background have to take one semester of biology, chemistry, and intermediate algebra before entering. Credits are counted toward an associate's degree if students want to continue.

But the payoff should be considerable. The MiraCosta credential programs will place students on career ladders with many higher rungs. With additional biotechnology course work and general education courses, a certificate holder will be able to earn an associate's degree at MiraCosta; and having Biogen Idec's new facility only a mile from the college should help employees to combine work and school. With an associate degree in biotechnoloy, Biogen Idec says a worker in a production career track will qualify for a lead operator position. Beyond that, associate degree completers can enter a bachelor's degree program at the nearby California State University campus at San Marcos, which gives MiraCosta students full credit for their associate's degree course work.

Creating several points of entry into biotechnology and related industries means that workers can start at different levels, depending on their skills and credentials. The idea is being pressed by the managers of the San Diego area's Workforce Investment Board, which invested $678,546 into

---

AA in Biotechnology

• **Certificate of Competence**	• **Certificate of Achievment**	• **Certificate of Competency**
• **Biotechnology Manufactur-**	• **Biotechnology Lab Assistant**	• **Biotechnology Research and**
ing Operator	• **(two semesters) 18–21 units**	**Development Technician**
•**(three semesters) 28–29 units**		• **(two years)**

| Science and applied courses that prepare students as production technicians. | Entry-level training provides basic foundation in science and mathematics needed for support personnel. | Technicians at this level gain proficiency in using scientific methodology for problem solving in manufacturing, quality control, or quality assurance, product de- |
| Tasks: operate and maintain equipment; grow cells and recover the proteins they produce; follow good manufacturing practices | Tasks: solution and media prepara- tion; inventory and order supplies; support for routine tasks | velopment, and analytic testing.

Tasks: implement lab procedures; use specialized lab equipment |

Figure 5.1. MiraCosta Community College biotech certificates and degree.
Source: Developed by author from MiraCosta brochures.

several activities to support workforce development in biomanufacturing. For its part the board identifies and screens candidates, who have been dislocated from other industries, for an accelerated biomanufacturing course at MiraCosta. The college received $197,000 to train two cohorts of twenty-two individuals in an accelerated job-training program. The grant pays half the salaries of students while they are working in a six- to ten-week internship. The first class is comprised mostly of displaced manufacturing workers from San Diego's semiconductor and electronics industries. Biogen Idec and Beckman Coulter committed to take on interns from this program.

Despite such grants, awards, and donations, it has been an ongoing challenge for California's community colleges to obtain the resources needed to build the highly specialized facilities required for hands-on biotech training. In 1990, several years before the Applied Biotechnology Initiative began, San Diego City College (a community college) opened a training facility with funds awarded by the state headquarters of the community college system.[45] But soon more labs and classroom space with up-to-date equipment were needed to keep up with the growing labor force requirements of the biotech industry. Given the long wait for funding for any proposal on the state's list of community college construction projects, Chancellor Gallego decided to go directly to the public. He succeeded. The

City of San Diego passed a $685 million bond initiative to construct a mul-
titude of buildings, including four new buildings for academic programs in
science, math, and high technology. One of the buildings, which opened at
Miramar College in the fall of 2004, includes space that is dedicated to
biotechnology programs.

MiraCosta College, however, had to struggle for several years to obtain
funds to expand its training facility to accommodate its new certificate programs in biotech manufacturing, even though they are sure to have enough
students to justify the investment. The college has been offering a biotechnology degree for fourteen years, so there is certainly demand for the graduates. In 2001 the college's president, Tim Dong, approved plans to convert
a 3,500-square-foot building that once housed a now defunct machine
tooling program into a biomanufacturing training facility. The price tag was
approximately $1.2 million. The Arts and Sciences dean Ric Matthews
worked with Schwalen and others at Biogen Idec to design the facility. But
before their plans were completed, the state announced community college
budget cuts that eliminated funding for the project. Matthews formed a
steering committee composed of members of the San Diego chapter of the
International Society for Pharmaceutical Engineers, and the steering committee members have donated considerable time and resources from their
own companies to the building project. The architectural and engineering
firms that designed Biogen Idec's new manufacturing facility donated
design services. A construction company that was dismantling a biotech
research lab retrieved lab benchware (autoclaves, dishwashers, and such)
for the college's use. In 2004, with $80,000 worth of services and equip-
ment donated, Matthews started a capital campaign to raise the rest. In
2004 the college agreed to finance $600,000 and received a $250,000 dona-
tion from Biogen Idec. Although $200,000 short of the goal, the bidding
process has started. Meanwhile, classes are going forward in existing science
facilities without the hands-on equipment needed for grounding students
in the practical aspects of cell production and purification.

San Francisco

The Bridge to Biotech program helps people like me who have no prior experience
prepare themselves for jobs in the industry. I sharpened my math skills, learned the
language of biotechnology, and some laboratory practices used in the industry.
The prospects look good for me to work in the biotech industry today because I took
the time and because there was a program available to teach me the skills to get in the
door.

JOHN THOMAS, graduate, Bridge to Biotech Program

The City College of San Francisco (CCSF) was one of the two original regional centers designated under California's Applied Biotechnology Initiative. It was given the task of coordinating the economic development activities of the ten other community colleges in the area that have technician programs in this field.

Like the San Diego community colleges, CCSF has been committed for some time to the biotech industry. It is the headquarters of Bio-Link, a National Advanced Technological Education Center for Biotechnology funded by the National Science Foundation to improve and expand programs to train technicians in this field.[46] City College of San Francisco has one of the largest biotech programs in California, with two hundred students enrolled. With two different certificate tracks, the program currently graduates about forty students a year. One of the tracks, a two-semester certificate program, prepares students for technician positions in biomanufacturing such as bioprocess, media-prep, or pharmaceutical manufacturing technicians, or as pharmaceutical materials specialists. The other, a four-semester advanced certificate program for lab technicians, prepares students for jobs in quality control and entry-level R&D. Students who complete the first certificate are encouraged to take the more advanced certificate while they are working. By adding about another year's worth of general education courses, students can transfer to complete a bachelor's degree.

These programs were designed to meet the needs of a wide variety of companies and had direct input from professionals at Genentech and Chiron. A core of six or seven companies participated in developing the curriculum. More important, according to the co-directors of CCSF's Biotechnology Program Edie Leonhardt and Phil Jardim, employers suggest updates to the curriculum on an ongoing basis as standard techniques and processes change.

About 70 percent of the students enrolled in the two certificate programs already have a four-year college degree and just need the practical experience the programs provide. But CCSF is also trying to reach people who have fewer skills at the start, and it appears to be making more of an effort than any other community college in the country to help minorities get on a biotech career ladder.

In 2003 the college opened its Bridge to Biotech program to provide residents of neighboring low-income communities, as well as displaced workers from the larger region, with the background they need to qualify for the certificate programs. The semester-long Bridge integrates biotechnology, language, and mathematics instruction. In its first semester thirty-five students started the course, and twenty-five completed it. In the second semester thirty-four of the forty-three who started the program completed it. The program does not have accurate records on this cohort, but Lewis estimates that about 25 percent took jobs. Of the thirty-four completers, thirty-one enrolled in the one-year certificate program. If the program continues at this rate, it will achieve its goal of providing a point of entry for minorities into the biotech field. Lewis estimates that about 75 percent of enrollees are minorities; about half are African American, 40 percent are Asian, and 10 percent are Latino. He is currently doing outreach to increase Latino enrollment.

For students who need intensive instruction in math and science before they can even start the Bridge program, a workforce development intermediary called SFWorks, which was founded by the San Francisco Chamber of Commerce, offers preparation. The clients of SFWorks are low-income, unemployed and underemployed individuals, and Lori Lindburg, the vice president of Program Development there, thought that they probably could not meet the ninth-grade reading and math levels expected of students entering the Bridge program. So SFWorks put together the On-Ramp Biotechnology Training Program to reach people with sixth-grade reading and math skills. (Like Bridge students, On-Ramp participants must have a high school diploma or a GED.)

The On-Ramp is a nine-week, part-time introduction to the life sciences with three components: a three-hour weekly lab taught by an instructor from a biotech company; a mathematics course taught by a community college instructor, which presents math concepts in the lab context; and a "professional development" segment, which is included in all SFWorks training. Lindburg explains that most welfare-to-work programs would refer to the latter segment as a "soft skills" course. Using the term "professional development," she believes, instills the idea that students have to become responsible for their own career development. In this segment On-Ramp students meet weekly with a coach, either individually or in groups, to identify their barriers to employment and advancement, and to create a plan for overcoming them. By the end of the nine-week course they have developed resumés and have practiced interviewing.

The On-Ramp is a noncredit program, but the community college has agreed that students who complete it successfully can move directly into the Bridge program. While enrolled in the Bridge program, On-Ramp students continue to get coaching, and they also work as interns in biotech firms for fifteen hours a week, earning $10.00 an hour. SFWorks pays $7.50 of that, and the companies pay the rest. Lindburg hopes that the companies will pick up more of the tab as they see the value of these interns.

Although still in its infancy, the On-Ramp program has experienced considerable success. Thirty students have graduated from three program cycles. Ninety-five percent of On-Ramp trainees have transitioned into CCSF's Bridge to Biotech program; 75 percent of enrollees have graduated, successfully completing both the Bridge program and a 180-hour laboratory internship; 75 percent of On-Ramp graduates are working in bioscience jobs, the majority earning $11 to $17 an hour and working as laboratory assistants, biomanufacturing technicians, clinical trials study coordinators, animal care technicians, and so on. Eighty percent of On-Ramp graduates have enrolled in additional postsecondary education, the majority in CCSF's Biotech Certificate program.

The National Science Foundation has recently recognized the success of these partnership programs and is funding pilot replication of the Bridge at two other community colleges, Santa Ana College and Austin Community College. NSF support will allow SFWorks to offer the On-Ramp program at CCSF's predominantly Latino Mission Campus; and SFWorks is currently planning to pilot the On-Ramp at other NCBC community colleges, beginning with Contra Costa College in Richmond, a predominantly African American community.

Like the San Diego community colleges, the campuses of CCSF are finding all this very expensive. The college invested about $80,000 in developing the Bridge curriculum, and it costs about $60,000 per year to maintain it. Much of the lab equipment has been donated by local firms. The success of the programs has led to an NSF grant to expand them elsewhere, so start-up costs will be minimal for these sites. It will be some time before we can estimate the program's per-student cost, since program development costs are higher in the first years and lessen over time. Further, the extent to which program costs are justified will depend on the long-term employability of graduates.

The Impact on Employment

In California workforce development is not as central a part of the state economic development effort as it is in North Carolina. Nonetheless the California community college system has clearly made regional economic development a priority mission. The regional centers allow the community colleges to collaborate on, rather than run, duplicate programs in the same region, and they also provide a focus for industry collaboration. Currently the regional centers are helping employers find the employees they need. It remains to be seen whether the education infrastructure will convince other biotechnology companies to locate their manufacturing locally when they are ready to make that move.

City College of San Francisco, through its Bridge program and its links to the SFWorks On-Ramp, has been successful in training residents of nearby low-income neighborhoods. The enrollments are relatively high for this type of course, as are the completion rates. As suggested by the National Science Foundation grant, it may be the nation's most effective program for creating more diversity on the biotech career ladder.

What Makes Career Ladders in Biomanufacturing Work

Biotech manufacturing is, by definition, high-road manufacturing, and thus the industry is well aware of its need to attract, train, and retain highly skilled workers. It is also a new industry, in need of workers with new and changing types of training. Both factors make for an unusual openness to the notion of career ladders. The industry is heavily involved in workforce development projects, and just about every biomanufacturing plant that I looked at had its own internal career ladder connecting learning (usually on-the-job) to career advancement. Many companies were also willing to make unconventional hiring decisions.

Nonetheless it is not entirely clear how—or even whether—public agencies should go about seizing this opportunity and pursuing the development of biotech career ladders. Some critical questions still need to be answered in three areas. First is the issue of money: Who should be spending the money, and how much of it should be spent, to train biotechnology workers and set them on a path of career mobility? The second area concerns the matter of skills: Will biotech manufacturing be characterized by consistent and portable clusters of skills, which can be ordered into career ladders and delivered by public workforce development agencies? And third is the issue of access: Can career ladders bring the opportunities of the biotech industry to the neediest workers?

Money

Providing job training for the biotech industry is very expensive. In North Carolina and California the public has spent millions to build an education infrastructure to serve this industry, and much more must still be spent—on faculty and on specialized training facilities—if the community colleges in these two states are to fulfill the mission assigned to them.

Biotech employers, too, have invested in training programs run by community colleges. Employers have donated tens of thousands of dollars worth of equipment to each of the programs examined in this chapter. They have put time and expertise into developing curricula and have often provided instructors as well, an in-kind contribution the value of which should not be underestimated. (Almost all the community college program directors and administrators with whom I talked reported difficulties retaining biotech instructors, who typically could earn much more working in industry jobs.)

The industry's investment in community college courses makes sense, since it is in the companies' interest that new workers be familiar with up-to-date equipment and manufacturing methods. And it is fair to assume that the companies are contributing no more than they expect to gain. But is the public, too, receiving a payoff adequate to justify its spending? The answer to that question is not at all clear. Even in North Carolina, Massachusetts, and California, where the biotech industry is ensconced and likely to continue developing, the public investment in workforce training (and other inducements) to lure biotech industry has been high relative to the number of jobs created so far. For example, in 2003 North Carolina expected to add between twenty-two hundred and thirty-three hundred jobs in biotechnology a year through 2005, and the North Carolina Biotechnology Center responded to such predictions by instituting a $45 million plan to bolster training efforts.[47]

Moreover, even in these three states, biomanufacturing remains a volatile industry, which adds to the expense and reduces the benefits of serving it. Keeping up with the changing needs of such an industry strains the resources of community colleges. They have to keep eliminating existing courses and faculty to free funds for new programs with new start-up costs and new teachers. Meanwhile, the unpredictability of research trials, FDA approvals, and other factors can leave a college that has gone to all this trouble with nothing to show for it but an expensive program with suddenly unneeded capacity. In Massachusetts, for instance, just as the BEST program was gearing up to meet a demand predicted by biotech firms for at least one thousand workers, the economy soured. As a result, only three rounds of the course were offered at Middlesex and Roxbury community colleges, and now this credential program is on hold at both. As for associate's degree programs in biotechnology, Middlesex, for all its efforts, is currently graduating fewer than ten students a year, and Roxbury has put its associate's degree program on hold.[48]

In North Carolina Joann Steiner of Novozymes has concluded that certificate programs like BioWork are appropriate when a company needs to hire a large number of employees at once, but they cannot be maintained to supply the few hires per year that most companies make on a continual basis. In the Boston area BEST was offered only when employers had accumulated enough new hires to constitute a cohort or class. Could such intermittently used programs be worth the public expenditure required to develop and offer them? At the moment there is no way to know. Better systems of accountability are needed to determine the actual return on these investments.

For all the millions that states plow into economic development, they currently do little to accurately calculate the effects of their efforts. If they measure anything, states focus on the number of jobs created in the wake of a new economic development initiative and the increase they see in their tax base. Based on such evidence, researchers have concluded that North Carolina's economic development strategy—with its heavy reliance on education and training subsidies—has been successful in reducing unemployment in rural areas and creating new, nonagricultural employment in the pharmaceutical and biotechnology industries.[49] But, if so, the specific mechanisms are unknown. Few community colleges have kept accurate records of even the initial job placements of their graduates, let alone the graduates' subsequent advances from entry-level positions. No colleges seem to keep track of the number of certificate completers who are readmitted into higher academic programs (e.g., certificate graduates who enter associate's degree programs). For the most part, program effectiveness is judged informally in conversations between a community college's program staff and an employer's HR staff.

Keeping better records would cost money, but the failure to keep records leaves states unable to determine which, if any, of these expensive educational programs are achieving what they intended to achieve—which, if any, are facilitating career advancement and stimulating the growth of target industries—and at what cost.

Skills

In the three states considered in this chapter, community college leaders are trying to develop biotech curricula that can be replicated throughout the college system—and portable biotech credentials that will qualify graduates for jobs throughout the state. Indeed, the goal is to create a seamless statewide system of higher education, which biotechnology and biomanufacturing employees can enter and reenter as career demands dictate. It is a goal that incorporates all the best of the career-ladder approach to workforce development. But designing lifelong learning opportunities for an industry that does not yet have—and may never have—nationally recognized credentials for different positions, or even standardized manufacturing processes and jobs, may be difficult.

The task is further complicated by the fact that the skills biomanufacturers require vary with the size of the company, its products, and the regulatory regime under which it operates. A large firm may have as many as seven levels of technicians, each requiring different skills, while a small firm will have only two or three levels and an entirely different configuration of skills. Similarly the manufacturing practices that regulators require of a drug manufacturer are quite different from those required of a manufacturer whose product comes under food regulations.

In addition, in most of these companies, manufacturing processes are continually advancing and changing. Workers, as a result, need ongoing training, which the company provides. Indeed, employers seem to expect certificate programs—and even degree programs—to provide their employees with only a basic foundation upon which the company itself then builds job-specific skills. But my conversations with biomanufacturing HR representatives suggest that company-provided training often gives workers only the new skills and information they need to perform their current jobs, and not the skills they need to advance or to change jobs. Continuing education or tuition reimbursement funds are provided in most biotech companies for this purpose, but not all employees are able to take advantage of them because of family responsibilities.

The current organization of the industry thus seems to encourage a lot of continuing education but with no guarantees in the form of job advancement or higher wages. And with so much training going on as part of the job, workers may well be disinclined to pursue college degrees on top of it. Yet, in the three states studied here, community colleges, supported by industry representatives, are developing curriculum under the assumption that career ladders in biomanufacturing go from a bridge program to a certificate program to an associate's degree to a bachelor's degree, each rung associated with a job advancement. It may be well advised for the colleges to pause in new curriculum development until the industry matures and patterns of advancement can be discerned. It is too soon to tell whether biomanufacturing will be characterized by consistent and portable skill clusters that can be ordered into career ladders. Current career ladders also vary according to the maturity of the companies in their progression from research and development to large-scale manufacturing.

Access

One of the main purposes of creating career ladders is to provide paths that people who start out with little education and few skills can follow to better jobs and wider opportunities. In the biomanufacturing industry, where even entry-level employees must have considerable scientific knowledge and mathematical skill, people with very low skill levels are likely to have difficulty getting to the first rung. North Carolina, Massachusetts, and California are all trying to skirt this difficulty and provide wider access to biotech jobs by offering short-term certificate programs. But even for these, applicants are required to have a high school diploma and eighth-grade mathematics and reading levels. And even students who meet these requirements may not be getting enough training.

The entry-level programs in North Carolina and Massachusetts, BioWork and BEST, each require about 128 hours of classroom training, the former offered part-time over three months and the latter full-time over four weeks. Each approach has both advantages and drawbacks. For example, some students who had not been in school for a while could not get used to the fast pace of BEST classes. A report evaluating the BEST program quotes one student as saying, "People felt scared . . . the course was too fast-paced . . . people were having trouble understanding."[50] Like any course offered for the first time, BEST had to be adjusted to accommodate such student concerns while maintaining the academic integrity of the program.

California's certificate programs are more extensive, and, to get into them, applicants must know some science and algebra as well as meet basic reading and mathematics requirements. Thus, even the Bridge to Biotech and the On-Ramp programs, which prepare people for the certificate programs, are longer-term than BioWork and BEST. The On-Ramp is a nine-week program whose graduates are expected to then enter the semester-long (twelve-week) Bridge program. In addition, On-Ramp students receive extensive professional development counseling, which continues when they enter the Bridge program.

None of these programs has yet brought a significant number of students into biomanufacturing, but all of them need to operate for a few more years before we can judge them. Also worth watching is another Massachusetts initiative that targets low-skilled workers in adult education programs. Massachusetts is one of eight states that received a grant in 2003 from the the Pathways to Advancement Academy of the National Governors Assocation, to expand access to postsecondary education for this population. Known in Massachusetts as the Reach Higher Initiative, the program is being planned by a team led by Commonwealth Corporation. The team hopes to move more people from adult education programs into postsecondary education, particularly into training programs for health care and high-tech occupations, by providing them with guidance, mentoring, and support.

Access may also improve as biotechnology research firms mature and become more aware of certificate programs and associate degrees. Mary Schwalen at Biogen Idec explains that the former Idec Pharmaceuticals saw a real shift in thinking on this as it moved to large-scale manufacturing. In its R&D phase, in which the majority of employees have graduate degrees, executive management staff found it hard to imagine hiring an employee, even in manufacturing, who did not have a bachelor's degree. But as manufacturing grew in scale and more community colleges developed programs tailor-made to fit their needs, that view has changed.

Biotechnology jobs may end up being too much of a stretch for underserved groups, or even perhaps for certificate graduates. (Several HR directors told me that they only consider certificate graduates when applicants with associate's degrees are not available. One explained that three-month certificate graduates do not have a sufficient understanding of basic science to be good problem solvers.) On the other hand, experience is teaching the industry that it is unwise to hire people with bachelor's degrees for operator positions at manufacturing plants, because they become bored and have a high turnover rate. When all the different access efforts are sorted out, the perfect fit for entry-level biomanufacturing jobs may be a blend of certificate and associate's degrees.

The Center on Policy Initiatives, a think tank critical of San Diego's economic development strategy, argues that, by targeting biotechnology and other high-tech industries to receive subsidies and other encouragement, San Diego may be increasing inequality in the region, since women and nonwhites are under-represented in high-tech occupations.[51] Residents of low-income communities have the same concerns. When Mayor Thomas Menino declared an area in Boston's poor Roxbury community a biotech corridor, community residents and organizations protested that there would be few jobs for people in the neighborhood.[52] They also protested the dangers that biotech labs might bring to the neighborhood.

While this critique may have merit, the better response is not to focus less on high tech but instead to focus more on providing access to these good jobs for minorities and women. If entry-level biotechnology jobs are too much of a stretch for adults with low skills, we should be reaching down into high schools and junior high schools to get minority youth and young women started on high-tech career paths. North Carolina Central University, a historically black school in Durham, is doing just that with its

Early College High School, a program that exposes junior high school students to science jobs in the field and lets high school students take science courses on the college campus. The goal, ultimately, has to be to create better school programs to reduce the need for second chance programs.

Chapter 6

Manufacturing

For most Americans, biotechnology represents the new economy and manufacturing epitomizes the old economy. Yet, as discussed in chapter 5, it is in manufacturing where much of the growth in biotechnology employment will occur. But biotechnology is only one small sector within manufacturing. A paradox confronts many manufacturing industries in the twenty-first century: on the one hand, rising productivity and global competition have rendered many jobs vulnerable to capitalism's famous "creative destruction." A seemingly robust company with a growing demand for workers can be marked virtually overnight for downsizing, relocation, or acquisition, or it can be overtaken by new technology. This institutional uncertainty undermines workforce training efforts in the manufacturing sector. But, on the other hand, even though training is a risky business, the most dynamic and competitive of manufacturing enterprises—those worth preserving and expanding—need skilled workers to produce new, high-tech goods as well as old goods using new, high-performance methods. Indeed, without skilled workers these industries will move offshore.

The new economy is, in fact, poised to create a significant number of new jobs in manufacturing, jobs that pay relatively well and offer good advancement possibilities. For example, the Bureau of Labor Statistics has forecast that, between 2002 and 2012, more than ninety thousand jobs in metals and plastics work will open up, more than ten thousand in machinist work, and more than twenty-two thousand in molding work.[1] These categories represent just a portion of manufacturing job openings in which people with less education than having earned a college degree could be and ought to be trained, and career-ladder programs for the manufacturing sector may well be the best way to go about it. What becomes important is identifying the sectors within manufacturing where enough replacement or new jobs are available around which to build career-ladder programs. But can these programs be designed to circumvent the dangers of the new economy and take advantage of its opportunities? This chapter examines this question. What becomes clear is that sectoral career-ladder programs in manufacturing can only succeed if they are embedded in a broader economic development strategy. State and local economic development practitioners need to make strategic decisions regarding which sectors to focus on so as not to invest too little or too much in training.

Why Manufacturing Still Matters

Manufacturing has many pockets of new growth. Our concern is that the United States will not be able to fill the growing demand for skilled technicians because of outdated negative perceptions of manufacturing jobs.

PHYLIS EISEN, vice president, Manufacturing Institute, National Association of Manufacturers

One of the greatest difficulties facing those who would like to offer training for jobs in traditional manufacturing industries is convincing people that such jobs are worth the trouble. The view that manufacturing is dead in America is so entrenched that business leaders in Milwaukee threatened not to participate in a citywide economic development project if the manufacturing sector was included as one of its targets. In the early 1990s African American community organizations in Chicago objected when the community college system proposed focusing its programs more on workforce training in areas such as manufacturing rather than academic transfer, on the grounds that it tracked students out of college. In city after city my own studies have found that few young people want to enter blue-collar occupations, even occupations that pay well and are rarely dirty. They assume that manufacturing no longer offers long-term job stability, and, of course, that is true in many instances. The manufacturing sector has been under siege since the 1970s.[2] The number of manufacturing jobs in America peaked in 1978 at 18.9 million (18.5 percent of the labor force) and by 2002 was down to only 15.3 million, or 10.6 percent of the nation's employment.[3] Over the two recession years of 2001 to 2003, manufacturing jobs dwindled by 14 percent—a loss of about 2.5 million jobs—and average employee earnings in this sector declined (in real dollars) by 9 percent.[4]

Yet manufacturing remains an essential part of the economy. It produces 64 percent of the nation's exports, on which our ability to conduct global commerce depends, and almost one-fourth of our total economic output.[5]

Indeed, manufacturing output has been *increasing* in recent years, despite declining employment in the sector, a feat made possible by a productivity growth rate of 4 percent—almost twice that of the rest of the economy.[6] It is true that we can no longer compete with low-wage countries in the assembly of most consumer goods, but our economic well-being as a nation depends on our ability to compete in the production of more advanced goods, such as semiconductors, electronic equipment, pharmaceuticals, and the machinery used to manufacture other products.[7] The industries producing these goods are not new and exotic; they are generally classed as traditional manufacturing. But these are goods that companies will continue to produce in advanced countries, even though wages are higher here, because their manufacture requires standards of high quality, sophisticated technologies, and a highly skilled labor force.[8] In these industries there are also competitive advantages to keeping manufacturing facilities close to research and development labs, since easy communication between the two means that new goods and new technologies will get into production more quickly.[9] The United States, in other words, has both a need and an opportunity to maintain and even expand its manufacturing capability in these high-end industries.

It makes sense to put effort into strengthening a variety of other manufacturing businesses as well, simply because they can provide good jobs for as long as they remain globally competitive. Indeed, the American manufacturing sector overall continues to pay relatively high wages, often with full benefits, to people without a college degree who otherwise would be stuck in the low-wage service sector. Fourteen percent of manufacturing jobs were unionized in 2002 (however, this figure has been halved since 1984, when there was a 28 percent unionization rate).[10] Even after the recent drop in average pay in manufacturing, the total compensation (including benefits) of full-time manufacturing workers is still about 20 percent greater than that of the average U.S. worker.[11] Advancement rates among manufacturing workers are higher than in jobs in retail trade or the services sector generally.[12] And contrary to the perception of the general public, there are many manufacturing jobs to be had. So, because of public perceptions about the nature of jobs and a shortage of quality training programs, employers are finding it hard to replace workers who are reaching retirement age. More than half the nation's manufacturers say that they are experiencing shortages of qualified candidates for jobs they need to fill. Many complain that they cannot find workers who have basic math and reading skills and also "soft" skills (e.g., punctuality, conflict management abilities, regular attendance, and the like).[13]

These are all good reasons for state and local governments to focus their economic development strategies on traditional manufacturing industries.[14] But not just any old assistance to any old manufacturer will do. There are different paths to profitability in any industry. In manufacturing, two commonly identified paths are the "low-road" and "high-road." Low-road producers compete on the basis of cost (paying lower wages), and, when they invest in technology, it is to compensate for a lack of it or to replace skilled labor.[15] High-road manufacturers compete by improving quality or productivity or both by reducing order-to-delivery time lags or product- and process-design lead times[16]—in other words, by adopting more advanced manufacturing methods. High-road manufacturers rely on skilled and committed employees working in fairly autonomous decision-making and problem-solving teams.[17] Innovations not just in technology, but also in workplace practices (the use of production teams, broad job definitions, and training incentives, for example), are needed to make a high-road path bring productivity gains.[18]

Within any given industry both high-road and low-road producers can be profitable.[19] Massachusetts-based New Balance produces sports shoes competitively as a result of its high-road partnership with MIT and other universities developing advanced manufacturing techniques. The low-road strategy is illustrated by Nike and Reebok, which have outsourced production to low-wage countries where they hire unskilled labor and use less sophisticated production technology. But while such a strategy may result in manufacturer profits, it is not a strategy for maintaining a competitive American manufacturing base or a well-paid American labor force.[20] The long-term health of the U.S. economy requires more manufacturers to take the high road.

The task for a community wishing to encourage high-road manufacturing is twofold: to supply industry with workers adequately trained for high-road manufacturing jobs, and to help companies to adopt manufacturing practices that require and attract skilled workers. The two approaches are, in fact, inseparable. For many firms, particularly small ones, the high road to profitability is out of reach simply because they do not know how to modernize production. Meanwhile, traditional workforce development activities—job-training programs that look only at filling slots and not at improving the kind of employment available—have proved grossly inadequate in the manufacturing sector. A smart development strategy, for any community interested in maintaining or expanding traditional manufacturing industries, is thus a multi-pronged one.

A growing group of economic development experts has been urging much the same thing, arguing that the best development strategy is a "sectoral strategy," in which a state or community identifies specific industries with particular growth potential in the region, focuses on those industries only, and tries to address *all* their needs.[21] The idea is to use not just the usual economic development tools—helping companies with facility siting, infrastructure development, and financing. The effort should also encompass workforce training, technology adoption, and the upgrading of manufacturing practices. The best development initiative, these strategists say, will create an alliance of businesses, labor unions, colleges, development agencies, community organizations, and so on, which together are capable of solving the whole variety of the targeted industries' problems. And the most effective alliance will rely on intermediaries to coordinate the effort. Two highly regarded sectoral development initiatives of this type are the Garment Industry Development Corporation in Brooklyn and the Jane Addams Resource Corporation, which provides hands-on training to prepare low-income residents and incumbent workers for jobs in metalworking firms on the north side of Chicago.[22]

As to the job-training component of any such strategy for strengthening manufacturing industries, career-ladder programs would seem to have much more to recommend them than traditional job-training activities. Career-ladder programs address both the training of workers and the design of jobs. Furthermore, they have the potential to provide workers with portable credentials, which would be particularly useful in a sector that is currently characterized by institutional impermanence and a fluctuating demand for labor. The advancement opportunities built into a good career-ladder program should convince more workers to get the kind of training that high-road manufacturing methods require. And the training itself, by placing manufacturing workers on a path of lifelong learning, should greatly enhance the nation's ability to compete in the high-end manufacturing businesses that are central to our success in the global economy.

Designing the career ladders, however, is a challenge. It is no easy task to figure out what the logical patterns of career advancement are in industries which, for the most part, have never adopted standard job descriptions or consistent skill requirements—and which, in any case, may now have to make significant changes in their manufacturing practices. There is no comparable problem in, say, health care, an industry in which a ladder of occupations, most of them defined by state-level credentials and exams, is already well established. For that matter, there would be no comparable problem designing manufacturing-industry career ladders in Europe, where manufacturers over the years have been forced by unions and government to take a good look at industry-wide labor force needs.[23] But as Bob Ginsburg, the director of the Center on Work and Community Development in Chicago, points out, U.S. manufacturers rarely acknowledge the shared needs of their own departments, let alone what they have in common with other companies. This industrial habit has stymied community colleges and other training providers in the past. If it is now to be overcome, employers—just like workers—will have to be shown that it is in their economic self-interest to participate in career-ladder programs.

Can sectoral development alliances accomplish all that? Can they forge an agreement on the design and implementation of career ladders in industries that have resisted uniformity in the past? Can they get workforce training agencies and economic development agencies to cross long-standing boundaries and provide multi-pronged support for high-road manufacturing? Can they increase the supply of skilled workers and good jobs in their communities? This chapter discusses the two cities that have gone furthest in such efforts: Milwaukee and Chicago. In both places it is clear that public and private organizations are beginning to take the responsibility of workforce development very seriously. But the efforts of both cities to upgrade and sustain manufacturing industries also illustrate how difficult the task is.

Wisconsin Regional Training Partnership

The workforce programs of WRTP are increasingly recognized as an important asset for economic development in targeted industries throughout the greater Milwaukee area.

JULIA TAYLOR, president, Greater Milwaukee
Committee

The Wisconsin Regional Training Partnership (WRTP), based in Milwaukee, is one of the largest and longest-running sectoral development alliances in the country. It grew out of the AFL-CIO's involvement in a job center that provided retraining and other services to the large number of workers displaced in the 1980s. But in 1992, with manufacturing employment picking up again in the region and an aging workforce starting to retire, manufacturers found themselves faced with a severe shortage of the skilled workers they needed in order to succeed in the global economy. Employers were suddenly willing to work cooperatively with unions to adopt high-performance manufacturing methods and teach workers the skills such methods require.[24] The Worker Center remade itself into the WRTP, a partnership of unions and twenty union-represented workplaces, which was dedicated to maintaining competitive companies and well-paid jobs in the region. WRTP incorporated as a nonprofit organization in 1996, and by 2003 it had grown to include 125 companies (mostly in manufacturing), which invest about $25 million a year in worker training.[25] Member firms include Allen Bradley, Harley Davidson, John Deere,

Navistar, and Peterbilt. All told, the partner firms employ about 60,000
workers (out of a total of 178,000 manufacturing workers in the metropolitan area).[26] About 40 percent of these workers are women, and 25 percent
are minorities.[27]

The WRTP strategy was conceived by three men: Phil Neuenfeldt, the
original director of the AFL-CIO Worker Center; Joel Rogers, a professor
at the University of Wisconsin–Madison and the director of the university's
Center on Wisconsin Strategy (COWS); and Eric Parker, then a COWS staff
member and now the executive director of WRTP. Their dual-customer
approach to job training—serving both employers and employees (potential and existing)—was unique at the time and remains the exception. This
is also true of their approach to plant modernization: WRTP puts together
a labor-management team to decide what changes would improve a
company's competitiveness and then provides the technical assistance to
make those changes. (Elsewhere workers are rarely asked to participate in
such efforts, which is one reason that worker training and the redesign of
jobs get short shrift in many industry modernization strategies.) Beyond
providing technical assistance for its partner firms and training for current
employees, WRTP also coordinates programs to reemploy dislocated
workers, prepare low-wage workers for better jobs, strengthen career
ladders, minimize temporary employment, and reach out to youth. As
described by Parker, WRTP combines the industry knowledge of a staffing
agency with the social mission of a community organization.

It works as follows:

Firms that join WRTP agree to help develop education and training programs on-site or at community colleges, which all partners can access. They
also agree to devote a certain percentage of payroll to education and training, and provide employment opportunities for unemployed adults and
youth.[28] In return, they receive modernization assistance—at below-
market rates—from experts employed by WRTP and from the staff of the
Wisconsin Manufacturing Extension Partnership (WMEP), which is part of
the national Manufacturing Extension Partnership program of the
federal National Institute of Standards and Technology. Since 1996 the two
organizations have provided technical assistance—including development
of quality-control systems, assessment of plant layouts (and recommendations for redesign), and training of production teams—to five hundred of
the four thousand manufacturing firms in the four-county Milwaukee
region.

The WRTP member firms contribute to employee training in various
ways. Several of the largest firms provide on-site workplace learning
centers, and firms that cannot support such an undertaking offer on-

the-job training, apprenticeships, or tuition reimbursement, or all three forms of assistance, for workers attending community college. WRTP itself acts as a training broker. It receives federal job-training funds (from the local agencies responsible for distributing this money) and, in turn, subcontracts the actual training work to local technical colleges. As Parker explains, WRTP is thus able to maintain control over course content and ensure that the needs of actual businesses are the starting point of all training programs.

WRTP has worked with two schools, Milwaukee Area Technical College (MATC) and Waukesha County Technical College. Both now offer training for a basic skills certificate, a two-hundred-hour course that qualifies its holders for entry-level production jobs and also gives them credit toward the entry-level manufacturing skills (ELMS) certificate (two hundred hours), a technical or process skills certificate (one thousand hours) or an associate's degree (a two-year program, with credits from certificates counting toward it). The ELMS certificate is a WRTP innovation, offering not only job training but a manageable first step toward higher certificates and degrees, which are nationally recognized.[29] Getting WRTP member firms to agree that a common set of skills is needed for entry-level work at just about any manufacturing plant is one of the organization's more significant accomplishments. Even member firms that provide their own basic training are now sending their on-site instructors to WRTP "train-the-trainers" courses, and they are following the WRTP-developed basic-training-certificate curriculum in their on-site programs.

WRTP thus has laid the groundwork for a manufacturing career path. But the organization had no success when it tried to interest employers in further steps along a WRTP-designed career ladder. The WRTP staff identified six credentials and their corresponding occupations, which comprised what WRTP called the Mature Certification System (see table 6.1).[30] But most member firms did not accept it. In unionized companies it is particularly hard to introduce the idea of advancing workers based on what they have learned (on the job or in school) rather than based on seniority. Moreover, each unionized plant in the WRTP partnership has its own internal career ladder, set by its collective-bargaining agreement, and employers have seen little benefit for themselves in adjusting those ladders to fit into a standardized, sector-wide system.

By the mid-1990s Parker and his colleagues on the WRTP staff had decided to stop pressing employers on credentialing, and little headway has been made since, even in coming to a consensus about whether apprenticeships or community college programs better prepare workers for advancement. Although WRTP continues to collaborate with the local col-

TABLE 6.1
WRTP mature certification system

Level	Credential	Occupations
1	Basic Skills Certificate	machine operators and other production jobs
2	Process Skills Certificate	machine operators and other production jobs
3	Technical Skills Certificate	production machinist, cell technician, and related jobs
4	Journey Work Card[a]	tool and die maker, maintenance mechanic, and other trades
5	Associate's Degree	CAD technician, engineering technician, and other technicians
6	Bachelor's Degree	design, purchasing, manufacturing and other engineers

Source: Parker and Rogers 2003.
[a]Workers can complete the first three certificates in consecutive order or move from 1 to 2 or 1 to 3.
Workers can also start directly in apprenticeships. Apprenticeships typically are for three to five years, during which time workers train on the job for four days and at a technical college one day a week.

leges on credential-oriented courses, it has otherwise sidelined this issue. This decision, however, by leaving WRTP more flexible, may be helping the organization to reach its primary goal of keeping well-paid jobs in the Milwaukee region. Although hiring slowed in the recession years after 2000, WRTP was able to prevent several plants from closing during the downturn. One company, Oilgear, a manufacturer of hydraulic equipment and systems, announced in 2002 that it was considering moving its Milwaukee operation to Texas. The WRTP staff worked with Oilgear's union and management to improve performance, and the company ended up moving work from its Texas plant to Milwaukee. When Milwaukee Cylinder, a family-owned producer of pneumatic and hydraulic cylinders, was bought out by Actuant in 1997, the new owners considered closing the plant. Again, WRTP helped union and management to jointly devise strategies for improving performance. The Milwaukee plant is now the company's most productive, and the company is expanding employment there. Union-management cooperation has also kept Milwaukee Brush, a German-owned manufacturer of a wide variety of brushes (e.g., paint brushes, brooms, and industrial equipment), in the city. In each of these cases, it was not a low-road strategy of wage reductions that saved the business; it was the ability of WRTP to find a high-road solution to the company's problems.

WRTP has also avoided the most widely criticized flaw in the nation's traditional job-training programs: under the federal Job Training Partnership Act, training providers have tended to "cream" off the most employable applicants in order to meet the placement quotients required by performance-based contracts.[31] Creaming is a problem when there are no alternatives or second chances for those not accepted—about 90 percent of the eligible population.[32] WRTP also screens applicants, but with the goal of placing all of them on a path to employment and advancement.[33] Included in the current WRTP partnership are not just unions and employers but also community organizations whose mission is to help the unemployed get through such screens. Staff members at these community organizations act as case managers and employment counselors, guiding people to appropriate preparation for training programs. The organizations also offer courses in employment readiness, basic math, English literacy, and preparation for the GED.

Over the years WRTP has won increasingly wider support for its multipronged strategy for getting low-income people into good jobs. It is a strategy of junctures: joining workplace modernization and workforce training; joining economic development efforts and workforce development efforts, which traditionally have been handled by wholly separate agencies; and also joining disparate training and pre-training programs into climbable career ladders. Indeed, it is hard to keep track of all the different community coalitions that WRTP (itself a coalition) has been part of.

In 1995 WRTP became part of a broad partnership called the Milwaukee Jobs Initiative, whose purpose was to reform traditional job-training systems to better serve low-income residents at a regional level. The Jobs Initiative was one of six similar projects across the nation initially funded by the Annie E. Casey Foundation. It brought many of the community's most powerful institutions into the effort (see table 6.2), and they remain involved now, even though the name "Milwaukee Jobs Initiative" was officially retired in 2003 and the organization was folded into WRTP.

Since 2001 WRTP has also been involved in a project called the Milwaukee Initiative for a Competitive Inner City (ICIC). This coalition of many of the same and additional community institutions is organized to bring good jobs to the city's poorest residents. Like the Milwaukee Jobs Initiative, the ICIC is one of several similar projects across the country funded by a single foundation—in this case, the Helen Bader Foundation. The Milwaukee ICIC surveyed local employers and found that many manufacturers in plastics, chemicals, food processing, and machine parts were seeking to expand but saw a variety of barriers to expanding in the inner city.[34] The ICIC will try to remove those barriers through brownfield remediation, land assembly, and workforce development. WRTP is responsible for the workforce development part of the project. In addition, WRTP is planning to open and operate a Workforce Training Center, a facility slated to open in the summer of 2004. The new Training Center will centralize resources for assessing low-income residents, preparing them for training,

TABLE 6.2
Milwaukee Jobs Initiative partners

Partner	Role
WRTP	Identifies employer technical assistance and workforce development needs; selects training and job candidates referred by community organizations and workforce development boards; assists technical colleges and other training providers in developing curriculum
Employers	Hire and advance workers; invest in workforce training and modernization
Unions	Appoint one-third of the board; assist with needs assessments; assist with internal training program development; participate in mentoring networks
Community Organizations (partial list) • Community Service Job Corp. • Community Justice Center • Northeast Milwaukee Industrial Development Corporation	Recruit, refer, and provide supportive services for unemployed adults; appoint one-third of the partnerships board of directors
Government Agencies • Milwaukee Housing Authority • Wisconsin Correctional Services • Job Centers (One-Stops)	Recruit, refer, and provide supportive services for unemployed adults
Educational Institutions • Milwaukee Area Technical College • Waukesha Technical College	Provide entry-level training customized to meet the needs of specific employers, higher-level certificates, and associate's degrees
Center on Wisconsin Strategy (COWS), University of Wisconsin, Madison	Provides technical assistance to partnership manufacturing firms and labor market analysis to the organization as a whole
Wisconsin Manufacturing Extension Partnership	Provides modernization assistance to manufacturing firms
Greater Milwaukee Committee (a council of local business, labor, and education leaders)	Appoints one-third of the board; helps raise funds from corporations and foundations

Source: Compiled by the author from Milwaukee Jobs Initiative documents.

placing them in training programs, finding them entry-level jobs in the targeted industries, and then creating advancement plans for them within those industries. The Center will be located in downtown Milwaukee, accessible by public transportation.

Creating these coalitions has not been easy. Several business executives from the Greater Milwaukee Committee at first objected to joining the Milwaukee Jobs Initiative because the coalition included the left-leaning Campaign for a Sustainable Milwaukee, which was then campaigning for a living-wage ordinance. More businesspeople balked after a *Wall Street Journal* article reported that the Greater Milwaukee Committee was being "bamboozled" by the living-wage group.[35] And several government agencies joined the Jobs Initiative but without much enthusiasm for its agenda of revamping the way they delivered services. To genuinely help in the development of new training programs and to actually coordinate services for low-income residents and the unemployed would have required a considerable investment of the agencies' time. Steven Holt, who was the director of the Milwaukee Jobs Initiative, says that some agencies, particularly the state and city workforce development agencies, were not fully committed to expending that effort, partly because they saw the initiative as an intrusion by outsiders, namely, the Casey Foundation and Joel Rogers of COWS, the think tank in Madison. In the end, however, the hard work of nurturing and sustaining community partnerships has paid off, according to WRTP's Eric Parker. The organization's current links, he says, demonstrate the consensus that has been achieved among business, labor, community, and civic leaders. The Milwaukee ICIC, WRTP's latest joint venture, is now creating a master board to coordinate economic development and workforce development policy. There is no question that the activities of WRTP have greatly increased the interest of Milwaukee's business and political leaders in workforce development—and in the bottom rungs, at least, of career ladders.

Beyond that, however, WRTP's achievements so far are mixed. It has not been able to get manufacturers in the region to sign on to a more extensive training system based on standardized career ladders, nor have the region's traditional workforce development players bought into the concept. Working instead on a plant-by-plant basis, WRTP has facilitated union-management efforts to modernize work processes and improve worker training at many of the community's largest manufacturing firms, thus raising the productivity of the big companies. The $25 million in training that firms invest annually reaches about seven thousand non-supervisory workers a year, 21 percent of whom are minorities.[36] We cannot know what the extent of business investment in training would have been without the intervention of WRTP, but the organization has certainly played a role in guiding and encouraging investment. Yet smaller manufacturers have been less willing to participate even in plant-by-plant training programs. And although it makes sense for the WRTP to focus on large unionized companies, which are more likely to employ high-performance work practices and which usually have the money and the contractual obligation to offer training, it is also true that the bulk of Milwaukee's manufacturing employees work at smaller companies. Leaving them out is a serious loss.

Thus far, WRTP's efforts on behalf of unemployed and displaced workers have also had mixed results. In the first five years of the Milwaukee Jobs Initiative, between 1995 and 2002, WRTP was only able to place 1,400 people in new jobs. On the positive side, those jobs were largely in manufacturing and did pay enough to support a family. The average starting wage of the workers placed by WRTP in those years was $10.55 an hour—$2.00 more per hour, on average, than at their previous jobs. Most of the jobs also offered benefits, a critical addition. In 2002, the last year for which data are available, WRTP placed 202 people in jobs with benefits, at an average hourly wage slightly over $11.00. These workers averaged a $1.44 hourly wage increase after one year on the job. But the total number of placements was still small, and, reflecting the impact of the 2002 recession on manu-facturing, about half the jobs were in health care, a sector that tends to have lower wages for low-rung jobs than manufacturing does.[37] Once the new Workforce Training Center is open, the plan is to place about 500 workers per year—still a fairly limited return on an investment of millions of public and private dollars in WRTP.

The Funding of WRTP

When WRTP started in 1992, it was supported by small grants from the local private industry council and technical colleges. By 1996, before the Annie E. Casey Foundation began funding the Milwaukee Jobs Initiative, WRTP had a budget of about $200,000 a year for brokering training funds. In 1997 the Casey grant—about $700,000 per year for planning and imple-menting the Jobs Initiative—provided about $250,000 to WRTP, which enabled Eric Parker and his board to greatly expand the scope of WRTP. The organization grew: many more employers were included, more tech-nical assistance was provided to manufacturing firms, the amount of job-training funds it brokered increased, and a pilot project was expanded. The goal for this first year was to fill ten job openings at ten companies paying wages of at least $10.00 per hour. This goal was achieved.

Furthermore, WRTP was able to leverage its Casey grant to win addi-tional funding from other foundations, government job-training contracts, and businesses. After developing a successful prototype in manufacturing between 1997 and 2000, WRTP received a demonstration grant from the U.S. Department of Labor to adapt the model to construction and health care. By 1999 WRTP's total budget was about $1 million, and about 70 percent of it came from the Annie E. Casey Foundation. By 2003, with a total budget of $1.2 million, only 25 percent came from the foundation. (The Casey grant was reduced to $300,000 in 2003 and will end in 2004.) By 2003 government contracts for workforce development made up half the WRTP budget.

The next round of funding from the Helen Bader Foundation for the ICIC project will allow WRTP to expand its level of services once again.

The Initiative for a Competitive Milwaukee of the Greater Milwaukee Committee has endorsed WRTP's plan to create a Career Center to assess, prepare, and place community residents in targeted sectors. The goal is to raise $500,000 per year from the private sector by 2006.

Two clear conclusions can be drawn from the WRTP experience: (1) that the organization's expansion and achievements would not have been possible without major investments from foundations; and (2) that even with significant foundation funding for more than a decade, it is difficult to change a workforce development system.

Work Chicago

If developing a career-ladder system in manufacturing is possible anywhere, it should happen in Chicago. In Cook County, which includes Chicago, more than 400,000 workers are employed in manufacturing. The city has effectively focused its economic development efforts on manufacturing. A wide network of community organizations is involved in business-retention and workforce-development activities. Several of the city's community colleges have developed effective training programs, and one of these programs, at Richard J. Daley College and its affiliated West Side Tech, offers a certificate in manufacturing technology, as well as associate's degrees and links to a bachelor's degree program in the same field.[38] Community organizations have created bridge programs to prepare people for community college certificate and degree programs. One offered by Instituto del Progresso Latino, for example, links students to the West Side Tech manufacturing program. And the demand for skilled manufacturing workers in Cook County—many more of them than current training programs are providing—is clear to all.[39] About 10,500 new workers have been and will be needed annually between 1996 and 2006, over 92 percent of them replacement workers.[40]

In this promising environment, an opportunity to create a coherent system of workforce development based on nationally recognized credentials emerged in 2000 when the Chicago Federation of Labor (CFL) and the Center for Labor and Community Research (CLCR) received a $750,000 grant from the U.S. Department of Labor to create a blueprint for a manufacturing career path. The initiative, which was called the Manufacturing Workforce Development Project, certainly seemed to have the political support it needed to succeed. The entire Illinois congressional delegation, the governor, the mayor, the president of the Cook County Board of Commissioners, the president of the Chicago Chamber of

Commerce, and the president of the Illinois Manufacturers' Association had supported the CFL/CLCR application. But although the labor federation and the CLCR succeeded in designing a unified training system based on career ladders, they could not implement it. Several foundations and training organizations withdrew their support from the undertaking, and this made it impossible to proceed systemwide. The CFL and CLCR were reduced to trying to institute job-training reforms on a much smaller scale. The story of this initiative reveals that, even in the best of circumstances, developing a unified new approach to job training can be a slow-going and highly political process, particularly if it involves many organizations that previously have been operating independently.

The goal of the Manufacturing Workforce Development Project was to identify weak links in the region's job-training system, target key manufacturing industries with the potential to take a high road to competitiveness, examine their workforce needs, and create a better job-training system that would be capable of meeting those needs. The new workforce development system would be designed to make use of

- industry-recognized standards,
- certified training providers,
- performance-based credentials, and
- career-advancement paths not limited to individual firms.

Because the career paths would be developed around clusters of jobs and skills, the new system would be able to respond to multiple manufacturers, and it would be able to offer workers the flexibility to move from one company to another. With support from foundations, the plan was to create an intermediary organization, called Work Chicago, which would implement the new system. But that last step never happened. And now the question is not whether the Work Chicago model is as good as it looked on paper but whether smaller-scale efforts can build the high-road manufacturing economy it envisioned.

The research done to come up with career-ladder proposals for Work Chicago was extraordinary. The CLCR researchers focused on thirty-seven industries, each of which employed more than one thousand workers and was expected to add at least a hundred workers per year. Collectively these industries accounted for three-quarters of the projected new manufacturing jobs in Cook County. The thirty-seven industries were then organized into thirteen clusters, and the research team identified the skill needs and hiring practices in each by conducting a survey, individual interviews, and focus groups. The researchers then proposed career ladders, asked employers and training providers to review them for accuracy, and revised them. Charts of the career paths were further refined by CLCR staff with knowledge of current manufacturing processes and machines, as well as current credentials and training programs.

The result was thirteen career ladders, each with occupational training needs grouped into foundation, core, and advanced skills. (Figure 6.1 is the career ladder for metals, machining, and electrical occupations.) The design of occupational-training curricula for each level was tied to nationally recognized standards. Metalworking programs, for example, were built around National Institute of Metalworking Skills (NIMS), which include tests and hands-on performance standards in thirteen metalworking occupations.[41] The researchers also made use of WorkKeys, a testing product developed by ACT, Inc. to test job-performance skills. With WorkKeys, anyone from high school students to incumbent workers could be placed in an appropriate training program or job.

The researchers' final report recommended building (or filling gaps in) a progression of credentials that could be obtained from high schools and community colleges—or from community-based training providers, unions, or trade organizations.

The researchers also studied the use of federal and state workforce training funds in Chicago—almost $98 million was spent on training for jobs in manufacturing in 2000—and concluded that the money was being spent, for the most part, ineffectively.[42] Several high schools, all seven of the colleges in the Chicago City Colleges system, the Illinois Institute of Technology, and at least fifty community organizations were offering training programs in manufacturing at the time of the report, with almost no coordination among them. Moreover, they were meeting only about half the local demand for manufacturing workers.[43] The report laments: "Supply-chain theory would assume that there is some central list of all available manufacturing education and training programs (there is not) and that public school systems and community colleges would introduce demand-targeted programs in coordination with one another (they do not)."[44]

Work Chicago was supposed to start with three key manufacturing industries: metalworking, food, and printing. The CLCR executive director Dan Swinney says that the research team and the project's advisory board recognized that only a powerful intermediary organization could overcome the zero-sum thinking and the turf jealousies that characterized the job-training scene in Chicago. The researchers proposed Work Chicago as an intermediary that would build partnerships between manufacturers,

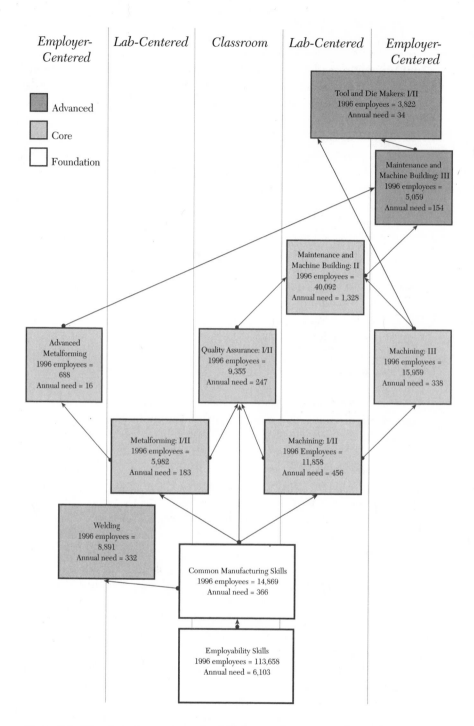

Employer-Centered   **Lab-Centered**   **Classroom**   **Lab-Centered**   **Employer-Centered**

Advanced

Core

Foundation

Tool and Die Makers: I/II
1996 employees = 3,822
Annual need = 34

Maintenance and
Machine Building: III
1996 employees =
5,059
Annual need =154

Maintenance and
Machine Building: II
1996 employees =
40,092
Annual need = 1,328

Advanced
Metalforming
1996 employees =
688
Annual need = 16

Quality Assurance: I/II
1996 employees =
9,355
Annual need = 247

Machining: III
1996 employees =
15,959
Annual need = 338

Metalforming: I/II
1996 employees =
5,982
Annual need = 183

Machining: I/II
1996 Employees =
11,858
Annual need = 456

Welding
1996 employees =
8,891
Annual need = 332

Common Manufacturing Skills
1996 employees = 14,869
Annual need = 366

Employability Skills
1996 employees = 113,658
Annual need = 6,103

Figure 6.1. Manufacturing career paths skill clusters diagram: metals, machinery, electrical manufacturing. The lines between the boxes show career paths for advancement. For ease of reading, the chart contains two columns for employer-centered training and two for lab-centered training

Source: Chicago Federation of Labor and Center for Labor and Community Research 2001.

training providers, and other organizations; would assign specific roles to each; would hold each responsible for meeting standards of quality and coordination; and would do continuing research, exploring new strategies for retaining jobs in Chicago and promoting state-of-the art technology and management techniques. The level of performance accountability that the researchers were contemplating was unprecedented, as was the level of cooperation and the level of funding. Implementing Work Chicago at the scale proposed would have required $1.2 million a year in foundation support.

The Decision to Support Incremental Change

From our perspective, the hardest work was completing our investigation, developing a very specific critique of the workforce development system, and identifying steps to move forward. It was certainly frustrating not to be able to implant our approach on a grand scale. But once we began to move our work forward on a smaller scale in the food sector we immediately began to gain strength based on the application of our approach, proving our point.

DAN SWINNEY, executive director, CLCR

The local and national foundations that initially had expressed interest in the project were not willing to fund it at that level. Part of the reason was stock market losses; foundations everywhere were cutting back. But, in addition, some of the foundation officers were not convinced that a single entity could coordinate all the certification and training activity envisioned, especially given the history of turf battles among Chicago's various training providers. Further, the foundations had been hearing concerns about Work Chicago from several organizations, some of which were on the project's advisory board. Some of these organizations thought a new intermediary would simply replicate work that had either been done already or was currently being done. Others believed the price tag was too high. Still others considered the Work Chicago approach to be too "top down," and that it should be based instead on previous system-building efforts. And still others would have preferred to integrate Work Chicago into the existing Chicago Workforce Board, which oversees the city's job-training activities under the Workforce Investment Act. There were also organizations that thought the career paths leaned too far toward German and Danish apprenticeship models; others thought they were too vague. Some of the organizations questioned whether the CFL and CLCR were the right organizations to lead Work Chicago. This last concern was exacerbated when Don Turner announced his retirement as president of the Chicago Federation of Labor.

Several advisory board members worried that the new CFL leadership might not have the same commitment to workforce development that Turner had.

It is hard to tell how much of the criticism was personal or was based on historic rivalries among workforce development organizations. The bottom line is that enough doubts were expressed by various individuals and organizations to make the foundations leery of fully funding an initiative that depended on wide support.

When the foundations' final commitment came in at $400,000, a third of what CLCR had asked for, Swinney decided to withdraw the proposal. He believed that an insufficiently funded effort would have simply created a weak organization with little ability to leverage additional resources. Such a limited organization, he claims, would have found itself competing with existing organizations rather than coordinating their efforts; it could not have overcome the problems identified in the report. As to why groups that seemed to be supportive of Work Chicago in the beginning came to express doubts in the end, Swinney commented, "When proposing system change, a new level of accountability, broader partnerships, and greater coordination, it's no surprise that some—particularly those in the field who are part of the system that was effectively critiqued as a 'non-system'— were resistant. This resistance to change is common in Chicago and elsewhere."[45]

One alternative to a full-scale overhaul of workforce development activities in Cook County was to try to implement the ideas on a smaller scale with the hope of incrementally building up to a system like Work Chicago. Swinney's withdrawal left this option to others, and the Chicago Workforce Board stepped up to the bat.

In February 2003 the Board contracted with the Center on Work and Community Development, an independent research and consulting group headed by Bob Ginsburg, the former director of research on the Work Chicago project, to create a credentialing system for the metalworking, machining, and electrical trades. The credentials were to be based on the career path that had been prepared for this cluster of industries in the Work Chicago report. This one-cluster project, called the Manufacturing Career Path Pilot, is now proceeding. A second project that is moving forward from groundwork laid in the Work Chicago report is Food Chicago, which is promoting a career-ladder approach in the food-manufacturing industry.

A Pilot in the Metalworking, Machining, and Electrical Trades

In the first year of the Manufacturing Career Path Pilot, the main effort was to convince employers and training providers of the value of using nationally recognized credentials based on NIMS and adopting an industry-wide career ladder. Ginsburg and his team met with manufacturers to demonstrate to them that they had common training needs and to persuade them to buy into the common occupational classification and training system that the team had created. Ginsburg explains that it was a difficult job to get employers who were convinced that their machines and manufacturing processes were unique to invest in the concept of portable skills; for the career-ladder concept to succeed, that culture of individuality would have to be changed. Moreover, while many manufacturers had already accepted that different types of jobs had different skill requirements, they had never agreed to a career path in manufacturing with a *sequence* of job titles and descriptions. Nevertheless the effort was successful. In the first year of the pilot project twenty-five manufacturers made a commitment in writing to hire workers with the entry-level credentials identified in the career ladder, to adopt job descriptions that reflected those credentials, and to support the new job-training system by donating instructors or funds. The project team continues to enlist employer and union involvement.

The project is preparing to open a credentialing center to provide different job-training organizations with the resources to prepare students for NIMS tests and certification. At the time of this writing, the up-to-date machinery needed for the first rung of training and tests had been donated by employers. The plan is to obtain additional machines with the tolerances required for other NIMS credentials in coming years. When fully operational, the credentialing center should be able to serve new labor market entrants and incumbent workers throughout the metropolitan area. It is located in the North Lawndale neighborhood, which has been underserved with manufacturing training. To date, about $200,000 has been raised from foundations to get the facility up and running.

Meanwhile, the Chicago Workforce Board organized a manufacturing workforce summit meeting in May 2003, which was attended by all of the region's eight workforce boards and several training organizations.[46] The boards agreed to establish joint policy priorities. And, based on the original CLCR research, they decided to focus on five sectors, including manufacturing. They adopted the goal of making job training in each sector more responsive to the needs of local industries. The first halting movement toward broader, if not yet systemwide, reform was under way. Food Chicago illustrates how such a sectoral approach might work.

Food Chicago

In 1996 CLCR started a project called the Candy Institute, with the goal
of improving productivity in Cook County's one hundred candy manufacturing companies and thus maintaining thirteen thousand good local jobs.
At the time neither the city's Department of Planning and Development
nor the Mayor's Office of Employment and Training was targeting particular industries, and most candy producers were so preoccupied with mere
survival that they did not see themselves in the context of a broader industry. But the Candy Institute persisted, and its training successes, coupled
with the Work Chicago report's compelling presentation of the career-path
concept, eventually captured the interest of other food manufacturers, of
local, state, and federal government, and of industry associations such as
the Illinois Manufacturers Association. With its expanding base, the Candy
Institute was renamed "Food Chicago" in 2003.

The Chicago area has 850 food-manufacturing firms, which employ
nearly 68,000 workers at an average hourly wage of $13.00. The industry
contributes $17 billion annually in sales and $2.6 billion in taxes to the local
economy.[47] The mission of Food Chicago is to increase the profitability of
this sizable local industry through production modernization, workforce
training, the use of industry-wide career ladders, and advocacy of supportive public policies.

Food manufacturing, however, does not even have consistently defined
occupations, much less nationally recognized skill standards. Thus creating
career pathways in the food industry is a difficult undertaking; it is even
harder to convince employers to define positions based on credentials they
may never have heard of.

It is noteworthy that Food Chicago invited neither employers nor unions
to its first meetings devoted to developing a career ladder and a standardized training system for the food industry. Instead, it brought together
representatives of the region's job-training providers and the Chicago
and suburban community colleges. This group reviewed all existing course
descriptions and food-manufacturing curricula; it identified the missing
pieces that would have to be added to the existing job-training system; and
it developed the career ladder shown in figure 6.2. The former executive
director of Food Chicago Friederika Kaider says that she wanted to move
forward quickly, and, for that reason, she chose to create a full training
system for the industry and then present it to employers for comments and
validation.

The Food Chicago career ladder begins with work-readiness instruction
for those who need that level of preparation for entry-level jobs and basic

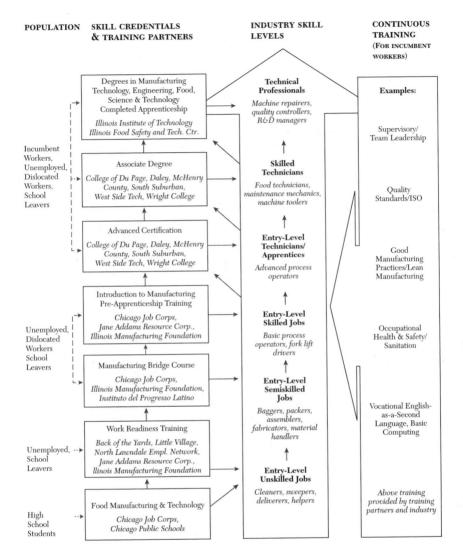

Figure 6.2. Food Chicago Career Path

Source: Based on Davis Jenkins and Tom DuBois, "Presentation to CWB Service Delivery Integration Committee," February 7, 2002, reprinted in Chicago Federation of Labor and Center for Labor and Community Research 2001.

training programs. The ladder includes vocational ESL (VESL) classes, which are needed by many new employees and incumbent employees as a first step toward advancement. (Approximately 40 percent of food industry employees in Chicago are Hispanic, the majority of whom have limited English skills.) Further training and additional certification allow employees (both new and incumbent) to move into higher-skilled, entry-level jobs and to prepare for more advanced training.

At least five companies that already had a training and advancement orientation (including Clyde's Donuts, Vie de France, and Kraft) quickly signed on to the project, as did three unions (the Bakery, Confectionery, Tobacco and Grainmillers Union; the Chicago Federation of Labor Service Employees International Union; and the Teamsters). In November 2003 Mayor Richard Daley endorsed the project and agreed to contact the eight largest food producers in the city and urge their support for Food Chicago's career ladder.

The career ladder was formalized as the Food Chicago Career Path Consortium in 2004. This group of training providers, unions, placement agencies, credentialing organizations, food companies, and contributors of funds has been encouraged to submit a proposal for funding by the U.S. Department of Labor. Each of the partners was working separately, but all have agreed to work with Food Chicago to better coordinate their efforts. To date, the training providers have signed agreements to work with food companies in the six-county metropolitan area and to teach nationally recognized or industry-wide credentials. The providers will market their programs collectively to high schools, One-Stop Career Centers, and community organizations. The Consortium will streamline recruiting and placement services to make it easier to match graduates with appropriate jobs. Using the information provided by the Consortium, companies will be able to hire workers at all levels with the appropriate skills.

As I write, Food Chicago is helping the unions to leverage public funds for incumbent worker training and to negotiate contracts that support training and career paths. It is also brokering training programs for participating firms—in increasing productivity, food safety and hazard analysis, sanitation, and computing. A pilot VESL program arranged by Food Chicago for a mid-sized candy manufacturer and its union has already been deemed such a success with its first thirty-one students that the company is contracting for seventy-one more employees to take the course. Swinney reports that 12 percent of the employees who participated in the program saw an average annual pay raise of $2,500. These outcomes resulted in the company undertaking a lean manufacturing training program for all three hundred of its employees, which has increased productivity by 30 percent, saving the company over a million dollars. This outcome, in turn, caused the company to reverse a considered move to Mexico.

In an effort to attract young people to the industry, Food Chicago and the Chicago Workforce Board have begun offering teachers and career counselors on-site visits to manufacturing facilities so they can personally see that many of the jobs are clean, pay well, and have advancement potential. The other side of the coin is that Food Chicago wants to be able to encourage start-up businesses in the fast-growing specialty-foods market and help them to adopt high-performance manufacturing methods. The organization has applied for a $2 million grant from the U.S. Department of Commerce to start up what the Food Chicago people are calling the Center for Business Innovation and Training, a facility that can be both incubator and home to fifteen or more small specialty-food producers at a time.[48] The Illinois Department of Commerce and Economic Opportunity has expressed interest in including the Center into the Chicago region component of the state's economic development plan.

It is too soon to draw conclusions about the effectiveness of either Food Chicago or the pilot project in metalworking, machining, and electrical trades. For now both have more plans than activities. But it is not premature to see that one aspect of the food-industry project is likely to have an important impact on the Chicago area's job-training system. CLCR's Food Chicago is committed to collecting data and analyzing the employer's return on investment for each of its job-training programs. Hard numbers of this kind could garner a great deal of support for the food-industry project, and for job training and career ladders more generally. In part, what convinced Cook County politicians and a handful of participating manufacturers to support Food Chicago in the first place were return-on-investment figures from Eli's Cheesecake, which were gathered in 2002 when that company contracted with the Candy Institute to deliver employee training.

Eli's Cheesecake keeps records of two types of errors that can occur in the production process: seconds and no-shows. Seconds are cakes that come out with minor flaws and are saleable only in outlet stores. No-shows are cakes that do not make it through the entire production process. As can be seen in figures 6.3 and 6.4, both types of errors declined noticeably as the company's workers completed classes over the course of the year in Good Manufacturing Practices and Food Safety.[49]

Jolene Worthington, the executive vice president of operations at Eli's Cheesecake, estimates that a 1 percent reduction in production errors saves the company about $150,000 every year. Using this figure, CLCR was able

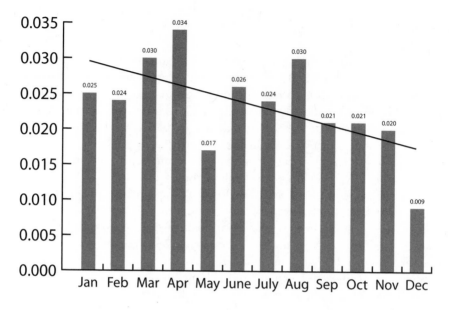

Figure 6.3. Percentage of seconds during the year of training, 2002
Source: Eli's Cheesecake and Food Chicago.

to demonstrate that $58,000 spent on job training resulted in a $550,000 savings to the company in 2002.[50] CLCR would like to be able to demonstrate soon that the basic strategy of upgrading manufacturing methods and worker skills in tandem can have just as clear a payoff.

A Tale of Two Cities

The Manufacturing Career Path Pilot and Food Chicago are two sectors identified in the original Work Chicago plan. Neither is content merely to provide training to some number of students and place them in jobs. Each aims for something larger: to increase the number of businesses in its industry that adopt high-road manufacturing practices and offer career-ladders with advancement opportunities for employees. This is the same link that WRTP is trying to establish in Wisconsin: a link between the Milwaukee region's economic development efforts and its workforce development efforts. However, the two cities illustrate quite different ways of making linkages.

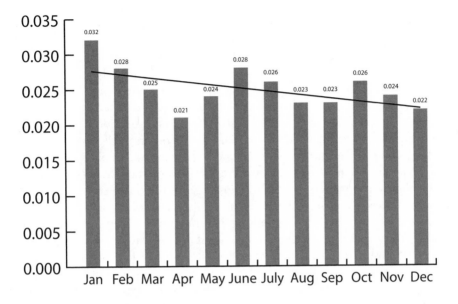

Figure 6.4. Percentage of no-shows during the year of training, 2002
Source: Eli's Cheesecake and Food Chicago.

Employers

In Milwaukee growing global competition convinced many of the city's large manufacturers of the need to adopt high-performance production practices and train workers accordingly. These employers also realized that union cooperation would be essential to the undertaking, and so they pursued a collaborative approach. The main accomplishment of WRTP so far has been facilitating that union-management cooperation. (The organization has had less success in reaching out to smaller companies that were not already sold on the idea.)

In Chicago, by contrast, few employers had a strong sense of the possible connection between worker training and company profitability. Food Chicago, as a result, did not even try to involve employers in its initial planning of a food-industry career ladder, and the number of employers involved in the project is still relatively small but growing. Bob Ginsburg expresses frustration over how hard it has been to convince manufacturers to accept even common job descriptions. "Historically, union and political pressures forced European and Asian manufacturers to view themselves and act as an industry," he says. "American individualism limits the ability of manufacturers to address global pressures." Chicago manufacturers,

Ginsburg says, are not together enough even to "fight political acceptance of the conventional economic wisdom that the demise of high-end manufacturing and the rise of services is okay."[51]

But the Chicago organizations have also found that employers will participate in a job-training and modernization program if they see that it serves their economic interests. As Bill Graham, the director of Workforce Development at Food Chicago, points out, many companies ask Food Chicago to provide vocational English, safety, and sanitation courses, and some of these companies will partially pay workers while taking these courses on site. But far fewer companies follow up with good manufacturing practices or lean manufacturing courses that would suggest ways to reconfigure production processes. Thus the task the organizations have set themselves is to convince employers of what so many Milwaukee businesses already believe. This is not something that traditional job-training programs have been concerned with to any significant degree. Most workforce development programs measure their success in terms of their effects on students—they measure students' completion rates, job-placement rates, and wage levels—but not their effects on employers. Typically job-training organizations look at the demand side of the employment equation only with occasional interviews of employers, asking whether they have hired program-trained workers, if they are satisfied with those workers, and if they would hire from the program in the future.[52] Food Chicago's documentation that worker training created productivity gains at Eli's Cheesecake went well beyond the usual and it seems to have won over other manufacturers. After the original CFL/CLCR report was released, the Illinois Manufacturers Association asked CLCR to complete an analysis of the state's manufacturing. The report recommended seeking state support for restructuring the Illinois workforce development system along the lines advanced in the original report and by Food Chicago. The Association and the Illinois AFL-CIO have made this objective and other high-road approaches part of their key policy and legislative goals for the next two years. The spread of career-ladder programs, which ask employers to offer workers more pay as they increase their skills, will probably require many more, similarly documented demonstrations and buy-ins by major industry associations—even in places like Milwaukee, where employers are already favorably disposed to job training.

Unions

Labor, too, has played different roles in Milwaukee and Chicago. In Milwaukee labor was committed to training and to high-performance manufacturing prior to the formation of WRTP; and in the WRTP's large, unionized member companies, labor works with management to decide which technologies and manufacturing methods to adopt and to make sure that workers receive the necessary training.

In Chicago, on the other hand, community organizations have been stronger advocates for workforce training over the last twenty-five years than unions have. The closure of many of the area's large, unionized plants in the 1980s left fewer opportunities for a jointly led, union-management initiative such as WRTP. The involvement of the Chicago Federation of Labor and its executive director at the time, Don Turner, in the discussion of how to frame a system of industry-wide career ladders may have been essential to getting the Work Chicago research funded and completed. However, the extent to which the Federation will stay involved in workforce development at this time, under its new leadership and with no large-scale project moving forward, is unclear.

In Chicago, where it is chiefly training providers, community anti-poverty organizations, and government leaders who are interested in career ladders, the supply of worker training and trained workers may end up driving the demand for them rather than the reverse.

Funding

Historically private foundations have played an important role in funding demonstrations of innovative approaches to job training. But they have played that role differently in these two cities. In Milwaukee funds from the Annie E. Casey Foundation enabled WRTP to solidify its work in manufacturing and expand the approach to the construction and health care sectors. Casey funding was significantly higher and longer term than most workforce grants, and, as a result, WRTP was able to leverage Casey funds to obtain additional support from other foundations, from state and local government, and from employers. While most workforce development initiatives struggle to find the foundation funding they need to survive, WRTP has reduced its dependence on foundation funding to about 25 percent of its total annual income. A new round of funding from the Helen Bader Foundation for the ICIC project may have the same effect for an expanded level of services, because the Bader funding, too, is a multiyear commitment to organization building.

Foundation support for job-training innovation also has been high in Chicago, but there it has gone mostly to smaller community organizations. With only a few exceptions,[53] foundation funding in Chicago has helped job-training providers, community colleges, and other agencies to improve their delivery of traditional services; it has not changed the way government workforce development systems operate. In Chicago, when the opportunity arose to fund a more thoroughgoing reform of a system that almost all who were involved acknowledge as inadequate, the foundations, for a range of reasons, let it slip by.

The element of foundation funding common in both cities, of course, is its time-limited nature. And federal job-training funds have never met more than a small percentage of the need in either city. Workforce development thus relies on funding from employers and increasingly from local government. In the latter category, Chicago has been particularly creative. It was one of the first cities to use tax increment financing (TIF) to finance workforce development in blighted areas.

TIF programs work as follows: When development in a blighted area of the city raises a property's value, the property tax on the parcel also increases. Instead of simply adding that extra property tax revenue to the city's general funds, the city designates the blighted area as a TIF district and sets the additional tax revenues aside to pay for improvements within the district.[54]

In Chicago, the TIF tool was overused. Community groups from poor neighborhoods complained, for instance, about a TIF district created in the Loop, Chicago's wealthy commercial district, which could hardly be called a blighted area. In fact, Chicago currently has 129 TIF districts, covering almost 30 percent of its land area, and about $400 million in funds.[55] In 1991 some thirty organizations interested in workforce development formed a task force, with funding from the Joyce Foundation, to ensure that at least some of that TIF money was used to benefit low-income residents.[56] After a year-long political battle, the city agreed to earmark close to 10 percent of future TIF revenues for job training for firms located in blighted TIF districts. The program, called TIFWorks, was started with a $5 million kitty, money that can be loaned to TIF districts that have a low or zero balance in their accounts so they can begin paying for training programs. The loans will be repaid out of the districts' future TIF revenues.

Creating a permanent funding base is one of the most difficult tasks that faces training providers. TIFWorks has the potential to offer just such a firm financial footing, but funding is still tied, as most traditional funding is, to the number of people trained and thus cannot be used for developing a more systematic approach to a job training system. The funding for TIFWorks, moreover, is still quite modest, which is one more reason that organizations working to create a career-ladder system in manufacturing in Chicago are likely to take even longer to achieve their goals than those in Milwaukee.

Community Colleges

Community colleges play a key role in WRTP and less of one historically in Chicago. The Food Chicago Career Path Consortium engages all seven of Chicago's City Colleges and it will be interesting to follow how this partnership changes the ways the colleges have of doing business. In Milwaukee WRTP is the region's largest training broker and all the training it brokers is provided by local technical colleges. WRTP staff negotiates with college staff over course content. As a result, employers' needs are getting met, and, in addition, considerable progress is being made in Milwaukee toward incorporating portable national standards into certification and degree programs. In Chicago, on the other hand, the two manufacturing projects that are on track are still fairly small, and most job training has been provided by community-based organizations rather than by community colleges. In Chicago the only guarantee that manufacturing skill standards would take hold is if the Workforce Board and the Mayor's Office of Employment and Training were to make contracts with training providers contingent upon teaching to the standards. And only such a step would force the Chicago City Colleges, which as a system has not been particularly responsive to employer needs, to change their curriculum. So far that is not happening, although Food Chicago has nine community colleges as members and aims to work with them in improving their performance.

Community colleges in both cities have a considerable amount of articulation in place to ease student movement from high school or a bridge program to a certificate program to an associate's degree program and, finally, to a bachelor's degree program in manufacturing, but this does not seem to be the key to creating climbable career ladders in manufacturing. Most community colleges do not maintain records that would shed light on the phenomenon, but it is clear that, throughout the country, few students move from one track to the other in manufacturing or in any other technical training field. Once students finish a certificate program and find a job, they seldom go back for an associate's degree, let alone a bachelor's degree. This suggests that the career ladder in manufacturing is one that starts with bridge programs and for most people ends with some college-level work, with a few needing an associate's degree or higher. And, as the wage data from WRTP and Food Chicago reveal, advancing this far on the career path leads to significant gains in income.

The Future of Career Ladders in Manufacturing

The City's partnership with the Candy Institute/Food Chicago will strengthen our food manufacturing sector. Food Chicago is the kind of public/private partnership that is good for our local companies and our local communities.

RICHARD M. DALEY, mayor of Chicago

The staffs of both the Milwaukee and the Chicago organizations are convinced that the best way to serve both employers and workers—and the best way to link economic and workforce development—is through career ladders. Yet neither Milwaukee nor Chicago has a career ladder in place in the manufacturing industry that is based on nationally recognized credentials and has been adopted by a large percentage of employers in the metropolitan area.

To change that, the Chicago projects are putting a lot of effort into convincing community job-training providers to build their programs around portable NIMS credentials—and convincing manufacturers that they would benefit from participating in such a system. The Manufacturing Career Path Coalition Pilot and the Food Chicago Career Path Consortium are demonstrating how this approach could work in different manufacturing industries. In contrast, WRTP has decided not to expend much effort convincing employers that they need to adjust their practices around industry-wide credentials. Rather, WRTP helps companies and their unions negotiate their own internal advancement ladders and worker-training benefits. At the same time WRTP is pressuring the local technical colleges to start linking their training programs to national standards, in the hope of getting career ladders started from that direction.

It is too soon to tell which strategy, if either, will be effective. In fact, we still have little hard data about either program. We know that the partner firms of WRTP, although they have not adopted industry-wide career ladders, are already creating better-quality jobs. And we also know that the two Chicago projects, although still very small, have the support of powerful political players such as Mayor Richard Daley. We know, too, that participating employers in both cities have agreed to hire low-income residents for good manufacturing jobs, which would not have happened without the intervention of an intermediary. This is all good news.

But if changing employer practices is important, the extent to which it is happening has to be measured. Additional evaluation criteria need to be considered by examining the following questions: How many firms have provided higher wages for participants in advanced training programs? How many employers have invested in the upgrading of skills? How many have established career ladders based on acquiring skills? To what extent have firms begun hiring from a more diverse and nontraditional labor pool? Evaluation of job-training efforts has to move beyond counting the number of placements achieved. We need quantifiable measures of the extent to which workforce development and career ladder initiatives are changing the practice and profitability of manufacturing, and the skills and job security of manufacturing workers.

Chapter 7

An Agenda for Moving Up in the New Economy

Investment in workers and in worker advancement systems is only one element of several necessary strategies if the overall objective is an economy that pays decent wages and allows opportunities for people to move up as they acquire more experience and skills. This concluding chapter examines the evidence accumulated throughout the book with regard to the three framing questions raised in chapter 1:

1. What does it take for career-ladder strategies to succeed at the immediate task of getting particular workers on a path to earnings growth and career advancement?

The programs presented in this book offer many examples of the best or the most promising practice. They also confirm the assumption that the reorganization of work is as critical a function of career-ladder programs as the provision of training. Unless a workplace is organized to accommodate career mobility, programs can do no more than just place people in jobs. Thus, where workplaces are not already structured for mobility, career-ladder programs must transform them. And for that to succeed, employers must not merely be the recipients of advice and services; instead, they must play as strong a role in career-ladder programs as do training organizations or workforce intermediaries.

Sometimes employers assume that role as a matter of enlightened self-interest, and the chief task of the career-ladder programs in this regard is to provide the enlightenment. At other times, regulatory or trade union pressures, or the carrot of government subsidies, must be brought to bear, and the key task of career-ladder programs is to lobby for it. The evidence indicates that some types of workforce intermediary are better at these tasks than others. The efficacy of any one type also varies in different industries and occupations.

2. Even if individual programs are successful, how much of a difference can the career-ladder strategy make?

My investigations suggest that the presence or absence of complementary regulatory, macro-economic, and demand-side policies are a crucial determinant of the strategy's impact even at the local level. For example, a relatively tight local labor market gives workers and advocates of worker advancement a measure of bargaining power, and, in most cases, that appears to be necessary in order to influence employer decisions concerning the structure of the workplace. A tight national labor market, anchored in a full-employment policy, would be all the more empowering. Further, in some industries wage regulation or wage-setting leverage from public payers is necessary to assure that career-ladder advancement actually produces rewards in pay.

The willingness of employers to restructure work can also be affected greatly by public policies. As we have seen, government worker training subsidies, if used strategically, can induce employers to provide pathways for advancement. Community colleges are also a form of public subsidy. Again, these public dollars can be used in a scattershot fashion in the hope that better-educated workers will necessarily be better-paid workers. Or community colleges can embark on deliberate partnerships aimed at producing career ladders. For instance, in North Carolina and California community-college training for positions in the bio-technology industry is part of a deliberate state government strategy to provide workers for manufacturing jobs, and to create career opportunities. In addition, public policies are required to protect the right to form trade unions, which in turn advocate for training, advancement systems, and better wages.

Finally, the level of funding for government job-training programs and the design of those programs will greatly affect the impact of a career-ladder strategy.

But even with complementary public policies in place, how much can be expected of career-ladder programs, and how many eggs, finally, should we put in this basket? These are questions that must not be ducked. And from the evidence of the programs in this book, it is clear that we need much better data before we can answer them.

3. How can the government job-training system and the public education system more effectively promote career advancement?

The present system of government job-training and worker-education programs supports career advancement only marginally. If we believe that workers can benefit immensely from lifelong career opportunities in order to advance—and the individual stories in this book confirm my belief that they can—then the present job-training system must be explicitly aligned with career-ladder strategies. How to accomplish that, how much to spend on it, and how to convince governments to invest in it are among the most important questions for career-ladder advocates to address at this time.

How to Get Career-Ladder Strategies to Succeed in Their Task

We have seen plenty of evidence that successful career-ladder programs can make a dramatic difference in the pay levels and the aspirations of low-wage workers. The existing literature provides guidance regarding the best ways to reach and serve job seekers, particularly low-income job seekers, and the kind of networking that is needed to do so. The evidence in this book suggests, however, that reaching employers is equally critical. Career ladders do not get constructed in the workplace or used unless either (1) employers are persuaded that such an approach is in their self-interest; or (2) external leverage from unions or government impels them to change practices. Formal credentials seem to be an important part of this process in some sectors, but less so in others Workforce intermediaries are, as expected, key to pulling all partners together to create the web of services needed. But the concept of the "intermediary" still lacks a political dimension, and this is needed to create systemic change to support career advancement.

More Willing Employers

Too few employers will spontaneously grasp the benefits of having skilled and loyal employees. Multiple structural changes in recent decades create an enormous temptation for employers to take a low road of low wages and high turnover. These include the weakening of trade unions, the "virtual" nature of the ever increasing number of business enterprises (a few core employees and lots of far-flung contract workers or temps); and the ease in a global, high-tech economy of cutting costs by relocating jobs.

However, this book, as well as other studies of employers, present many examples of employers who have changed the structure of work to include more opportunities for entry-level workers to advance into better-paying jobs. And these examples confirm that employers have considerable discretion in how they structure jobs and how they pay workers. When both high and low roads can be profitable, what factors determine the willingness of employers to take the high road and adopt career-ladder strategies? One factor is stability. Other researchers have found that businesses that are more likely to invest in training for their workers are those that cannot easily pick up and move elsewhere, offer employee benefits, employ new production technologies, and enjoy low turnover.[1] Hence it is not surprising that health care has been a particularly promising area for creating career ladders. The demand for workers in health care occupations (e.g., nurses, lab technicians) does not vary as unpredictably as the demand for workers in some other industries. And hospitals and nursing homes cannot relocate to Asia. Other locally rooted service-sector industries, which, like health care, are substantially underwritten by government, should also be good candidates for career ladders, and my research bears that out. These include child care and education.

Manufacturing industries and companies vary in stability. Many manufacturing jobs are relatively easy to relocate to lower-wage areas, and jobs are also vanishing as a result of increased productivity. Even a seemingly robust company with a growing order book may find itself downsized, relocated, acquired, or overtaken by new technology. And as we saw in Milwaukee, market forces may overwhelm even employers who choose the high road. This institutional uncertainty makes it difficult to sustain career ladders in some manufacturing industries, particularly those producing nondurable goods that can be made more cheaply in less-developed countries. On the other hand, manufacturers of high-tech products such as medical instruments—companies that need to remain close to customers and researchers—will often choose to take the high road, attracting, training, and rewarding skilled workers. In biotechnology, once a firm has won FDA approval for a production process at a particular location, the firm is unlikely to move. This has made biotechnology manufacturing a good focus for career-ladder initiatives. As we saw in chapter 6, biomanufacturers themselves expect to invest considerable time and resources in training their workers.

Firm size is also a factor in employers' willingness to create career ladders, because large firms are more likely than small ones to have internal labor markets with formal occupational classifications. They are thus more likely to provide training benefits.[2] And because of their size, their per-person training costs are comparatively low.[3] Large firms are also more likely to have human resource departments, which tend to advocate for investment in worker training.[4] The pattern can be seen in chapter 5. The larger, unionized firms in Milwaukee are better positioned to invest in training than small- and medium-sized companies. And possibly because investment in training is easier for them, they are committed to adopting high-performance work practices that can support internal career ladders.[5]

Size is also an issue in the service sector. In health care most nursing homes are too small to have their own training programs and need assistance through programs such as ECCLI, whereas larger hospitals not only have the resources to provide training but also have an array of jobs that trainees can advance into. Small nonprofit child care centers do not have resources to invest in training, nor do they have enough jobs to construct a multi-rung ladder. But even in larger centers reimbursement rates prohibit developing a tiered wage structure based on acquiring more education.

Employers' comfort with career-ladder strategies is thus a complex and highly nuanced issue. And when career-ladder advocates present them with a high-road alternative to their current organization of work, it has to suit the employers' particular circumstances. In Chicago we saw that many manufacturers were reluctant to adopt industry-wide job descriptions that would allow better coordination of job training and clearer pathways to advancement. Sometimes it is self-evident that the high-road alternative is in the employer's interest, but at other times it has to be made feasible (for instance, with government-subsidized modernization assistance) or imposed (by union negotiation, for example). In Chicago investment in training by the Chicago Workforce Board convinced some employers to adopt standard job descriptions and commit to identifying career advancement pathways. What convinced employers in Milwaukee to do so was both investment by the Jobs Initiative and union cooperation in adopting high-road production techniques as well as the training needed to implement them.

What Willing Employers Need to Do

We know a lot about how to design good education and training programs for people with low skills. Good programs offer a comprehensive approach to training that includes social support services, particularly child care; soft-skills training so that new workers know the norms of the workplace; post-employment services to help new workers learn how to respond to tough work situations—both technical and interpersonal skills; learning communities or support groups; curriculum developed in cooperation with business; and practice-based learning.

Typically job-training programs do not challenge ingrained styles of management. That would take a level of participation in the training of low-skill workers that most employers are not willing to provide. But career ladders do not seem to work in highly hierarchical work settings in which lower-level employees are treated as if they are not capable of thinking. Thus it seems that career-ladder programs must also address management styles.

The matter is further complicated in health care, child care, and education, where the professional-paraprofessional distinction carries with it a class distinction and often a racial or ethnic distinction. The influence of organizational hierarchy is greatest in health care. One of the biggest complaints of CNAs and home health aides is that they are not treated with respect. In nursing homes CNAs have the most contact with patients, but typically they are not part of the patient-care planning team. CNAs who have taken courses to increase their skills often report that they are treated the same afterward. Employers need to create an environment of respect if lower-skilled workers are to be accepted by their colleagues as the former advance. Whether at a nursing home or a hospital, career-ladder programs need to be accompanied by training or by discussions with workers at all levels to establish how all will contribute in care-giving teams. In Boston, Children's Hospital made sure this happened by selecting a "program champion," a term coined by Joseph Cabral, then manager of employment and diversity. The champion's role was to convince the other hospital staff members that creating opportunity for lower-level workers would benefit the organization as a whole. Although this specific role was only mentioned in hospital and nursing-home settings, probably any workplace participating in a career-ladder program would benefit from having a top-level point person to convey the importance of the program to all workers.

Some employers I visited had fully reorganized the work process to ensure that even the lowest-level employees were treated as valued members of a team working toward a goal. Other employers sent managers for training to learn how to interact more respectfully with the workers they supervise. The adoption of a team-based problem-solving approach at Apple Health Care nursing homes has resulted in changes in protocol that have made workers and residents happier and has saved the organization money. Such changes have value independent of career ladders, but they also are probably the necessary base for effective career-ladder programs. The staff at Bridges to the Future in Boston believe that a key to that program's success was that it started with training for managers, who then became advocates for the program with others.

Employers also need to work with community college staff on developing curricula. We saw this willingness in Bridges to the Future and several health care training initiatives. In manufacturing, WRTP worked with community and technical colleges on developing curriculum on behalf of its member firms. In biotechnology, employers are just beginning to figure out the skills they need and are working closely with community colleges in developing curricula for short-term training up to college degree programs.

Credentials

The notion of career ladders suggests formal job titles and credentials. But these seem to be more important in some sectors than in others. In health care the federal government has established minimum requirements for CNAs working in nursing homes, and some states have instituted additional training requirements. State governments have licensing requirements and exams for LPNs and RNs. This is a sector that is accustomed to a hierarchy of credentials, and it makes sense to follow the same form when adding new rungs to the career ladder. Thus the Extended Care Career Ladder in Massachusetts is attempting to create additional credentials within the CNA occupation, with the goal of standardizing the new grades across the state. This has not happened yet, but it will ultimately determine the degree to which the credentials are portable.

Child care, with its mish-mash of training programs, would benefit greatly from consolidation into a single system of nationally recognized credentials. Most states have devised education and skills-updating requirements for different occupational categories in this field, but the requirements and the categories differ significantly from one state to the next. The child care industry needs pathways for advancement, but right now too many are being created. Chapter 3 identified four distinct pathways being developed for a three-rung career ladder (teacher aide, teacher, center director): state-mandated, short-term course requirements; Child Development Associate credential programs; associate's degree programs in early childhood education; and U.S. Department of Labor apprenticeships. Much effort is wasted at the state level in identifying individual requirements, when we have nationally recognized credentials that could be used by all. The child care field may need to create levels under the CDA for child care assistants—like the new rungs for advancement within the CNA category, which ECCLI is establishing—but these, too, could be nationally standardized. The military's system of child care credentials, which is well established and has been replicated successfully in Washington state, offers a model for a national credentialing system.

The case for standardized credentials is less clear in manufacturing. Several nationally recognized credentials exist in different industries. The National Institute of Metalworking Standards is one example. While NIMS standards are sometimes used in developing training program curricula, individual manufacturers still do not typically use job descriptions that correspond to them. This is why WRTP did not push employers to adopt common job descriptions when employer resistance became evident. In contrast, both the Manufacturing Career Path Pilot and Food Chicago are identifying the skill requirements that go with common occupational titles and are asking employers to adopt them.

For workers, the advantage of basing jobs and advancement on nationally recognized credentials is greater portability of skills. In an environment in which even profitable plants can be bought out or closed with little notice, the ability to transfer one's skills to another employer is essential. Career ladders need to reflect the American worker's new "psychological contract"—the change, discussed in chapter 1, from the old pursuit of job security to today's pursuit of employability security. However, in some of the most high-wage and advancement-oriented industries, credentials may be beside the point. Biomanufacturing, for instance, is so new that, even within a single company, job titles and possible advancement pathways are often still in flux.

Measurement and Accountability

To obtain public financial support for career-ladder programs, advocates will have to demonstrate that the nation as a whole gets a worthwhile return on its investment. This means more than just showing that poor people get jobs, which is all that most programs currently do. According to the late Cindy Marano and Kim Tarr at the National Network of Sectoral Partners, 70 percent of workforce intermediaries do not keep data on advancement. Among those who do, the outcomes are sketchy. Their national survey of 243 workforce intermediaries found that among the seventy-three programs that kept any data at all on this, nineteen reported that they could document career advancement promotions for between 10 and 25 percent of their clients one to three years after placement, sixteen could document the same for between 25 and 50 percent of clients, eighteen for 50–75 percent of clients, and nine for more than 75 percent of clients.[6] We do not know the type of advancement, how much client wages increased, or how these results compare to those of people placed through One-Stop Career Centers. The efforts of CLCR's Food Chicago to collect and analyze data on employers' return on investment for each of its job-training programs is an approach that more programs should attempt.

Union-run career-ladder programs present another kind of accountability issue. New York City's teachers union, for example, has negotiated a contract that requires the school district to pay employees for taking courses. The union sees this benefit as a way for workers to advance but also to get an education in any area they desire. Management, on the other hand, questions whether the school district and the public can afford to provide education benefits for employees that are not used to directly improve the quality of education received by children. A similar debate is taking place at Cape Cod Community Hospital, where management wants more restrictions on how education benefits can be used.

The economic development programs examined in this book also lack accountability. There is little public questioning of state and local governments that cumulatively spend billions of dollars on a variety of subsidies to private firms—all in the name of economic development. Development agencies are rarely required to document that the public is getting a reasonable—or, indeed, any—return on its investment. Most studies of these expenditures conclude that, for the most part, money is spent to pay businesses for what they would have done anyway and is an unwise use of public funds.[7] To be sure, there are times when it does make sense for states and cities to make investments to build strength in particular industries. There is no doubt that biotechnology will create cures for many diseases; on this ground alone, public investment may be wise. But how much can be justified and in which states? After all, while a few companies will make millions from patented medications, only a limited number of jobs or other spin-offs will occur and only in a limited number of places. The issue is too complex to be resolved with simple cost-benefit accounting, but decision makers have to be sensitive to overspending on a sector with questionable payoff and under-spending in areas of well-established payoff.

It is no accident that we do not have better data on employment and training outcomes. Training funds are adequate for analysis of placement, if that, and long-term evaluation of retention and advancement only occurs if private foundation funds are available. State agencies want to demonstrate to the public that they are proactive on the economic development front. In evaluating customized training outcomes in one state, I found that every worker trained was classified as a job saved.[8] Employers are happy to get subsidized training, state government is seen as being proactive, and the public does not ask a lot of questions about outcomes. The audience for accountability, unlike in elementary and secondary education, is rather small. To evaluate spending and payoffs, better data are desperately needed.

Workforce Intermediaries—the Right Frame?

As discussed in chapter 1, reliance on workforce intermediaries is widely considered to be the best way to bridge the critical structural gap between employers who may not appreciate the value of providing opportunities for their workforce and workers who may not know how to use the career opportunities provided. There is good cause for this enthusiasm. Although their programs are small, many workforce intermediaries have achieved high training-completion rates, job-placement rates, and even starting wage levels. They have been successful in connecting a small portion of the country's low-income workers to better jobs than people have generally been able to find using the government's One-Stop system.[9]

However, in the course of researching this book I have become somewhat skeptical about the standard notions of what constitutes a workforce intermediary and how effective intermediaries can be in achieving more equitable regional labor markets, more advancement opportunities for low-skilled workers, and broad changes in the government's workforce development system. These other functions, and not the organization's job-matching activities, are what make the workforce intermediary worth distinguishing from other types of job-placement outfits. Yet in these other realms, little change has occurred. My research suggests that few workforce intermediaries have the leverage to initiate or catalyze change at such a level.

The term "workforce intermediary" conflates a variety of organizations that have very different institutional agendas. The nation has about 243 workforce intermediaries, the majority of which (73 percent) are nonprofit organizations. The most common workforce intermediary is the community-based organization. Some intermediaries are part of the government employment and training system: Workforce Boards and One-Stop Career Centers. Educational institutions, including community colleges, are viewed as intermediaries, as are economic development organizations, business associations (including chambers of commerce), and unions.[10] It is hard to imagine such a disparate group mobilized toward the common end of creating more equitable labor markets and advancement paths for low-skilled workers. The U.S. Chamber of Commerce and many industry associations, for instance, are on record as opposing increases in the minimum wage, opposing legislation that would facilitate union organizing, and favoring the repeal of the Davis-Bacon Act. Community-based organizations have strong credentials in working to achieve better job opportunities, but their ability to influence employers and labor markets is quite limited. So what exactly is the common agenda of a chamber of commerce, a community organization, and a labor union? It exists only to the extent that they depoliticize the workforce intermediary role.

But presenting the intermediary's role as a seemingly technical function—putting workers together with opportunities in the most effective manner—elides the fact that many of the key issues in structuring or restructuring work are deeply political. The political questions include how much money low-wage workers are to be paid; what levels of taxation will support which kinds of wage and training subsidies; what regulatory constraints employers should face; and whether workers are permitted to exercise their right to form unions.

The workforce-intermediary frame tends to focus attention on the "dual customer" approach of organizations, emphasizing that their services are "employer driven." This means that intermediaries—community colleges, for example—consult with businesses to identify their labor force and skill needs, and to ensure that trainees meet them. But if we are to take seriously the career-ladder goal of influencing employers to improve the quality of jobs and create more internal advancement opportunities, then these sorts of neutral, "dual customer" consultations are hardly sufficient. Given the goals of the career-ladder strategy, questions of power invariably arise, and workforce intermediaries have to be evaluated in those terms. Are they forces for deeper structural change? Or are they co-opted by their "partner" role?

The demand-side results of a workforce development program typically are measured only by occasional interviews with employers asking them whether they are benefiting from the program, have hired workers, are satisfied with workers, and would hire from the program in the future.[11] But additional demand-side criteria need to be considered: How often has the intervention of intermediaries resulted in establishing higher wages or benefits for participants? How often has it spurred employer investment in upgrading skills and creating career ladders? How often has it changed hiring practices? How often has it resulted in the creation of new jobs? To what extent has it encouraged firms to support a diverse and frequently nontraditional labor force?[12] And to what extent has it mustered worker or legislative power to achieve these things?

The evidence assembled in this book suggests that few intermediaries without union connections have a strong track record on such questions. And unions, by definition, are different creatures from other kinds of workforce intermediaries, because their essential mission is worker empowerment, not serving employers. Among their other activities, unions push back against employers who seek to suppress wages and eliminate benefits, including education benefits. They often pro-actively work to persuade employers to structure career opportunities. WRTP, working with unionized firms, is one of the few workforce intermediaries that can document increased employer commitment to adopting high-performance production techniques and training workers for higher-level jobs. On the other hand, WRTP has not had much connection to, or influence on, the area's One-Stop system, and therefore its reach, even in the Milwaukee region, remains limited.

Many community colleges have an equity agenda but are stymied by inadequate government investment and cumbersome restrictions on their use of funds, as well as their own ambivalences about whom they should serve. Some community colleges have a good track record in preparing low-income and low-skill job seekers for entry-level jobs with advancement potential. As discussed in the previous chapters, they need more support in doing this. But it is not at all clear that community colleges can be agents of fundamental change in local labor markets, employer practices, or the government training system. Community colleges can do a fine job of providing technical assistance and the customized training that businesses want, as well as creating remedial and technical programs for students. But to call them a workforce intermediary is an exaggeration, if the term implies promoting systemic changes and not just providing services.

Despite this set of caveats, I credit some remarkable organizations with maximizing the intermediary role. One intermediary that has had an impact on labor markets, employer practices, and government policies is the Paraprofessional Healthcare Institute. The three home care cooperatives it has created provide low-income women with a higher level of training than most aides receive, and they have attempted to change their local labor markets by creating a better-quality service with workers who are paid at a higher rate. Further, PHI has influenced state policy in Massachusetts by advocating for, and developing a broad constituency to support, passage of the Nursing Home Quality Initiative discussed in chapter 2. The initiative requires long-term care facilities to create new job titles for two additional levels of CNA and to attach permanent wage increases to them. Although the initiative is not pushing wages up significantly, it is a step in the direction of using public policy to bolster career ladders and the wages of low-wage workers.

It is hardly surprising that such success stories are rare, given the current political climate. If an entire living-wage and career-opportunity strategy is to be built around intermediaries, some further thinking is needed about what kinds of intermediaries are up to the task.

2. How much of a difference can the career-ladder strategy make?

It is heartening to hear about CNAs overcoming multiple obstacles to become LPNs, displaced workers finding well-paying jobs in biomanufacturing, and the paraeducator who becomes a teacher. But the more typical path is moderate advancement over a slow period: CNAs or paraeducators advancing into newly created levels within the same occupation or entry-level production workers advancing a few grades. These are not insignificant moves. Even this level of tinkering around the edges of the profound

forces that are bifurcating the American labor market can make a difference for thousands of low-wage workers. But no matter how successful,
these programs cannot make significant inroads into the nation's extreme
income inequality. Most career-ladder programs graduate fewer than 100
people per year, some considerably fewer. The largest-scale programs presented in this book are WRTP, which has provided training for about 6,000
workers in its eight years, and the 1199c Training and Upgrading Fund,
which has advanced 103 CNAs into LPN positions in three years. The need
is vastly greater. There are 64.2 million American workers making less than
$15,000 a year. Only a much larger effort could have a significant economic
impact. And that would require a much greater investment in training and
a much broader national commitment to high-road employment practices
and increased wages.

Even at the local level, the impact of career-ladder programs seems to
depend to a great extent on public policies that affect the demand side of
the program—that is, on public policies that increase the willingness of
employers to adopt career-ladder goals. In New York City a union negotiated with the city for education benefits. In Chicago the Workforce Board
is encouraging employers to adopt standard job classifications and career
ladders. In Seattle the Economic Opportunity Institute is still trying to
find ways for city government to support the state's career-ladder
demonstration.

If the goal is to have a society, or even a community, in which work pays
a living wage and there are plentiful opportunities to advance, then career-
ladder programs are a useful tool. But how much difference they make at
either level seems to depend on our political will—on what we choose to
do politically: increase wage supports and wage regulation, create an environment that supports unionization, and fund and configure training programs in a context of low unemployment.

Wage Regulation and Subsidy

Public policy influences the structure of wages in multiple ways. For
example, laws regulating wages and hours (The Fair Labor Standards Act)
provide a basic floor (although it has never had an adequate system of
enforcement.) In particular industries, most notably construction, government policy (the Davis-Bacon Act) mandates that employers with federal
contracts pay "prevailing" (usually union) wages. And government, albeit
intermittently, subsidizes some of the costs of working, such as child care
and job-training expenses. Government also sponsors a system of
unemployment compensation, which modestly increases the bargaining

power of workers to hold out for a decent wage. In addition, government subsidizes wages, mainly through the Earned Income Tax Credit. Liberals and conservatives agree that the EITC is the best anti-poverty program we have, because it rewards work and ensures an income floor.

This set of policies, however, does not add up to a national policy to make work pay. Nor does it produce systematic opportunities to advance in a profession or career, especially at the low end of the labor market. To achieve that goal, it would be necessary to raise minimum wages (the last increase was in 1996), increase spending on income supports, and use the leverage of government contracts to raise wages and support the structuring of career ladders, not just in construction but also in other industries where government directly or indirectly pays much of the wage bill, such as health care and child care.

The Support of Unions

As institutions of worker voice and empowerment, unions have significant impact on workers' wages and advancement potential. Unions monitor employer compliance both with wage and overtime agreements, and with health and safety regulations. They often force employers to be more explicit about their internal labor markets and their structures. And many of them have long experience thinking explicitly about career ladders. Historically the nation's oldest career-ladder program is the union apprenticeship.[13] Union-sponsored apprenticeships in the building trades have created access to well-paying jobs with benefits for hundreds of thousands of workers (but also, historically, have excluded minorities and women). Unions, more than any other single organization, create a workplace culture that values education and advancement. The relatively new service-sector unions, such as the Hotel Employees and Restaurant Employees, 1199, and the Service Employees International Union, not only bargain for the traditional goal of better wages and working conditions, but have been among the more creative forces on behalf of programs for career advancement. As a result of persistent organizing, the hotel industry in Las Vegas, for example, has been a surprisingly fertile ground for career ladders and improbably generous pay scales as well.

In the health care field, unionized facilities are more likely than nonunion facilities to offer education benefits that low-income workers can actually use. (Non-unionized facilities are more likely to offer tuition-reimbursement benefits, if they offer education benefits at all, and these do not help low-income workers who cannot front the tuition and are not given time off for attending classes.) The career-ladder program at Cape Cod

Hospital is one example of the many training and advancement programs that have been won through contract negotiation. The 1199C Training and Upgrading Fund in Philadelphia shows the power of coordinating the union education benefits of multiple employers in one training facility. Yet maintaining the benefits for any given workplace is an ongoing struggle. Workers at one of the major hospitals affiliated with the Fund lost education benefits in 2003 contract negotiations.

Unionization of home care workers in California resulted in pay raises and education and training benefits. The nascent unionization movement in the child care field may offer similar hope for improving working conditions and promoting professionalism. In Seattle some child care employers see unionization as a way to force higher government reimbursement. However, the inability to find a permanent funding stream for Washington's Early Childhood Education Career Development Ladder remind us that, when the government is ultimately the paying customer, union efforts need to be complemented by a public-policy commitment to pay living wages and support professionalism.

The ability of workers to organize unions, in turn, reflects three basic variables: the state of worker consciousness and militancy; the willingness of government to enforce the right of workers to organize and join unions, free from employer retaliation; and the ease with which a given company can relocate or outsource the work. Of these, the one that public policy can most readily affect is enforcement of the right to unionize.

How Can the Government Job-Training System and the Public Education System Better Promote Career Advancement?

Lifelong learning has been the mantra of the workforce development world for some time. In theory it sounds great. All Americans should have the opportunity to continue their education in order to improve their life circumstances. Those who failed or who were failed by the public education system should have a second chance to earn credentials to land a decent-paying job. The idea is that adults should be able to get on and off the education pathway as personal choice and life circumstances permit. But, in practice, what would it take to reframe the nation's primary job-training program and the states' community college systems to truly support lifelong learning and career advancement?

The National Workforce Training System

As many advocates have noted, we cannot create a skilled workforce "on the cheap." Federal and state governments and employers have to increase the number of people for whom job training is available. In 2002 only 206,000 people were trained under the nation's primary training program, the Workforce Investment Act (WIA) of 1998.[14] If all Department of Labor funds are totaled, we spend about $7 billion a year on job training for adults and youth, but this only amounts to about $50 per eligible adult and $300 per eligible youth[15]—hardly enough to pay for one course at a community college. Investing to meet the coming shortage of skilled labor will require billions more than what we are currently spending. The Bush administration proposal for FY2004 is to maintain the 2003 WIA spending level, which was below 2002. This is not sufficient funding to address the nation's skills gap or to keep the American economy competitive globally.

Furthermore, if career advancement, rather than just placement, is the goal, then the WIA system has to provide training for the upgrading of incumbent workers as well as the unemployed. The current system does not allow local boards to adapt services to the needs of different groups: initial job seekers, displaced workers, and low-wage workers. States can use discretionary funds (15 percent of a state's total WIA allocation) for training programs directed specifically at incumbent workers, and several states are doing so, but the results are far from meeting national needs. Indeed, almost all the career-ladder programs described in this book receive most, if not all, of their funding from sources other than WIA.

Most of the responsibility for upgrading the skills of working adults now falls on the states, and all but two have some sort of program for training incumbent workers. These are mostly connected to economic development initiatives to retain existing, and develop new, industries. Many states would like to follow North Carolina's lead of providing free training through the state's community college system to firms that are expanding. But state funding for such workforce training has been hard to maintain over the past few years. A recent survey of thirty programs in sixteen states found that funding is declining for 75 percent of programs and that future budget cuts are expected.[16]

A dozen states fund incumbent-worker training programs by designating for that purpose a small portion (less than 1 percent) of employer contributions to unemployment insurance (UI).[17] The UI funds provide about $15 million in worker training funds in Massachusetts. With an amendment to Federal Unemployment Tax Account regulations, the federal government could provide matching funds or return some small percentage of UI

funds to states that use UI funds for the training of incumbent workers in
key industries. Similarly federal WIA funds could be used to match state
customized training programs, a funding strategy advocated by Jobs for the
Future, a leading non-profit research, consulting, and advocacy organization in the field of education and workforce development. These
approaches give federal and state government and employers mutual
responsibility for skills upgrading.[18]

Beyond that, incentives for employers and individuals to invest in
upgrade training could be increased through lifelong learning accounts—
individual savings accounts, with employee contributions matched by
employers, for use in upgrading job skills. The Center for Adult and
Experiential Learning is currently supporting a demonstration project
involving 350 workers at three sites (Chicago, Northeast Indiana, and San
Francisco) and advocating for national and state policies to support such
accounts.[19] In the demonstration project, the individual employee's
donations are matched dollar for dollar by employers to an established
cap. Employees are required to develop a learning plan with the help of
career and education advisers and can use the funds only for courses that
advance them toward their career goals. The intent of CAEL is to motivate
employers who would not otherwise invest in education and training for
lower-level workers. While raising funds for a much broader demonstration, CAEL is advocating for a new tax law that would make the individual
accounts tax-exempt to the employee and provide tax credits to contributing employers.

Workforce investment boards, the local policy-making organizations
under WIA, can also gear programs more toward skills upgrading for
existing workers. Although the WIA reauthorization of 2003 has not
passed, it contains new performance requirements that move away from its
current emphasis on placement to rewarding local boards that emphasize
retention and advancement. The Chicago Workforce Board's funding of the
Manufacturing Career Path Pilot illustrates how local boards can now
promote coordinated training for incumbent workers in a metropolitan
area.

About 16 percent of the U.S. population over the age of twenty-five has
less than a high school education. If the only job openings for them are for
CNAs or security guards, then the people who take those jobs need to have
ongoing opportunities to gain skills that would qualify them for better-
paying work. Otherwise they will never earn a decent wage. Under the
present job-training system, neither the appropriate training nor the other
supports and services that would enable this population to use training programs are now widely available.

Community Colleges

In just about every economic sector, community colleges are the key education and training link for career-ladder strategies. In every chapter of this book, we saw community colleges providing training at many levels—from basic literacy, ESL, and remedial courses to technical courses for college graduates. But few of these programs are specifically designed to be part of a career pathway for low-wage workers or low-skilled job seekers. This is a population that needs to be able to interrupt school or training in order to go back to work and then take up school or training again when there is an interruption of work—or to attend school and work at the same time. It is a population that also may need to progress through a full sequence of education programs:

Pre-bridge→Bridge→Certificate→Associate's Degree→Bachelor's Degree

For the most part, community colleges are not attending to either of these needs effectively.

Typically a community organization provides the pre-bridge program, as we saw with San Francisco Works' On-Ramp program in biotechnology and the Instituto del Progresso Latino's program in manufacturing. In theory community colleges take over from there and are the link to four-year institutions. But things seldom work that way. Most community colleges have little interest in collaboration and coordination with community organizations and little success in articulation with four-year colleges. The colleges seem to need incentives and directives pointing them in both directions, and they require more funding if they are to serve the number of students in need of lifelong educational opportunities. State budgets, which typically provide about 60 percent of community college revenue, have recently cut community college funding dramatically. Nationwide, community college tuitions were raised an average of 11.5 percent in 2003, in response to state budget cuts. California's community colleges increased tuition a whopping 60 percent in 2003.[20] States will have to restore and increase community college funding dramatically if they want to increase the skill levels of the workforce. Any increased funding, however, has to be more closely tied to performance.

For instance, community college students in remedial or noncredit certificate programs currently advance into certificate or degree programs at a very low rate. Bridge programs were designed to improve those outcomes by imparting basic skills appropriate to particular occupational settings. Preliminary evidence suggests that bridge programs are largely effective in preparing students for certificate programs, the next rung up. We saw this with the SF Works On-Ramp and the manufacturing bridge program in Chicago. But there is not much evidence of advancement into associate's degree programs. The bridge programs do create opportunity where it did not exist before, but it takes a lot of time and resources to get bridge programs up and running. The manufacturing bridge program in Chicago, for example, took years of planning, funded by hundreds of thousands of dollars from foundations and state government. On average, the cost of putting a student through a 320-hour bridge program is $1,200 (not including development costs and overhead). And the recruitment, case management, and job-placement services typically provided by community organizations add another $3,500 per student.[21] This is not a high price tag for getting someone into a decent-paying job. But if the goal is for people to move on to associate's degrees and advance, it is not yet clear that bridge programs are doing that.

Current funding policies typically skew the priorities of community colleges in other directions. Community colleges receive lower or no reimbursement for students in noncredit courses, like those for bridge programs. Their incentive, therefore, is to focus on other programs. Increasing numbers of high school graduates are attending community college for the first two years of college in order to save money. And, per student, this population costs less to serve—and brings in more revenue—than low-income students who need remedial work before they can even enter certificate programs. Also more financially attractive are the college graduates and other adults who attend community colleges as course takers (not degree seekers) to pick up job-related technical skills. These courses are either paid for by the students or their employers. These are students who do not need remedial, noncredit training before they can take classes—as we saw in most of the biotechnology certificate programs.

Further skewing the priorities of the colleges is the fact that low-income students often have WIA vouchers to pay their tuition, and the colleges say that the vouchers come with burdensome paper work and reporting requirements. Many community colleges refuse to accept them.[22]

Community colleges also have an economic development mission, which some fulfill better than others. Most rely on independent units to provide technical assistance and on customized employee training under contract to particular businesses in their service areas. Evidence indicates that incumbent workers do increase their earnings as a result of such short-term training.[23] But because most states do not fund these noncredit classes, most colleges cannot afford the staff and overhead required to maintain them. Of the three states discussed in the biotechnology chapter, California and

North Carolina have three sources of funding for workforce development—state funds that are part of an ongoing community college appropriation, state funds from other agencies, and nonstate funds. Massachusetts has no regular appropriation for workforce development but does have access to the other two sources. The inconsistency in available funding is why John Lederer, the longtime director of adult education and employer outreach at Shoreline Community College in the Seattle area, argues that "one of the best ways to promote lifelong learning and college-business partnerships is to support contract and non-credit education with the same funding that for-credit education receives."[24]

Better upward linkages to four-year institutions would also support lifelong learning and career advancement. Although community colleges in some states are set up to provide the first two years of a bachelor's degree, in most places few students move on to a four-year college.[25] The programs studied for this book suggest several different ways to improve on these outcomes. Kentucky, Oklahoma, and Texas use a common course numbering system at community colleges and universities to facilitate movement from one to the other—a step in the right direction. North Carolina is attempting to build programs in specific industries, such as biotechnology, which start with a certificate and continue through the bachelor's degree. Colleagues in Caring works with higher education institutions in several states to avoid unnecessary course duplication for nursing students who move from one school to another.

Linking community colleges to four-year institutions seems to be not as much a funding issue as one of connecting institutions with very different cultures and student bodies. Faculty at four-year institutions are rewarded for research and publication, not for facilitating linkages with community colleges. Thus it is likely that articulation agreements will have to be put together at the state level by specially designated committees.

Community colleges have not been subject to the same accountability pressures as the K-12 education system, so there are many unanswered questions about what they do well.[26] We need some of these questions answered before forging ahead under the assumption that our educational institutions can support lifelong learning for low-income workers. The bridge approach has been tried in manufacturing, biotechnology, and information technology, but results, with some notable exceptions, have not been well documented. To justify the cost of developing additional bridge programs, we need more evidence that a sufficient number of students in bridge programs end up in decent-paying jobs. Conversely we need evidence that a bridge to college is actually needed. As we saw in both manufacturing and biotechnology, going back to school for the AAS degree may not be necessary for advancement, if businesses offer on-the-job training. In addition, we have to critically assess whether the types of courses created for bridge programs should carry college credit. In most disciplines there is a delicate balance between making the course work for certificates relevant and maintaining college-level standards.

In one other important respect, our current job-training and educational system is not supportive of adult learners. The country's main source of college funding, the Pell grant, is essentially inaccessible to working adults enrolled in community colleges. The Pell Grant Program (Title IV of the Higher Education Act) distributes about $9.5 billion a year in grants to income-eligible college students (another $42 million is available in loans). But the grants are available only for studies leading to an academic degree, not for studies leading to a technical certificate or degree, and not for bridge and other short-term programs such as BioWork or BEST. Further, to meet the Pell Grant Program's requirement of satisfactory progress toward a degree, the grantee must be in school almost full-time, something working adults cannot manage. Senators Hillary Clinton (D-NY) and Bob Graham (D-FL) introduced the Non-Traditional Student Success Act in 2004 to increase financial aid to working adults and to provide incentives to schools that take measures to accommodate their needs. But this bill still would leave the Pell Grant's degree requirements in place. And working students who attend school less than half-time still would not be eligible. A job-training and educational system supportive of career ladders would change those restrictions—and make the same changes to the Hope and Lifetime Learning Tax Credit programs as well.[27]

In sum, there are a number of measures that would make the country's job-training and education programs more supportive of the career advancement efforts of employed adults. It is not clear how much money should be spent on them. But it is safe to say that in an economy of precarious jobs—an economy in which employability may be the only route to financial security—we must greatly broaden access to education and training.

Economic Development or Public Welfare?

Ultimately the amount of funding that goes into creating career advancement opportunities for low-skilled, low-wage workers is a function of whether the public sees such spending as an investment in the economy or as public welfare. Even though the payoff is not clear, Americans tend to support programs like North Carolina's, which link economic and workforce development by providing free training to new or expanding firms in targeted industries. Most people see the logic of attracting new growth industries. Landing a business with subsidies makes big headlines, but few notice when the promised jobs do not materialize several years later.[28] But spending money to give poor people second and third chances to complete a GED and job training is more politically controversial, particularly when the poor people are predominantly minorities and immigrants.

Under some circumstances a constituency can be developed for investing in low-wage workers. Direct-care workers in health care (particularly in nursing homes), child care, and, to some extent, education have a middle-class constituency that can be mobilized on their behalf. The Massachusetts Nursing Home Quality Initiative came about because the Paraprofessional Healthcare Institute was able to mobilize broad support among people who had experienced substandard care of their family members and understood the connection between quality of work and quality of care. Likewise Washington state's Early Childhood Education Career Development Ladder was the result of a campaign by the Economic Opportunity Institute and child care advocates. They mobilized middle-class parents, who made the same connection concerning child care. It seems that if low-wage workers do not have a union, then they better have a middle-class constituency advancing their cause.

Conclusion

This review of career-ladder strategies suggests several policy conclusions. First, using public policy to encourage the more explicit structuring of career paths so that relatively less-skilled workers can look forward to economic advancement over the course of their lives is a very worthwhile goal. It would benefit not only individuals but also our national productivity. Second, however, career ladders cannot be the only national strategy for "making work pay" because many occupations have very narrow pyramids of advancement. Work needs to pay a living wage, even outside the context of paths to advancement. Career ladders are a very useful part of an overall living-wage strategy but not a silver bullet. Third, career advancement strategies are practically impossible to achieve in more than token fashion unless they are complemented by generally tight labor markets and friendly regulatory policies, in some cases mandatory ones. Fourth, the existing employment and training system promotes career ladders only in passing, and needs to be restructured, as discussed above, to make advancement, not just placement, an explicit systemic objective. And the entire system also needs more adequate funding. And, finally, although the concept of workforce intermediaries is promising, unless these several changes are put in place the entire approach could meet the fate of other promising foundation-funded initiatives that languish at a token or demonstration level and never achieve their potential. America's low-wage workers deserve better—they deserve a chance to move up in the new economy.

NOTES

1. The Potential and Limitations of Career Ladders

1. Bernhardt et al. 2001.

2. Mishel, Bernstein, and Schmitt 1999. In September 2000 the Census Bureau defined the poverty level for a family of four as below $17,062. A survey of economists concurred that $25,000 is a more accurate amount to enable a family of four to fulfill basic needs (see Uchitelle 2001).

3. Osterman 1993; Leigh 1989.

4. In 1995 the General Accounting Office identified more than 160 federal job-training programs run by fifteen separate government agencies, putting pressure on Congress to consolidate the system.

5. Holzer and Waller 2003.

6. See Kuttner 1997; Harrison and Bluestone 1988.

7. Freeman 1996.

8. See Harrison and Bluestone 1988. Although considerable methodological debate emerged over these and other findings, Karoly compared several methods of examining inequality in family earnings and concluded that inequality had indeed increased since the late 1960s (see Karoly 1993). See also Danzinger and Gottschalk 1993, 19–98.

9. Inequality of wealth (net assets) also increased in the 1990s. See Wolff 1996.

10. Wright and Dwyer 2002. Using data from the *Current Population Survey* of the U.S. Census, Wright and Dwyer found that in the 1990s about 40 percent of total net job expansion came from the worst job quality deciles and the best job quality deciles.

11. Wright and Dwyer 2002.

12. Aspen Institute Domestic Strategy Group 2002.

13. Mishel, Bernstein, and Schmitt 1999.

14. Dalaker 2001, 9.

15. Acs, Phillips, and McKenzie 2001; Kazis and Miller 2003, 21–44.

16. Meisenheimer 1998, 22–47.

17. Mishel, Bernstein, and Schmitt 1999.

18. Sylvestri 1993.

19. Dinardo, Fortin, and Lemieux 1996; Howell 1994; Freeman 1993; Danziger and Gottschalk 1994; Freeman and Medoff 1984.

20.   Bluestone and Harrison 1999.

21.   Freeman 1996. Freeman identifies several other studies employing different methodologies and samples, and over different time periods, that produce almost identical findings.

22.   Lafer 2002.

23.   Mishel, Bernstein, and Boushey 2003.

24.   See Bernhardt et al. 2001; Cappelli 1999; Cappelli et al. 1997; Diebold, Neumark, and Polsky 1997; Gittleman and Joyce 1996; Farber 1995; Rose 1995; Cappelli et al. 1997.

25.   Mishel, Bernstein, and Allegretto 2004.

26.   Wright and Dwyer 2002.

27.   Bernhardt et al. 2001. The study compares two longitudinal samples of men over two fifteen-year periods, 1966 to 1981 and 1979 to 1994.

28.   Schrammel 1998, 3–9. This study uses *Current Population Survey* data.

29.   Duncan, Boisjoly and Smeeding 1995, 6. The cutoffs used were $11,521 in 1993 dollars for the poverty level and twice the poverty level, $23,042 for the middle class.

30.   Duncan, Boisjoly and Smeeding 1995, 15. This is not to say that education doesn't matter. The income gap between workers with low and high levels of education has been increasing since the 1960s, and education is still the best single predictor of income (Katz and Murphy 1992). According to the College Board, in 1997 the median annual household income by education level was as follows:

Less than 9th grade	$16,154
High school graduate	$34,373
Associate degree	$48,604
Bachelor's degree or more	$66,474
Doctorate	$84,100

But a disturbing finding of comparisons of the employment patterns of workers entering the labor market in the 1960s and 1980s is that education is not as much a predictor of wage growth as one would expect. In 2001 almost 35 percent of low-wage workers had a high school diploma and close to 30 percent had completed some college (see Mitnik, Zeidenberg, and Dresser 2002). Higher levels of education are necessary, but no longer sufficient, to guarantee good earnings and patterns of steady advance—because of structural changes in the labor market (see Reich 1991). It is not surprising that people with only a high school education or less are more likely to be stuck in low-wage jobs. But it is surprising that 22 percent of low-wage workers with children have some postsecondary education. Workers with some college now have earnings less like college graduates and more like high school graduates (Bernhardt et al. 1999, 157).

31.   Cappelli 1999, 63.

32.   Piore and Sabel 1984.

33.   Cappelli and O'Shaughnessy 1995.

34.   See Harrison 1994.

35.   Applebaum 1989.

36.   Cappelli 1999, 74.

37.   Stone 2001, 519–661.

38.   For a review of this system, see Cappelli 1995, 563–602.

39.   Conference Board 1997.

40.   Stone 2004, 2001.

41. Pink 2001, 82.
42. Cappelli 1994, 94.
43. Benner 2002.
44. Carnoy, Castells, and Benner 1997; Saxenian 1996.
45. Arthur and Rousseau 1996.
46. Lawler 1994.
47. Saxenian 1996.
48. Batt and Keefe 1998.
49. Cappelli 1999; Quotations in text from Sugalski, Manzo, and Meadows 1995.
50. See Rose 1995.
51. Cappelli 1995, 583.
52. Bernhardt and Marcotte 2000.
53. Carré and Rayman 1999.
54. Bluestone and Rose 1997.
55. See Hirsch and Shanley 1996.
56. See Groshen 1991.
57. Ballantine and Ferguson 2003.
58. Bartel, Ichniowski, and Shaw 2003.
59. Heaphy 1999.
60. Needleman et al. 2001. The results varied by type of complication and hospital unit, but the findings hold overall.
61. Moss, Salzman, and Tilly 2000.
62. Low wages are associated with low levels of labor market attachment (see Strawn and Martinson 2000). Workers who earn better wages have more of a stake in keeping their jobs. A longitudinal study of welfare recipients in the state of Washington from 1988 to 1992 found that wage levels influence how long former welfare recipients remain off assistance. Of those welfare recipients who were earning hourly wages of $9.50 or more, 67 percent remained off assistance three years later. For those who earned less than $6.50 an hour, only 32 percent remained off assistance for three years (see Lidman 1995). Oregon's experience is similar (see Scrivener 1998). One of the largest demonstration programs that examined strategies for improving job retention among former and current welfare recipients, the Post-Employment Services Demonstration (PESD), found that people whose first jobs were higher-paying and offered benefits were more likely to stay employed and to advance into better jobs (see Rangarajan, Schochet, and Chu 1998). Analysis of employment patterns from the National Longitudinal Study of Youth reveals that once women find good jobs they stay in them regardless of characteristics such as former welfare use, education, race, or number of children (see Rangarajan, Schochet and Chu 1998; Pavetti and Acs 1997). These studies suggest that it is not simply that more qualified people find better-paying jobs but that better-paying jobs motivate people to stay employed.
63. Burtless 1999.
64. Fitzgerald 1999.
65. Cappelli 1999, 192.
66. Card and Krueger 1995.
67. Kazis 2004; Fitzgerald 2000.
68. In a study of New Jersey's REACH program, Hershey and Pavetti (1997) found that 43 percent of clients cited child care, along with health problems, pregnancy, and family problems, as key reasons for losing jobs. They also argue that women with formal child care stay employed more consistently than those with informal arrangements.

69.   See Meléndez 1996; Harrison, Weiss, and Gant 1997; Meléndez and Harrison 1998; Harrison and Weiss 1999; Lautsch and Osterman 1998.

70.   More general information on JARC can be found on their website, http://www. jarc.org.

71.   See Fitzgerald, Jaffe, and Perry 2002; Fitzgerald and Leigh 2002.

72.   Allsid et al. 2002; Fitzgerald 2000; Jenkins 1999.

73.   See Alssid et al. 2002; Fitzgerald and Jenkins 1997.

74.   This description draws from Fitzgerald and Carlson 2000.

75.   See Alssid et al. 2002; Fitzgerald 2000, 1998.

76.   See Meléndez 1996; Harrison, Weiss, and Gant 1997; Meléndez and Harrison 1998; Harrison and Weiss 1999; Lautsch and Osterman 1998.

77.   Dawson and Surpin 2001.

2. Health Care

1.   The terms "nurse aide" and "nurse assistant" are used interchangeably. The term "certified nursing assistant" (CNA) refers to those aides who have taken a certification examination. Federal law requires nursing homes and other long-term care facilities to hire certified aides, whereas hospitals can fill nurse aide positions in any way they choose.

2.   American Association of Colleges of Nursing 2003.

3.   Bureau of Labor Statistics 2003.

4.   Kaiser Commission on Medicaid and the Uninsured 1999.

5.   Approximately half this population is elderly; the rest are mentally retarded, mentally ill, physically incapacitated, or have other chronic medical conditions (see Hagen 1999).

6.   Harrington et al. 1999.

7.   National Academy of Science, Institute of Medicine 1996.

8.   Scanlon 2001.

9.   Ibid.

10.   A 100 percent turnover rate means that of one hundred workers on the job today, anywhere from zero to twenty will be on the job in a year.

11.   Feuerberg 2001.

12.   This figure is from the On-Line Survey and Certification System (OBRA), a survey used by state agencies to check compliance with federal regulations. The Health Care Financing Agency did time studies in 1995 that arrived at 4.17 hours. Both studies are discussed in National Academy of Sciences, Institute of Medicine 2000.

13.   See ibid., 191.

14.   Bowers and Becker 1992.

15.   Frank and Dawson 2000.

16.   *Consumer Reports* 1995.

17.   Leonard 2001.

18.   Eaton 2000a.

19.   Dawson and Surpin 2000.

20.   Wunderlich, Gooloo, and Kohler 1996.

21.   Miller, and Luft 1994.

22.   Cornerstone Communications Group 2001.

23.   Gordon 2000.

24.   American Association of Colleges of Nursing 2000.

25. Ibid.

26. Shifting from nursing home to home and community care could actually increase costs, since people who might forgo long-term care would use home-care services (see Wiener and Stevenson 1997).

27. The HCFA reports that Medicaid paid a projected 9.3 percent, private insurance 18.9 percent, and self payers 28.1 percent of home-care services in 2000. Available online at http://www.nahc.org/Consumer/hcstats.html.

28. Wunderlich, Gooloo, and Kohler 2001.

29. Averaged for nurse aides working in all four settings identified in table 2.1.

30. The SEIU is the largest health care union in the country, representing more than seven hundred thousand members.

31. This section draws from an interview with the SEIU organizer David Rolf, reported in Meyerson 1999.

32. Seeley 1999.

33. Haefele 2000.

34. The wages are set by each county, and the wage negotiated is matched from state and federal government funds. The federal government shares about 40 percent of the county's wage costs. The remaining amount is split, with the state paying 65 percent (up to a maximum, which, in 2003, was $9.50) and the county paying 35 percent. So, although the wage in San Francisco is $10.35, the state contributes only up to $9.50—and the county has to be able to come up with difference.

35. Pearce 2000.

36. Available online at http://www.paraprofessional.org/Sections/Sites/CHCA.htm.

37. Apple, a $100-million corporation, has 21 homes with a total of 1,750 beds.

38. This average was $9.83 as of May 2003, according to BLS Occupational Employment Statistics. Available online at http://stats.bls.gov/oes/2003/may/oes311012.htm.

39. Interview with Susan Misiorski.

40. Available online at http://www.commcorp.org/cwi/programs/eccli/results.html.

41. Interview with Barbara Frank.

42. Wilson, Eaton, and Kamanu 2002.

43. Ibid., 64–75.

44. Ibid., 70.

45. Name changed to protect the confidentiality of the student.

46. AFSCME 1199, the national union of hospital and health care employees, represents people in occupations from nurse aides to dentists and medical doctors.

47. The CNA-training program for welfare-to-work students, called Project CARRE (Creating Access, Readiness, and Retention for Employment), lasts sixteen weeks and includes life and work-readiness skills (timeliness, anger management, communication, and the like). It also includes an internship, which allows students to gain on-the-job experience and determine whether they are suited to the field. The program director Afeefa Murray reports a 70 percent job retention rate among Project CARRE's first class of graduates, which is considerably higher than most CNA programs. Murray attributes this success to post-employment services offered at the Breslin Center and to what she calls "preventive retention." Murray describes two elements of the preventive retention curriculum: teaching students to pull back when in an explosive situation and giving them practice at making choices. Students are presented with potential situations that may encounter when working, such as, "What do you do if you get a call at work that your child is sick?" Students write down the options and explore the likely consequences of each. They then write a plan for how they would deal with the sit-

uation. In addition, Project CARRE provides its graduates with free monthly transportation passes and full-tuition scholarships for the LPN program. The Department of Labor grant also includes funds to match a graduate's savings that are earmarked for buying a car, to provide driving lessons, and to help pay for insurance and car repairs.

48.   The School of Practical Nursing was created when the Philadelphia Public School system closed its practical nursing program in 1998 because of funding cuts. The public school program had enrolled more than one hundred students a year, and it was the place where Local 1199 sent its CNAs for their LPN training. Even with a clear need, it was not easy for the union to create a replacement. Jim Ryan, at the time the director of the 1199C Training Fund, notes that it took two years to convince the State Board of Nursing that a union could run such a program, even though 1199C had been designated as an eligible education agency when it won federal vocational education funding. The new School of Practical Nursing cannot be accredited until it has achieved a track record, but it is now approved by the State Board of Nursing.

49.   In some cases NLR (National Labor Relations board) regulations stipulate that LPNs are supervisors and thus cannot be members of bargaining units. This is more commonly true in nursing homes than hospitals. Even if not in the bargaining unit, the increase in wages is substantial in the move from CNA to LPN.

50.   The sites were Georgia, Iowa, Maryland, Minnesota, North Dakota, Rhode Island, South Carolina, and Texas. The Cleveland, Ohio, site dropped out shortly after the program started.

51.   The sites relied on different sources for funding. In New York many of the participating hospitals were unionized, and the unions supplied funds for tuition, books, and supplies, and also worked with the hospitals in selecting participants. The state Department of Labor also helped hospitals in covering replacement wages. In other states insurance companies, community organizations, and churches donated funds.

52.   McNally 1999.

53.   A list of states is available on the Colleagues in Caring website: http://www.aacn. nche.edu.

54.   Rice and Rapson 1997.

55.   Rapson 2000.

56.   Interview with Mary Fry Rapson.

57.   For Cleveland, see Lenberg 1997. For Maryland, see Rapson 2000.

58.   Interview with Alda Melo, SEIU 2020, January 2005.

59.   Griffen 2001.

60.   Mentors go through an eight-hour class that covers confidentiality, what to talk about, how to listen, and conflict resolution.

61.   Cabral has since become the director of career services at New York Presbyterian Hospital.

62.   Interview with Joseph Cabral.

63.   Boston Health Care and Research Training Institute 2004.

64.   As part of the confidentiality agreement, employers do not reveal their turnover rates.

65.   Through the Boston Neighborhood Jobs Trust, developers in certain areas of the cities must provide either workforce development or housing. A developer of medical space in the Longwood area is donating the office space as part of this linkage agreement.

66.   Dawson and Surpin 2000, 19 (quote is slightly paraphrased).

67.   American Federation of State, County, and Municipal Employees 2000; "Summary

and Impact of the Medicare, Medicaid, and SCHIP Balanced Budget Refinement Act of 1999," available online at http://www.ppsv.com/issues/mmdoc.htm.

68. Paraprofessional Healthcare Institute 2000.

69. North Carolina Division of Facility Services 2000. The states are Arkansas, Colorado, Massachusetts, Missouri, Oregon, California, Illinois, Maine, Rhode Island, South Carolina, Texas, Virginia, Washington, Michigan, Montana, Minnesota, Kansas, and Wyoming. There is a table on the website that summarizes what every state is doing to improve retention and wages for CNAs.

70. North Carolina Division of Facility Services 1999.

3. Child Care

1. The mean wage of child care workers in 2000 was $7.86; that of parking lot attendants was $7.69. The mean wage of nonfarm animal caretakers was $8.46 (Bureau of Labor Statistics 2000).

2. Fullerton 1999.

3. Wolfe and Vandell 2002.

4. A national survey conducted in 1998 reported that "82% said they were 'extremely' or 'somewhat concerned about child care availability, 78% said the same about its cost, and 83% about its quality" ("YMCA Survey Reveals Child Care to be Major National Concern"; available online at http://www.ymca.net/presrm/research/ccconf.htm.

5. Reynolds et al. 2001; Vandell and Wolfe 2000; Devaney, Ellwood, and Love 1997.

6. Danzinger and Waldfogel 2000.

7. Olson 2002.

8. http://nccic.org/pubs/cclicensingreq/threshold.html.

9. http://nccic.org/pubs/cclicensingreq/cclr-famcare.html.

10. Child Care Aware. Available online at http://www.childcareaware.org/en/care/centers.html.

11. The states are California, Connecticut, Georgia, Maryland, Michigan, and Washington. Children's Defense Fund, "Child Care Basics: April 2001," http://www.childrensdefense.org/earlychildhood/childcare/basics.aspx.

12. Mezey et al. 2002.

13. Bowman, Donovan, and Burns 2000.

14. EarlyChildhood.Org;   http://www.earlychildhood.org/standards/descriptions.cfm; http://www.beginningschildcarecenters.org/standards.html.

15. Available online at http://www.naeyc.org/accreditation.

16. Nelson 2001.

17. Center aides are called "child care workers" in U.S. Department of Labor statistics, which can cause some confusion. In this chapter the term "child care workers" refers to all who are involved in child care occupations at any level.

18. Laverty et al. 2001, 3.

19. Career Guide to Industries 2001.

20. Available online at http://www.common-sense.org/?fnoc=/common_sense_says/00_nov.

21. Vandall and Wolfe 2000. The NICHD Study of Early Child Care examination findings for U.S. child care centers (for ages fifteen to thirty-six months) are 8.1 percent,poor;

53.2 percent, fair; 29.6 percent, good; and 9.0 percent, excellent. Available online at http://aspe.hhs.gov/hsp/ccquality00/tables4–13.htm#t9.

22.   Helburn and Morris 1996; Helburn 1995; Galinsky et al. 1994. The scores are based on the Observational Record of the Caregiving Environment (ORCE), which includes counts of caregiver actions (e.g., responds to vocalization, asks questions, speaks negatively) and qualitative ratings of caregiver responsiveness over time. The observations take place during four forty-four-minute observations over two days. Observers use 4-point ratings scaled from 1 to 4 to assess the overall quality of care. ORCE rates the quality of care on the following scale: less than 2 indicates poor; 2 to 2.9 indicates fair; 3–3.4 indicates good; and 3.5 or higher indicates excellent. See Vandell and Wolfe 2000.

23.   Campbell et al., 39.

24.   Ibid.

25.   This section draws from interviews with Sue Russell, the executive director of Child Care Services Association (Child Care Services Association 2000, 2001).

26.   Sue Russell correspondence, July 2004.

27.   Smart Start is a statewide organization with local branches in every North Carolina county. The local partnerships fund an assortment of programs to promote early childhood education. Not every county has a WAGE$ program. See http://www.smartstart-nc.org/.

28.   The course work required for a CDA credential includes eight content areas: planning a safe and healthy learning environment; steps to advance children's physical and intellectual development; positive ways to support children's social and emotional development; strategies to establish productive relationships with families; strategies to manage an effective program operation; maintaining a commitment to professionalism; observing and recording children's behavior; and principles of child growth and development.

29.   The 1999 awardees were Colorado, the District of Columbia, Indiana, Iowa, Kansas, Nevada, New Hampshire, New York, Vermont, Washington, and Wisconsin. The 2000 awardees were Alaska, Arkansas, California, Connecticut, Maine, Montana, Oklahoma, Rhode Island, South Dakota, and Tennessee. The 2001 awardees were Delaware, Idaho, Illinois, Maryland, Massachusetts, Mississippi, North Carolina, North Dakota, Pennsylvania, West Virginia, and Wyoming. Sources include Salzman et al. 2003 and an interview with Suzi Brodof, ACDS Coordinator, West Virginia, June 9, 2004.

30.   This grant was extended until February 2005.

31.   Hardt 2004.

32.   From 2002 Statistical Abstract of the United States.

33.   Laverty et al. 2001; Whitebook et al. 2001, vi. Child care experts note that children feel more secure when they become accustomed to the same caregivers. As aides and teachers come to know children better, they are better able to respond to their needs.

34.   Whitebook and Sakai 2003; Shonkoff and Phillips 2000; Whitebook 1998; Whitebook and Berlin 1999; Sakai and Howes 1997.

35.   Whitebook, Howes, and Phillips 1998.

36.   The wages are 9.5 percent higher ($6.79 vs. $6.20) for the lowest-paid assistants and 16 percent higher (8.52 vs. 7.34) for the highest-paid assistants; they are 17.4 percent higher for the lowest-paid teachers and 33.7 percent higher for the highest-paid teachers.

37.   Whitebook et al. 2001.

38.   Phillips et al. 1996; Helburn 1995; Whitebook et al. 1990.

39.   National Council of Jewish Women 1999.

40.   Bureau of Labor Statistics 2001.

41.   Gornick and Meyers 2001.

42.   In 2003 more than 200,000 children were served in 800 centers employing about 15,000 child care workers. These figures include facilities for school-age children, as well as 437 child development programs for preschool-age children (interview with Barbara Thompson, policy analyst, Office of Children and Youth, U.S. Department of Defense, July 23, 2003).

43.   Campbell et al., 12.

44.   States vary, some requiring inspection of regulated child care providers more than once a year, others only once in five years. In many states inspectors have caseloads that make thorough inspections impossible and enforcement of violations only minimal. In 1999 inspectors in twenty-two states carried caseloads of more than 125 child care facilities each. Only eleven states met the federally recommended standard of 75 facilities per inspector. See U.S. General Accounting Office 2000.

45.   Cited in Campbell et al. 2000, 15.

46.   U.S. General Accounting Office 1999.

47.   Military Family Resource Center 2000.

48.   Campbell et al. 2000, 26.

49.   Of the total expenditure, 73 percent ($257 million) goes to child development centers, 12 percent ($43 million) to family child care homes, 11 percent (#38 million) to the care of school-age children, and 4 percent ($14 million) to resource and referral (Campbell et al. 2000).

50.   Interview with Barbara Thompson, policy analyst, Office of Children and Youth, U.S. Department of Defense, June 15, 2004.

51.   Campbell et al. 2000.

52.   Zellman and Johansen 1998.

53.   Ibid.

54.   Burbank and Wiefek 2001.

55.   Typical certificate requirements are illustrated in this curriculum from Bellevue Community College:

Course No.	Course Name	Credit Hrs.
ECED 171	Introduction to Early Childhood Education	5
ECED 172	Fundamentals of Early Childhood Education	5
ECED 181	Children's Creative Activities	5
ECED 191	Practicum in Early Childhood Education	5
ECED 192	Practicum in Early Childhood Education	5
ECED 193	Practicum in Early Childhood Education	5
ECED 201	Parent Involvement in Early Childhood Education	5
ECED 204	Child and Health Safety	3
HLTH 292	First Aid and CPR	4
HOMEC 256	Child Development and Guidance	3
TOTAL		45

56.   Boyd and Wandschneider 2004.

57.   Ibid.

58.   It was projected that approximately 260 centers would be able to participate. There are approximately 650 licensed child care centers in Seattle. For details of the espresso tax, see http://www.realchangenews.org/pastissuesupgrade/2002_07_10/features/taxing_espresso. html.

59.   Teachers were granted emergency licensing in order to meet the demand, meaning

that child care teachers with a bachelor's degree could move into these jobs quickly and earn certification while working.

60. For distribution among counties, see http://uwba.org/uw_impact/w4cc/w4qcc_caresmap.htm.

61. San Francisco's living wage law was passed in August 2001. It requires city service contractors and leaseholders at San Francisco International Airport to pay workers at least $9.00 an hour. This wage increased to $10.00 in 2002 and will increase by 2.5 percent for three additional years. Covered workers also must receive twelve paid days off and ten unpaid days for family emergencies. See http://www.livingwagecampaign.org for more information on living wage campaigns in San Francisco and other cities.

62. The surplus funds were the result of a state decision to match funds the city had committed to supplement wages of in-home supportive service workers above the level paid by the public authority.

63. Stipulations are taken from the Notification of Availability of Funding (NOFA) for the Child Care Center WAGES Plus Program of the City and County of San Francisco.

64. Crane 2004.

65. It is important to note that while in many cases Head Start programs provide a good model for child care programs, it is hard to make the argument that this is a federal model that should simply be expanded. Head Start is locally administered and does not provide a single career ladder in part because it is operated under the auspices of many other organizations. Moreover, it has been argued that policy initiatives around child care are more likely to emanate from and be supported by the state and local levels and that local/state programs are designed as responses to specific needs identified within the area, as seen with WAGES Plus. See Whitebook and Eichberg 2002; Twombly, Montilla, and DeVita 2001.

66. Crane 2004.

67. The percentage is based on 68,055 four-year-olds served (interview with Tiffany Gibson, Georgia Office of School Readiness, June 14, 2004).

68. Information in the text box is derived from the National Child Care Information Center, U.S. Department of Health and Human Services, 2003. Guidelines prepared by the Georgia Office of School Readiness 2003 and Gallager, Clayton, and Heinemeier 2001.

69. Available online at http://www.highscope.org/EducationalPrograms/EarlyChildhood/homepage.htm (accessed 7/12/04).

70. Office of School Readiness. Online at http://www.osr.state.ga.us/TrainingSchedule03_04.pdf.

71. Office of School Readiness 2002–2003, School Year Summary of Pre-K Program Changes. Online at http://www.osr.state.ga.us/forms/prek/summarychanges.pdf.

72. Georgia Department of Education 2003a and 2003b.

73. Gornick and Meyers 2001; Schulman 2000.

74. See Mitchell, Stoney, and Dichter 1997.

75. Wolfe and Vandell 2002, A20.

76. U.S. Department of Health and Human Services 2000. "New Statistics Show Only Small Percentage of Eligible Families Receive Child Care Help" (press release, December 6). Online at http://www.hhs.gov/news/press/2000pres/20001206.html.

77. Cited in Whitebook et al. 2001, 59.

78. Hewlitt and West 2001.

79. See England and Folbre 1999.

80. See National Child Care Information Center 2004c for a summary of this research.

81.   Wolfe and Vandell 2002, A20. The studies included are the Perry Preschool Project, Carolina Abecedarian Project, and the Chicago Child-Parent Centers.

82.   Park-Jadotte, Golin, and Goult 2002.

83.   Burton et al. 2000.

84.   Laverty et al. 2001.

85.   *Online at* http://www.strategiesforchildren.org/eea/legislation/eea_legislation_home. htm.

86.   Bergmann 2001.

87.   Bowman et al. 2000.

88.   Gornick and Meyers 2001.

89.   Based on 2001 U.S. GDP of $10.082 trillion.

90.   Gornick and Meyers 2001.

4. Education

1.   Estimates of the teacher shortage vary. The problem is not an absolute shortage of applicants but a shortage in particular subjects and particular places (mostly urban and rural schools); see Darling-Hammond 2001. Shortages of special education, mathematics, and science teachers are especially acute, partly because these subjects have higher a turnover than others (see Cornett 1998; Boe, Bobbitt, and Cook 1997). Another aspect of the teacher short-age is that the least experienced teachers are more likely to teach in high-poverty schools that need more highly skilled teachers to work with underperforming students (see Haycock 1998).

2.   Over the last few years the term "teacher aide" has been largely replaced with "teacher assistant" or "paraprofessional."

3.   The ESEA is the law authorizing most federal elementary and secondary education programs. It was reauthorized as the No Child Left Behind Act of 2001 for fiscal years 2002–2007. Title I of the ESEA, which was started in 1965, is the major component of the legislation. In FY2002 it provided about $13 billion to local school districts. Title I funds provide additional academic support for improving the achievement of students in high poverty schools. These funds can be spent for hiring paraprofessionals.

4.   Estimates of the number of teacher assistants vary because of differences in the various settings that are included. Data here are from Bureau of Labor Statistics 2001.

5.   Approximately nine out of ten paraprofessionals work in the classroom, with the other 10 percent working largely in library settings. Of all teacher assistants, 75 percent work in elementary schools. See Leighton et al. 1997.

6.   Millsap, Moss, and Gamse 1993.

7.   American Federation of Teachers 2002. Accurate data on paraprofessional earnings are not available. Part of the problem is that districts use different occupational titles for similar jobs and that there are multiple titles for the various types of paraprofessionals. See http:// www.nrcpara.org/resources/stateoftheart/demographics2c.php (accessed February 18, 2003).

8.   See http://www.nrcpara.org/resources/stateoftheart/demographics2c.php. American Federation of Teachers 2002.

9.   Unionized paraprofessionals largely belong to AFT affiliates, NEA affiliates, and SEIU. In Los Angeles most of SEIU's twenty-eight thousand education members are teaching assistants. See http://www.ed.gov/pubs/Paraprofessionals/roles2.html (accessed December 9, 2002).

10.   Prior to the 2001 ESEA, credentialing requirements for paraprofessionals were set by the states, which still establish non–Title I education requirements. Thirty-one states have minimum education requirements (usually a high school diploma or equivalent), but only thirteen of these states have certification and credentialing requirements. The most comprehensive systems are in Kansas and Maine; each has a three-tiered system. Many of these systems were developed in the 1970s and 1980s, and do not reflect the changing scope of practice of paraprofessionals.

11.   Pickett 1986; U.S. Department of Education 1997.

12.   Millsap et al. 1992.

13.   Moshoyannis, Pickett, and Granick 1999; Pickett 1995.

14.   Becket 1998; Genzuk, Lavadenz, and Krashen 1994.

15.   Snyder, Hoffman, and Geddes 1998; Haselkorn and Fideler 1996.

16.   Clewell, and Villegas 2001.

17.   Ibid.; American Federation of Teachers 2002.

18.   Recruiting New Teachers, Inc. 2000.

19.   Ibid.

20.   Clewell et al. 2000; Connecticut State Department of Education 1997.

21.   Brief descriptions of some of these programs are available on the U.S. Department of Education website, http://www.ed.gov/pubs.

22.   The data in this and the following paragraph are from Clewell and Vellegas 2001.

23.   Educational Testing Service developed the three PRAXIS tests.

24.   Clewell and Villegas 2001, 21.

25.   Ibid.

26.   The handbook, *Ahead of the Class: A Design Handbook for Preparing New Teachers,* is available from the Urban Institute in Washington, D.C., or online at http://www.urban.org.

27.   Clewell, personal communication, 2004.

28.   Teacher assistants can obtain 2.5 hours per week of release time for attending classes worth five or more credits at any City University of New York (CUNY) campus or any of twelve private colleges. Paraprofessionals used to be able to take a leave without pay to finish a degree, but this benefit was eliminated because of budget cuts.

29.   The Paraprofessional Academy also maintains a website for paraprofessionals, http://www.parprofessionalacademy.org.

30.   All teachers must pass the California Basic Educational Skills Test (CBEST), a test of proficiency in reading, writing, and mathematics skills. Beginning teachers must complete the Professional Preparation Program, which is the equivalent of one year of full-time study. Teachers start as interns and in that capacity can teach, under supervision, for up to two years. At the end of the internship they earn Level 1 (preliminary) certification.

31.   All programs, however, provide some in-kind support, typically personal advising, e-mail accounts, computers, facilities, and staff development sessions.

32.   The new budget of $11.478 million was reduced to $6.5 million in FY2003–2004 owing to the state's fiscal crisis, and remained that amount in 2004–2005 (interview with Marilyn Fairgood, director, PTTP, August 11, 2004).

33.   Interview with Marilyn Fairgood, director, PTTP, August 11, 2004.

34.   Fairgood 2002.

35.   Ibid.

36.   Based on a nine-month school year.

37.   Interview with Seven Brandick, director, LAUSD Paraeducator Career Ladder Program, August 19, 2004.

38. The California State Universities are Dominguez Hills, Long Beach, Los Angeles, and Northridge.

39. Brandick interview.

40. Ibid.

41. Ibid.

42. Colvin 1998.

43. This one-year program prepares teachers for the state's subject matter tests and provides ongoing orientation to the classroom.

44. Online at http://207.166.53.39/questions/ma01.html

45. Beginning teachers without full credentials earn $36,000 and move to $41,000 when fully certified.

46. Brandick interview.

47. Rintell, Pierce, and Wurzel 2002.

48. Rintell included students pursuing master's degrees in the programs because of the increasing need for graduate degrees in education (for example, teachers pursuing "professional licensure" in Massachusetts must have a master's degree). Also, Salem State only offers graduate (and not undergraduate) degrees in special education, reading, and ESL.

49. Students' transcripts are evaluated by an international documentation center to determine their credit equivalent in the United States.

50. Interview with Ellen Rintell, August 12, 2004.

51. Rintell and Pierce 2002.

52. No statewide data on acceptance rates are available because of variance in local programs (interview with Marilyn Fairgood, director, PTTP, August 11, 2004).

53. Schulman 1990.

5. Biotechnology

1. U.S. Department of Commerce 2003. All biotechnology products are made using living organisms.

2. Biotechnology Industry Association 2003. Most biotech companies are small. Approximately one-third of biotech companies employ fewer than 50 employees. More than two-thirds employ fewer than 135 people.

3. Agres 2001. The educational distribution among North Carolina's biotech and biopharmaceutical workers in 2002 was as follows:

Degree / Area of Employment	HS	Cert.	AAS	BS	MS	Ph.D
Research and Development 10%	9%	1%	2%	44%	17%	27%
Validation 2%	11	12	9	59	7	2
QC/QA 17%	10	10	11	62	5	2
Manufacturing Support 14%	31	26	16	24	3[a] combined with Ph.D.	
Production 52%	75%	8	5	10	1	0

[a]Master's and Ph.D. degrees combined

4. The medical device industry includes (in descending order of employment) surgical and medical instruments, electromedical and electrotherapeutic apparatuses, surgical appliances and supplies, ophthalmic goods, irradiation apparatuses, in vitro diagnostic substances, and laboratory apparatuses and furniture.

5. Clayton-Matthews 2001.

6. The FDA assumes that if a company is producing successfully in one region, it can leverage the same effective management and quality assurance and control systems for the second facility. Scot Sarazen, the former senior vice president for Life Sciences at MassDevelopment who formerly worked for Genzyme, explains that any manufacturing plant is supported by many people who work in research and development, usually in a nearby location. Having already established that one manufacturing facility is well supported in a particular location, the FDA will more easily believe that another facility will be similarly successful.

7. Interview with P. Hewitt of the Tufts Center for the Study of Drug Development, cited in Eaton and Bailyn 2000. But one must be cautious about cost statistics, since they often do not identify the significant amount of government funding that they include; see Goozner 2004.

8. Grabowski 2003.

9. Grabowski, Vernon, and DiMasi 2002.

10. Determining exact employment numbers is complicated by the fact that different organizations and states define the industry differently. Some include only biotechnology, whereas others use broader categories such as life sciences or biosciences (see Cortright and Mayer 2002).

11. Ibid.

12. See http://www.ncbiotech.org/ncindustry/careers/jobresc/prepare.cfm#asdeg.

13. Commitment is particularly high when employees feel in control of their work situation and the company is seen as stable. See Eaton 2000.

14. Eaton and Bailyn 2000.

15. "The History, Current Status, and Future Direction for the California Community Colleges Biotechnology Initiative: Helping Meet the California Biotech Industry Need for an Operational Workforce," January 2004. *California Community Colleges' Economic and Workforce Development Program White Paper.* Online at http://www.cccbiotech.org/pdf/white_paper.pdf.

16. Rosenfeld et al. 2003, 4.

17. Ibid.

18. Ibid.

19. Ibid.

20. North Carolina Community College System 2003.

21. The eight areas are microbiology; QC/QA; analytical chemistry; cell culture; microbial physiology; purification; virology; and bench scale process development and recovery.

22. Reidy 2004. Amy Brockelman, the manager of Public Affairs at Biogen in Cambridge, Massachusetts, reports that Biogen's first manufacturing plant was built in Cambridge in the 1980s. In 1995 Biogen located its first manufacturing facility in North Carolina. This plant, with a capacity of 6,000 liters, is much smaller than the 90,000-liter plant started in North Carolina in 2003. Biogen currently employs more than 500 workers in North Carolina and will reach 680 by the end of 2004. More than 1,500 are employed in Cambridge.

23. The remaining funds will come from the state and the private sector.

24. The Massachusetts Alliance for Economic Development was created in 1993 to

provide information on available property for companies seeking to expand or relocate. It is a public-private consortium of utility and telecommunications companies, real estate associations, and the Massachusetts Office of Business Development.

25. Comings, Sum, and Uvin 2000.

26. Abel 2003.

27. Flynn 2003.

28. Ibid.

29. Protein-based biological drugs are made from living cells that are genetically engineered to produce or express proteins that mimic those proteins synthesized by humans.

30. The Collaborative is funded by the Education Development Center, Inc. (EDC), a private, nonprofit educational research and development organization. EDC's Center for Education, Employment, and Community (CEEC) facilitates partnerships between industry, education, and government to develop industry skill standards, curriculum, and training programs.

31. The occupations are process development associate, manufacturing technician, manufacturing instrumentation/calibration technician, aseptic fill technician, facilities technician, environmental health and safety technician, chemistry quality-control technician, microbiology quality-control technician, documentation coordinator, and validation specialist. Through workshops with experienced biomanufacturing technical workers from New Hampshire, Massachusetts, and Rhode Island, a modified DACUM (Developing a Curriculum) process was used to identify skill standards. The standards will be validated through a survey of employers throughout the Northeast. Gaps in existing community college curricula will be identified, and changes made accordingly.

32. Social Venture Partners was started by a group of high-tech entrepreneurs in Seattle in 1997. The concept was to create a philanthropic organization in which the partners would be highly engaged in the projects funded. The organization has expanded to twenty-three cities. Each partner contributes $5,000 to $6,000 annually to make grants that focus on capacity building among community-based and related organizations. A team is formed for each grant to provide technical assistance with the goal of the work being self-sustaining in a few years. SVP Boston has fifty-two partners (many of them married couples).

33. Ferrier 2002.

34. See http://www.bio.org/events/2004/media/sfbio.asp (accessed April 22, 2004).

35. Originally the money was designated for three institutes, but in 2001–2002 a fourth institute was developed and included in the budget. See "California's New Economy," 2001–2002 Governor's Budget Summary, California Department of Finance; Available at http://www.dof.ca.gov/HTML/Budgto1–02/CAecon-N.htm.

36. See http://www.qb3.org.

37. Gallego 2003.

38. Each of the six centers received a $178,875 grant, and there was an additional $152,500 grant to fund the position of state director. See http://www.cccbiotech.org/about-bio.html.

39. Huxley 2004.

40. SANDAG is the San Diego region's metropolitan planning organization. Created in the 1960s, SANDAG coordinates regional planning activity in economic development, transportation, solid waste management, and water supply and water resources management. For a history of the organization, see http://www.sandag.cog.ca.us.

41. County of San Diego 2001.

42. The San Diego Community College District includes three colleges: Miramar, City, and Mesa.

43. The Access Excellence project of the National Health Museum describes the production process: monoclonal antibodies are produced by fusing single antibody-forming cells to tumor cells grown in culture to create a hybridoma. Each hybridoma produces relatively large quantities of identical antibody molecules. When the hybridoma multiplies in culture, it produces a population of cells, each of which produces identical antibody molecules. They are called monoclonal, because they are produced by the identical offspring of a single, cloned antibody-producing cell. Once a monoclonal antibody is made, it can be used as a specific probe to track down and purify the specific protein that induced its formation. See http://www.accessexcellence.org/AB/GG/monoclonal.html.

44. Although Idec's headquarters are moving to Boston as a result of a merger with Biogen, the production facility is still being built.

45. See http://www.cact-sd.org/about-us.htm.

46. Bio-Link started in 1998 with funding from the National Science Foundation's Advanced Technological Education (ATE) Center program. The national center is housed at the Community College of San Francisco. There are four regional centers. See http://www.Bio-Link.org.

47. North Carolina Citizens for Business and Industry, "Biotech Training Center May Help Create 3,000 Jobs"; see http://www.nccbi.org/NCMagazine/2003/mag-07–03regionals. htm.

48. Klineman 2003.

49. Bleakley 1996.

50. Flynn 2003.

51. Marcelli, Baru, and Cohen 2000.

52. Schweitzer 2002.

6. Manufacturing

1. U.S. Department of Labor, Bureau of Labor Statistics, Office of Occupational Statistics and Employment Projections. See ftp://ftp.bls.gov/pub/special.requests/ep/ind-occ. matrix/ind_pdf/i310330.pdf.

2. A commonly cited reason for some of the loss is the short-sighted profit strategies in the 1950s and 1960s, such as licensing technology to foreign producers and moving to cheap labor countries. See Bluestone and Harrison 1982; Giffi, Roth, and Seal 1990.

3. The size of the 1978 labor force was 102.2 million; in 2002 it was 144.9 million (Bureau of Labor Statistics 2002a).

4. Bartik 2003.

5. Department of Commerce data cited in National Manufacturing Association, the Manufacturing Institute, and Deloitte and Touche 2003.

6. Popkin 2000.

7. The Center for Workforce Success makes the case that "tooling and machining supports the existence of virtually every other type of manufacturing industry by producing special tools, dies, jigs, fixtures, gauges, special machines, and precision-machined parts, usually custom designed and made for use as components in a larger intermediary product, or in production of final products by other manufacturers." See Center for Workforce Success 2001, 24.

8. In industries that rely on consistent high-quality production, other factors compen-

sate for higher labor costs. For example, the advantage of cheap labor cannot compensate one electrical blackout a year, a common occurrence in less-developed countries, for a silicon chip maker (See Fingleton 1999, 127).

9. Appelbaum et al. 2000; Cohen and Zysman 1987.

10. AFL-CIO. See http://www.aflcio.org/issuespolitics/manufacturing/revitalize.cfm.

11. The White House Office of the Press Secretary, February 5 2000. According to the National Association of Manufacturers, 70 percent of manufacturers provided employees with direct health care coverage in 1997, compared to less than half of other private-sector companies; see the National Association of Manufacturers 2003.

12. Holzer 2004.

13. Center for Workforce Success 2001.

14. Fingleton 1999.

15. Many industry case studies reveal how new technologies were used to reduce worker autonomy and control over the production process. On the printing industry see, Wallace and Kalleberg 1982. On the metalworking industry, see Cann, McGraw, and Forrant 1991. On the aerospace, agricultural implement, and auto industries see Shaiken, Herzenberg, and Kuhn 1986. On engine production, see Knauss 1997.

16. Gunn 1992.

17. Most evidence suggests that adopting high-performance work systems increases worker trust in employers, makes work more rewarding, and does not increase worker stress (See Appelbaum et al. 2000). In addition, retention rates are higher among firms using high-performance work systems (see Jenkins and Florida 1999; Arthur 1994).

18. Rubenstein 2000; Ettlie 1988; MacDuffie 1995.

19. Groshen 1991.

20. Still, the low-road strategy may be profitable in some manufacturing sectors. See Luria 1996.

21. See, for example, the National Network of Sector Practitioners at http://www.nedlc.org.

22. The National Network of Sector Practitioners promotes sectoral strategies and provides technical assistance to economic and workforce development organizations in implementing them.

23. Hamilton 1990; Haveman and Saks 1985.

24. Parker and Rogers 1996.

25. These figures are drawn from an article, "Workplace Change Comes to Wisconsin," that appears on the Center on Wisconsin Strategy website. A more detailed description is available at *http://www.cows.org*.

26. Ibid.

27. Wisconsin Regional Training Partnership 2002.

28. Luker, Layden, and Turner 1997.

29. The Manufacturing Skill Standards Council (MSSC), a national organization of businesses, labor unions, trade associations, and other organizations, has proposed standards in four broad areas: quality control, manufacturing processes, safety, and maintenance. The National Occupational Competency Testing Institute, a business that provides competency assessments in numerous occupations, has developed written and competency-based tests of the skills identified by MSSC. The Milwaukee Area Technical College is piloting the use of these tests in Wisconsin.

30. Parker and Rogers 2003.

31. For a review of this literature, see Fitzgerald and McGregor 1993.

32. Leigh 1989.

33. Meléndez and Harrison 1998.

34. The Milwaukee ICIC also concerns itself with three non-manufacturing industries with inner-city potential: health care, construction, and business processing.

35. McGroarty and Humphries 1995.

36. Wisconsin Regional Training Project 2000, 2002.

37. Parker and Rogers 2003.

38. Jenkins 2003.

39. Jenkins and Theodore 1997.

40. Chicago Federation of Labor and Center for Labor and Community Research 2001.

41. The main standards used were the National Skill Standards Project for Advanced High Performance Manufacturing (NACFAM), 1997; Manufacturing Skill Standards Council (MSSC) Standards, 2000; and the National Institute for Metalworking Skills (NIMS) Standards, 1997.

42. Jenkins and Theodore 1997.

43. Several of these programs are highly effective. One example is Jane Addams Resource Corporation (JARC), which is recognized nationally for its successful metalworking training programs for incumbent workers and for Chicago residents in need of work. Working with businesses in developing curriculum, JARC began the Metalworking Skills Training Program in 1991. The program offers two courses in six- to eight-week modules. The first combines math literacy with shop math and blueprint reading, and the use of measuring tools. In the second, students specialize in one of three areas: Advanced Blueprint Analysis, Measuring for Quality Control, or Trig for the Trades. A third level of training provides workers with hands-on instruction in the operation and setup of a punch press. In addition, JARC offers Business Software, Manufacturing Software (CAD, CAM, and CNC), and ESL classes. By 1996 JARC was operating the only die-setting apprenticeship program in the country registered with the U.S. Department of Labor's Bureau of Apprenticeship and Training (see Fitzgerald and Leigh 2002). JARC is part of the nation's largest foundation-led sectoral initiative, the Aspen Institute's Sectoral Employment Development Learning Project, funded by the Charles Stewart Mott Foundation (see Rademacher 2002).

A second highly regarded program is the Manufacturing Technology Bridge Program, which integrates basic math, literacy, and communication skills with technical training in manufacturing skills. The Bridge Program is a partnership of the University of Illinois at Chicago Great Cities, Daley College, Instituto del Progreso Latino, and the Illinois Institute of Technology. Students start with the sixteen-week bridge program and can advance to Daley College for a one-year certificate or a two-year associate's degree, and from there to a bachelor's degree in manufacturing at the Illinois Institute of Technology. Although few Bridge students get as far as the associate's degree, an evaluation by the Academy for Educational Development in 2001 found that Bridge students earn twice as much ($16,555 compared to $7,758) and are five times more likely to be consistently employed than a comparison group that had not been through the program (see Jenkins 2003).

44. Chicago Federation of Labor and Center for Labor and Community Research 2001, 76.

45. Interview with Dan Swinney, April 2004.

46. Chicago Workforce Board 2003.

47. Center for Labor and Community Research 2003a.

48. Center for Labor and Community Research 2003b.

49. Data for both figures were provided by Eli's Cheesecake to the Center for Labor and Community Research.

50. Cited in Graham 2004.
51. Interview with Bob Ginsburg, April 2004.
52. McGahey 2004.
53. See Fitzgerald 2004; Fitzgerald and Leigh 2002.
54. Klemanski 1989.
55. Neighborhood Capital Budget Group 2004.
56. Neighborhood Capital Budget Group 2002.

7. An Agenda for Moving Up in the New Economy

1. Frazis, Gittleman, and Joyce 2000.
2. Knoke and Kalleberg 1994.
3. Lynch and Black 1998.
4. Salzman, Moss, and Tilly 1998; Osterman 1995.
5. Ibid.
6. Marano and Tarr 2004.
7. Fitzgerald 2002; Bartlett and Steele 1998; Harrison and Kantor 1978. For an ongoing account of recent corporate subsidy deals, see http://www.goodjobsfirst.org.
8. Fitzgerald and Patton 1994.
9. See Giloth 2004.
10. Marano and Tarr 2004.
11. McGahey 2004.
12. Fitzgerald 2004.
13. Apprenticeships predated unions through craft guilds in the colonial period, but few apprentices established their own shops because they could not accumulate enough capital. Other apprenticeships were more indentures than career ladders; see Jacoby 1991.
14. The White House 2004.
15. Holzer and Waller 2003.
16. Mills and Biswas 2003.
17. Bidot-Cruz and Marano 2003.
18. Rubin, Seltzer, and Mills 2003.
19. For more detailed information, see the Center for Adult and Experiential Learning website: http://www.cael.org.
20. Evelyn 2003.
21. Jenkins 2003.
22. Javar and Wandner 2002.
23. Duscha 2002.
24. Lederer 2002.
25. Jenkins 2003.
26. Grubb 2001.
27. For details on how these programmatic changes could be made, see Bosworth and Choitz 2002.
28. Fitzgerald 2002.

Bibliography

Abel, Cora Beth. 2003. "MASSBIOED'S Overview Course Arms More Non-Scientists with Information Necessary to Lead Employment in Biotechnology." *Bioline* 17 (1): 4.

Acs, Gregory, Katherin Ross Phillips, and Daniel McKenzie. 2001. *Playing by the Rules But Losing the Game: America's Working Poor.* Washington, D.C.: Urban Institute.

Agres, Ted. 2001. "The Biotech Triangle." *The Scientist* 15 (21): 28–31.

Alssid, Julian L., David Gruber, Davis Jenkins, Christopher Mazzeo, Brandon Roberts, and Regina Standback-Stroud. 2002. *Building a Career Pathways System: Promising Practices in Community College Centered Workforce Development.* New York: Workforce Strategy Center.

American Association of Colleges of Nursing. 2000. *Nursing School Enrollments Continue to Decline, Though at a Slower Rate.* Washington, D.C.: American Association of Colleges of Nursing.

——. 2003. *Thousands of Students Turned Away from the Nation's Nursing Schools Despite Sharp Increase in Enrollment.* Washington, D.C.: American Association of Colleges of Nursing.

American Federation of State, County, and Municipal Employees. 2000. "The Staffing Crisis in Long-Term Care." *Health Focus* (April). http://www.afscme.org/publications/health_focus/focus400.htm.

American Federation of Teachers. 2002. *It Takes a Team: A Profile of Support Staff in American Education.* April. http://www.aft.org/psrp/reports/team2002.pdf.

Applebaum, Eileen. 1989. "The Growth in the U.S. Contingent Labour Force." In *Microeconomic Issues in Labour Economics*, ed. Robert Drago and Richard Perlman, 62–82. New York: Harvester Wheatsheaf.

Appelbaum, Eileen, Thomas Bailey, Peter Berg, and Arne Kalleberg. 2000. *Manufacturing Advantage: Why High Performance Work Systems Pay Off.* Ithaca, N.Y.: Cornell University Press.

Arthur, Jeffrey B. 1994. "Effect of Human Resource Systems on Manufacturing Performance and Turnover." *Academy of Management Journal* 37 (3): 670–687.

Arthur, Michael B., and Denise M. Rousseau. 1996. "Introduction: The Boundaryless Career as a New Employment Principle." In *The Boundaryless Career*, ed. Michael B. Arthur and Denise M. Rousseau, 3–21. New York: Oxford University Press.

Ballantine, John W., and Ronald F. Fergusen. 2003. "Plastic Manufacturers: How

Competitive Strategies and Technology Decisions Transformed Jobs and Increased Pay Disparity among Rank-and-File Workers." In *Low-Wage America: How Employers Are Reshaping Opportunity in the Workplace*, ed. Eileen Applebaum, Annette Bernhardt, and Richard Murnane, 195–228. New York: Russell Sage Foundation.

Barrington, Linda. 2000. *Does a Rising Tide Lift All Boats?* Washington, D.C.: Conference Board.

Bartel, Ann, Casey Ichniowski, and Kathryn Shaw. 2003. "'New Technology' and Its Impact on the Jobs of High School Educated Workers: A Look Deep Inside Three Manufacturing Industries." In *Low-Wage America: How Employers Are Reshaping Opportunity in the Workplace*, ed. Eileen Applebaum, Annette Bernhardt, and Richard Murnane, 155–194. New York: Russell Sage Foundation.

Bartik, Timothy. 2003. *Thoughts on American Manufacturing Decline and Revitalization*. Kalamazoo, Mich.: Upjohn Institute.

Bartlett, D., and J. B. Steele. 1998. "Corporate Welfare, Part One." *Time*, November 8, 9, 16, 23, 30, 38.

Batt, Rosemary, and Jeffrey Keefe. 1998. "Human Resource and Employment Practices in Telecommunications Services, 1980–1998." In *Employment Practices and Business Strategy*, ed. Peter Cappelli, 107–152. Oxford: Oxford University Press.

Becket, D. 1998. "Increasing the Number of Latino and Navajo Teachers in Hard-to-Staff Schools." *Journal of Teacher Education* 49 (3): 196–205.

Benner, Chris. 2002. *Flexible Work in the Information Economy: Labor Markets in Silicon Valley*. Oxford: Blackwell.

Bergmann, Barbara R. 2001. "Decent Childcare for Decent Wages." *American Prospect* 12 (1): 8–9.

Bernhardt, Annette, and Dave E. Marcotte. 2000. "Is 'Standard Employment' Still What It Used to Be?" In *Non-Standard Work: The Nature and Challenges of Changing Employment Arrangements*, ed. Françoise Carré, Marianne A. Ferber, Lonnie Golden, and Steve Hertzenberg, 21–41. Champaign, Ill.: Industrial Relations Research Association.

Bernhardt, Annette, Martina Morris, Mark S. Handcock, and Marc A. Scott. 2001. *Divergent Paths: Economic Mobility in the New American Labor Market*. 2001. New York: Russell Sage Foundation.

Bernstein, Aaron. 1996. "Is America Becoming More of a Class Society?" *Business Week*, February 26.

Bidot-Cruz, Alexandra E., and Cindy Marano. 2003. *The State of Workforce Investment: A Selected Review of State Level Financing for Training and Workforce Preparation*. Oakland, Calif.: National Economic Development Law Center.

Blank, Helen, Andrea Behr, and Karen Schulman. 2000. *State Developments in Child Care, Early Education, and School-Age Care*. Washington, D.C.: Children's Defense Fund.

Bleakley, Fred R. 1996. "To Bolster Economies, Some States Rely More on Two-Year Colleges." *Wall Street Journal*, November 26, A1, A12.

Blood, Margaret. 2000. *Our Youngest Children: Massachusetts Voters and Opinion Leaders Speak Out on Their Care and Education*. Boston: Strategies for Children/The Stride Rite Foundation.

Bluestone, Barry, and Teresa Ghilarducci. 1996. *Making Work Pay: Wage Insurance for the Working Poor*. Annandale-on-Hudson, N.Y.: Jerome Levy Institute of Bard College.

Bluestone, Barry, and Bennett Harrison. 1999. *Growing Prosperity*. New York: Houghton Mifflin.

Bluestone, Barry, and Stephen Rose. 1997. "Overworked and Underemployed." *American Prospect* 8 (3): 58–69.

Boe, E., S. Bobbitt, and L. Cook. 1997. "Whither Didst Thou Go?" *Journal of Special Education* 30:371–389.

Boston Health Care and Research Training Institute. 2004. *Report to the BEST Initiative.* Boston: Boston Health Care and Research Training Institute.

Bosworth, Brian, and Victoria Choitz. 2002. *Held Back: How Student Aid Programs Fail Working Adults.* Belmont, Mass.: FutureWorks.

Bowers, Barbara, and Marian Becker. 1992. "Nurse's Aides in Nursing Homes: The Relationship between Organization and Quality." *Gerontologist* 32:360–366.

Bowman, Barbara, M. Suzanne Donovan, and M. Susan Burns, eds. 2000. *Eager to Learn: Educating Our Preschoolers.* Washington, D.C.: National Academy Press.

Boyd, Brenda, and Mary Wandschneider. 2004. "Washington State Child Care Career and Wage Ladder Pilot Project." *Phase 2: Final Evaluation Report.* Pullman, Wash.: Washington State University, Department of Human Development.

Buerhaus, Peter I., Douglas O. Staiger, and David I. Auerbach. 2000. "Implications of an Aging Registered Nurse Workforce." *Journal of the American Medical Association* 283: 2948–2954.

Burbank, John R., and Nancy Wiefek. 2001. *Early Childhood Education Career Development Ladder.* Seattle, Wash.: Economic Opportunity Institute.

Bureau of Labor Statistics. 1998. "National Occupational Employment Data." http://www.bls.gov/oes/1998/oesnat98.htm.

——. 1999. "Labor Force Participation Rate of Fathers and Mothers Varies with Children's Ages." *Monthly Labor Review: The Editor's Desk* (June). http://www.bls.gov/opub/ted/1999/jun/wk1/art03.htm.

——. 2000. *National Occupational Employment and Wage Estimates.* Washington, D.C.: Bureau of Labor Statistics. http://www.bls.gov/oes/ 2000/oessrci.htm.

——. 2001. *Career Guide to Industries: 2000–2001 Edition.* Washington, D.C.: Bureau of Labor Statistics. http://www.umsl.edu/services/govdocs/ooh20002001/41.htm.

——. 2002a. "Contents of Labor Force Table." http://www.census.gov/statab/USA98/dd-lb.txt.

——. 2002b. *Washington State Occupational Employment and Wage Estimates.* Washington, D.C.: Bureau of Labor Statistics. http://www.bls.gov/oes/2002/oessrest.htm.

——. 2003. "Occupational Employment and Wages, May 2003." http://stats.bls.gov/oes/2003/may/oes291111.htm.

Burtless, Gary. 1999. "Effects of Growing Wage Disparities and Changing Family Composition on the U.S. Income Distribution." *Brookings Review* 17: 31–39.

Burton, Alice, Jessica Mihaly, Jennifer Kagiwada, Marcy Whitebook. 2000. *The CARES Initiative in California: Pursuing Public Policy to Build a Skilled and Stable Child Care Workforce, 1997–2000.* Washington, D.C.: Center for the Child Care Workforce.

Burton, Alice, Marcy Whitebook, Marci Young, Dan Bellm, Claudia Wayne, Richard N. Brandon, and Erin Maher. 2002. *Estimating the Size and Components of the U.S. Child Care Workforce.* Washington, D.C: Center for the Child Care Workforce.

Burwell, B. 1998. *Medicaid Long-Term Care Expenditures in FY 1998.* Cambridge, Mass.: MEDSTAT Group.

California Child Care Resource and Referral Network. 1999. *The California Child Care Portfolio.* Sacramento: California Child Care Resource and Referral Network.

California Department of Finance. 2002. "California's New Economy." 2001–02 *Governor's Budget Summary.* Online at http://www.dof.ca.gov/HTML/Budgt01–02/ CAecon-N.htm.

Campbell, Nancy D., Judith C. Appelbaum, Karin Martinson, and Emily Martin. 2000. *Be All That We Can Be: Lessons from the Military for Improving Our Nation's Child Care.* Washington, D.C.: National Women's Law Center.

Cancian, Maria, Robert Haveman, Thomas Kaplan, Daniel Meyer, and Barbara Wolfe. 1999. "Work, Earnings, and Well-Being after Welfare: What Do We Know?" In *Economic Conditions and Welfare Reform,* ed. Sheldon Danzinger, 161–186. Kalamazoo, Mich.: Upjohn Institute for Employment Research.

Cann, Elyse, Kathleen McGraw, and Robert Forrant. 1991. *Phoenix or Dinosaur: Industrial District or Industrial Decline.* Springfield, Mass.: Machine Action Project.

Cappelli, James. 1999. Quotations in text from Thomas D. Sugalski, Louis S. Manzo, and Jim. L. Meadows. 1995. "Resource Link: Reestablishing the Employment Relationship in an Era of Downsizing." *Human Resource Management* 34 (3): 389–403.

Cappelli, Lauri Bass, Harry Katz, David Knoke, Paul Osterman, and Michael Useem. 1997. *Change at Work.* New York: Oxford University Press.

Cappelli, Peter. 1995. "Rethinking Employment." *British Journal of Industrial Relations* 33 (4): 563–602.

———. 1999. *The New Deal at Work.* Cambridge, Mass.: Harvard Business School Press.

Cappelli, Peter, and K. C. O'Shaughnessy. 1995. *Changes in Skill and Wage Structures in Corporate Headquarters, 1986–1992.* Philadelphia: Working Paper, National Center on the Educational Quality of the Workforce.

Card, David, and Alan Krueger. 1995. *Myth and Measurement.* Princeton, N.J.: Princeton University Press.

Carnoy, Martin, Manuel Castells, and Chris Benner. 1997. "Labour Markets and Employment Practices in the Age of Flexibility: A Case Study of Silicon Valley." *International Labour Review* 136:27–48.

Carré, Françoise, and Paula Rayman. 1999. *Professional Pathways: Examining Work, Family, and Community in the Biotechnology Industry.* Cambridge, Mass.: Radcliffe Public Policy Center.

Center for Labor and Community Research. 2003a. *Center for Business Innovation and Training: A Concept Summary.* Chicago: Candy Institute/Food Chicago.

———. 2003b. *The Food Chicago Career Path.* Chicago: Candy Institute/Food Chicago.

Center for Workforce Success. 2001. *The Skills Gap 2001: Manufacturers Confront Persistent Skills Shortages in an Uncertain Economy.* Washington, D.C: National Association of Manufacturers.

Center on Wisconsin Strategy. 2002. *Milwaukee Jobs Initiative: Five Years of Better Jobs.* University of Wisconsin-Madison. http://www.cows.org/pdf/workdev/mji/ov-mji-2.pdf

Chicago Federation of Labor and Center for Labor and Community Research. 2001. *Creating a Career Path System in Cook County.* Chicago: Chicago Federation of Labor and Center for Labor and Community Research.

Chicago Workforce Board. 2003. *Summary of Manufacturing Workforce Summit.* Chicago, Ill.: Chicago Workforce Board.

Child Care Aware website. 2004. http://www.childcareaware.org/en/care/centers.html.

Child Care Services Association. 2000. *T.E.A.C.H. Early Childhood® Celebrating Ten Years.* Chapel Hill, N.C.

——. 2001. *T.E.A.C.H. Early Childhood.*® *Annual Report.* Chapel Hill, N.C..: Child Care Services Association.

Children's Defense Fund. 2001. *Child Care Basics.* http://www.childrensdefense.org/earlychildhood/childcare/basics.asp.

Clayton-Matthews, Adam. 2001. *The Medical Devices Industry in Massachusetts.* Boston: University of Massachusetts Donahue Institute, Economic Research and Analysis Division.

Cleveland, C.B. 1997. *Nursing Education Mobility Action Group Project (NEMAG), Evaluation Research Final Report.* Cleveland, Ohio: The Center for Health Affairs.

Clewell, Beatriz Chu, Katherine Darke, Thenoa Davis-Googe, Laurie Forcier, and Sarah Manes. 2000. *Literature Review on Teacher Recruitment Programs.* Washington, D.C.: Urban Institute.

Clewell, Beatriz Chu, and Ana María Villegas. 2001a. *Absence Unexcused: Ending Teacher Shortages in High Needs Areas.* Washington, D.C.: Urban Institute.

——. 2001b. *Ahead of the Class: A Design Handbook for Preparing New Teachers.* Washington, D.C.: Urban Institute.

Cohen, Stephen S., and John Zysman. 1987. *Manufacturing Matters: The Myth of the Post-Industrial Economy.* New York: Basic Books.

Comings, John, Andrew Sum, and Johan Uvin. 2000. *New Skills for a New Economy.* Boston: MassInc.

Common Sense Foundation. 2000. "Common Sense Says That Child Care Workers Should Earn a Living Wage." *Common Sense Says* 3, no. 11 (November). http://common-sense.org/pdfs/css_v3_i11.pdf.

Conference Board. 1997. *HR Executive Review: Implementing the New Employment Contract.* New York: Conference Board.

Connecticut State Department of Education. 1997. "Teaching Opportunities for Paraprofessionals." http://www.ed.gov/pubs/Paraprofessionals/conn.htm.

Consumer Reports. 1995. "Nursing Homes: When a Parent Needs Care." *Consumer Reports* 60, no. 8 (August): 518..

Cooper, Candy J. 1999. *Ready to Learn.* New York: French-American Foundation.

Cornerstone Communications Group. 2001. *Analysis of American Nurses Association Staffing Survey.* Warwick, R.I.: Cornerstone Communications Group.

Cornett, Lynn. 1998. *Quality Teachers: Can Incentive Policies Make a Difference?* Atlanta, Ga.: Southern Regional Education Board.

Cortright, Joseph, and Heike Mayer. 2002. *Signs of Life: The Growth of Biotechnology Centers in the U.S.* Washington, D.C: Brookings Institution Center on Urban and Metropolitan Policy.

County of San Diego. 2001. *Biotechnology Action Plan.* San Diego: County of San Diego.

Crane, Elise. 2004. *WAGES Plus, WAGES Plus Quality+, and WAGES+ Family Child Care.* San Francisco: City Colleges of San Francisco.

Dalaker, 2001. *Poverty in the United States: 2000.* Washington, D.C.: U.S. Census Bureau. http://www.census.gov/prod/2001pubs/p60-214.pdf.

Danziger, Sheldon, and Jane Waldfogel, eds. 2000. *Securing the Future.* New York: Russell Sage Foundation.

Danziger, Sheldon, and Peter Gottschalk, eds. 1994. *Uneven Tides: Rising Inequality in America.* New York: Russell Sage Foundation.

Darling-Hammond, Linda. 2001. "The Challenge of Staffing Our Schools." *Educational Leadership* 31 (3): 55–57.

Dawson, Steven L. 1998. *Confronting the Decline of Paraprofessional Care*. Presentation to the AARP National Conference: "Paraprofessionals on the Front Lines: Improving Their Jobs and Improving the Quality of Long-Term Care," September 11.

Dawson, Steven L., and Rick Surpin. 2001. "Direct-Care Healthcare Workers: You Get What You Pay For." *Workforce Issues in a Changing Society*. Washington, D.C.: Aspen Institute.

———. 2000. *Direct-Care Health Workers: The Unnecessary Crisis in Long-Term Care*. New York: Paraprofessional Healthcare Institute.

Dawson, Steven L., and Karen Kahn. 1999. *Quality Care Partners: A Case Study*. New York: Paraprofessional Healthcare Institute.

Devaney, Barbara L., Marilyn R. Ellwood, and John M. Love. 1997. "Programs That Mitigate the Effects of Poverty on Children." *Children and Poverty* 7 (2): 88–112.

Diebold, Francis X., David Neumark, and Daniel Polsky. 1997. "Job Stability in the United States." *Journal of Labor Economics* 15 (2): 206–233.

Dinardo, John, Nicole Fortin, and Thomas Lemieux. 1996. "Labor Market Institutions and the Distribution of Wages, 1973–1992: A Semiparametric Approach." *Econometrica* 64 (5): 1001–1044.

Direct Care Alliance. 2000. *National Survey on State Initiatives to Improve Paraprofessional Health Care Employment*. Bronx, N.Y.: Direct Care Alliance/Paraprofessional Healthcare Institute.

Duscha, Steve. 2002. *Jobs after Training: The Report Card for California*. Sacramento: Steve Duscha Advisories.

Duncan, Greg, and Jeanne Brooks-Gunn. 1997. *Consequences of Growing Up Poor*. New York: Russell Sage Foundation.

Duncan, Greg, Johanne Boisjoly, and Timothy M. Smeeding. 1995. *Slow Motion: Economic Mobility of Young Workers in the 1970s and 1980s*. Syracuse, N.Y.: Center for Policy Research, Maxwell School of Citizenship and Public Affairs, Syracuse University.

Early Childhood.org. 2004. *Comparison of Early Childhood Programs and Standards*. http://www.earlychildhood.org/standards/descriptions.cfm.

Eaton, Susan C. 2000a. "Beyond 'Unloving Care': Linking Human Resource Management and Patient Care Quality in Nursing Homes." *International Journal of Human Resource Management* 11 (3): 591–616.

———. 2000b. "The Emergence of a Social Contract: Evidence from the Biotech Sector Courts." MIT Working Paper 00–001." Cambridge, Mass.: MIT Industrial Performance Center.

Eaton, Susan C., and Lotte Bailyn. 2000. "Careers as Life Paths in Firms of the Future." In *Career Frontiers: New Conceptions of Working Lives*, ed. Maury Peiperl, Michael B. Arthur, Rob Goffee, and Tim Morris, 177–198. Oxford: Oxford University Press.

Ellwood, David, and the Aspen Institute Domestic Strategy Group. 2002. *Grow Faster Together or Grow Slowly Apart*. Washington, D.C.: Aspen Institute.

England, Paula, and Nancy Folbre. 1999. "Who Should Pay for the Kids?" *Annals, AAPSS* 563:194–207.

Ettlie, John E. 1988. *Taking Charge of Manufacturing*. San Francisco: Jossey-Bass.

Evelyn, Jamilah. 2003. "Tuition Is Up 11.5% at Community Colleges, Survey Finds; State Budget Cuts Are Blamed." *Chronicle of Higher Education*, September 26, 43.

Fairgood, Marilynn. 2002. *The California Paraprofessional Teacher Training Program, A Progress Report to the Legislature*. Sacramento: California Commission on Teacher Credentialing.

Farber, H. S. 1995. *Are Lifetime Jobs Disappearing? Job Duration in the United Statees*, 1973–1993. Princeton, N.J.: Industrial Relations Section, Princeton University.

Ferrier, Kay. 2002. *California Community Colleges Economic Development Program Annual Report, Fiscal Year 2000–2001*. Sacramento: California Community College Economic and Workforce Development Program.

Feuerberg, Marvin. 2001. "Appropriateness of Minimum Nurse Staffing Ratios in Nursing Homes." *Phase II Final Report*. Washington, D.C.: Centers for Medicare and Medicaid Services.

Fingleton, Eamonn. 1999. *In Praise of Hard Industries*. Boston: Houghton Mifflin.

Fitzgerald, Joan. 1998. "Is Networking Always the Answer? Networking among Community Colleges to Increase Their Capacity in Business Outreach." *Economic Development Quarterly* 12:30–40.

——. 1999. "Promoting Entrepreneurship among Inner-City High School Students: Does It Improve Student Outcomes?" *Urban Education* 34:155–180.

——. 2000. *Community Colleges as Labor Market Intermediaries: Building Career Ladders for Low-Wage Workers*. New York: Community Development Research Center, New School University.

——. 2002. "Retention Deficit Disorder." *City Limits* (April): 37–38.

——. 2004. "Moving the Workforce Intermediary Agenda Forward." *Economic Development Quarterly* 18 (1): 3–9.

Fitzgerald, Joan, and Virginia Carlson. 2000. "Ladders to a Better Life." *American Prospect* 11 (15): 54–60.

Fitzgerald, Joan, and N. Leigh. 2002. *Economic Revitalization: Cases and Strategies for City and Suburb*. Thousand Oaks, Calif.: Sage.

Fitzgerald, Joan, and Alan McGregor. 1993. "Labor-Community Initiatives in Worker Training in the United States and United Kingdom." *Economic Development Quarterly* 7 (2): 172–182.

Fitzgerald, Joan, and Wendy Patton. 1994. "Race, Job Training, and Economic Development: Barriers to Racial Equity in Program Planning." *The Review of Black Political Economy* 23:93–112.

Fitzgerald, Joan, David Perry and Martin Jaffe. 2003. *The New Metropolitan Alliances: Regional Collaboration for Economic Development*. Boston: CEOs for Cities.

Flynn, Erin. 2003. *BEST Initiative for Biotechnology: Preliminary Evaluation Findings*. Arlington, Mass.: FutureWorks.

Frank, Barbara, and Steven L. Dawson. 2000. *Heath Care Workforce Issues in Massachusetts*. Boston: Massachusetts Health Policy Forum.

Frank, Robert, and Cook, Phillip. 1995. *The Winner Take All Society*. New York: Free Press.

Frazis, Harley J., Mauray Gittleman, and Mary Joyce. 2000. "Correlates of Training: An Analysis Using Both Employer and Employee Characteristics." *Industrial and Labor Relations Review* 53:443–462.

Freeman, Richard B. 1996. "Labor Market Institutions and Earnings Inequality." *New England Economic Review* (May–June): 157–168.

Freeman, Richard B. 1993. "How Much Has De-Unionization Contributed to the Rise in Male Earnings Inequality?" In *Uneven Tides: Rising Inequality in America*, ed. Sheldon Danziger and Peter Gottschalk, 133–164. New York: Russell Sage Foundation.

Freeman, Richard, and James Medoff. 1984. *What Do Unions Do?* New York: Basic Books.

Freudenheim, M., and L. Villarosa. 2001. "Nursing Shortage Is Raising Worries on Patients' Care." *New York Times*, April 8.

Fullerton, Howard N., Jr. 1999. "Labor Force Participation: 75 Years of Change, 1950–98 and 1998–2025." *Monthly Labor* Review (December): 3–12.

Galinsky, Ellen, Carollee Howes, Susan Kontos, and Marybeth Shinn. 1994. *The Study of Children in Family Child Care and Relative Care: Highlights of Findings.* New York: Families and Work Institute.

Gallagher, James, Jenna Clayton, and Sarah Heinemeier. 2001. *Education for Four-Year-Olds: State Initiatives—Technical Report No. 2.* Chapel Hill: University of North Carolina, National Center for Early Development and Learning.

Gallego, Augustine. 2003. *Community Colleges and Economic Development.* San Diego: San Diego Community College District.

Genzuk, M., M. Lavadenz, and S. Krashen. 1994. "Para-Educators: A Source for Remedying the Shortage of Teachers for Limited-English Proficient Students." *Journal of Educational Issues of Minority Students* 14:211–222.

Georgia Department of Education. 2003a. *State Salary Schedule.* http://techservices.doe. k12.ga.us/admin/reports/SalarySchedule03.pdf.

———. 2003b. *Georgia Annual/Monthly Teacher and Administrator Salary Schedule.* http://www.doe.k12.ga.us/doe/finances/salaries.asp.

Georgia Office of School Readiness. 2002–2003. *Georgia Pre-K Program Guidelines.* http://www.decal.state.ga.us/prek/prekguidelines.html.

Giffi, Craig, Aleda V. Roth, and Gregory M Seal. 1990. *Competing in World-Class Manufacturing.* Homewood, Ill.: Business One Irwin.

Giloth, Robert, ed. 2004. *Workforce Intermediaries for the Twenty-first Century.* Philadelphia: Temple University Press.

Gittleman, Maury, and Mary Joyce. 1996. "Earnings Mobility and Long-Run Inequality: An Analysis Using Matched CPS Data." *Industrial Relations* 35:180–196.

Goozner, Merrill. 2004. *The $800 Million Dollar Pill: The Truth behind the Cost of New Drugs.* Berkeley: University of California Press.

Gordon, S. 2000. "Nurse, Interrupted." *American Prospect* 11 (7): 7.

Gormley, William T., and Jessica K Lucas. 2000. "Money, Accreditation, and Child Care Center Quality." *Foundation for Child Development*, Working Paper Series. New York: Foundation for Child Development.

Gornick, Janet, and Marcia K. Meyers. 2001. "Support for Working Families." *American Prospect* 12 (1): 3–7.

Grabowski, Henry. 2003. *Innovation and R&D Incentives for Orphan Drugs and Neglected Diseases.* http://www.earthinstitute.columbia.edu/cgsd/documents/grabowski.ppt.

Grabowski, Henry, John Vernon, and Joseph DiMasi. 2002. "Returns on Research and Development for 1990s New Drug Introductions." *Pharmacoeconomics* 20: supplement 3, 11–29.

Graham, William. 2004. *Tax Increment Financing Training Final Report with Productivity Information.* Chicago: Center for Labor and Community Research.

Griffen, Sarah. 2001. *Bridges to the Future First Year Report.* Boston: Jamaica Plain Neighborhood Development Corporation.

Groshen, Erica. 1991. "Five Reasons Why Wages Vary among Employers." *Industrial Relations* 30 (3): 350–381.

Grove, Rebecca, and Jennifer Anthony. 2002. *SaMCARES, San Mateo County: Matching Funds for Retention Program Implementation Study Report, Year I (2001–2002).* http://pace.berkeley.edu/QIS-San%20Mateo.pdf.

Grubb, Norton W. 2001. "Second Chances in Changing Times: The Roles of Community Colleges in Advancing Low-Wage Workers." In *Low-Wage Workers in the New*

Economy, ed. Richard Kazis and Marc Miller, 283–306. Washington, D.C.: Urban Institute.

Gunn, Thomas G. 1987. *Manufacturing for Competitive Advantage*. Cambridge, Mass.: Ballinger.

———. 1992. *21st Century Manufacturing*. New York: HarperBusiness.

Hagen, Stuart. 1999. *Projections of Expenditures for Long-Term Care Services for the Elderly*. Washington, D.C. Congressional Budget Office.

Hamilton, Steve. 1990. *Apprenticeship for Adulthood*. New York: Free Press.

Harms, T., D. Cryer, and R. M. Clifford. 1990. *Infant/Toddler Environment Rating Scale*. New York: Teachers College Press.

Harms, Thelma, Debby Cryer, and Richard M. Clifford. 1999. *Infant/Toddler Environmental Rating Scale*. http://www.fpg.unc.edu/~ecers/iters.html.

Harrington, Charlene, Helen Carrillo, Susan C. Thollaug, and Peter R. Summers. 1999. *Nursing Facilities, Staffing, Residents, and Facility Deficiencies, 1991–1997*. San Francisco: Department of Behavioral and Social Science, University of California. http://www.cms.hhs.gov/medicaid/services/nursfac97.pdf.

Harrison, Bennett. 1994. *Lean and Mean*. New York: Basic Books.

Harrison, B., and Marcus Weiss. 1998. *Workforce Development Networks*. Thousand Oaks, Calif.: Sage.

Harrison, B., Marcus Weiss, and Jon Grant. 1995. *Building Bridges: Community Development Corporations and the World of Employment Training*. New York: Ford Foundation.

Harrison, Bennett, and Barry Bluestone. 1988. *The Great U-Turn*. New York: Basic Books.

Harrison, Bennett, and S. Kantor. 1978. "The political economy of state job-creation business incentives." *Journal of the American Institute of Planners* 44 (2): 424–435.

Haselkorn, David, and E. Fideler. 1996. *Breaking the Glass Ceiling: Paraprofessional Pathways to Teaching*. Belmont, Mass.: Recruiting New Teachers, Inc.

Haveman, Robert H., and Daniel H. Saks. 1985. "Transatlantic Lessons from Employment and Training Policy." *Industrial Relations* 24 (1): 20–36.

Haycock. Kati. 1998. "Good Teaching Matters . . . a Lot." *Thinking K–16* 3, no. 2 (summer).

Health Care Financing Administration. 2001. *National Health Expenditure Projections: 2000–2010*. March. http://www.hcfa.gov/stats/NHE-Proj/proj2000/proj2000.pdf.

Heaphy, Emily, et al. 1999. *Case Study: The Patient Care Delivery Model at the Massachusetts General Hospital*, March. Boston, Mass.: Harvard Business School.

Helburn, Suzanne, ed. 1995. *Cost, Quality and Child Outcomes in Child Care Centers*. Denver: University of Colorado, Center for Research in Economic and Social Policy.

Helburn, Suzanne, and John Morris. 1996. "Provider Costs and Income." Unpublished manuscript. Denver: University of Colorado, Center for Research in Economic and Social Policy.

Hershey, Alan M., and LaDonna Pavetti. 1997. "Turning Job Finders into Job Keepers." *The Future of Children* 7:74–86.

Hewlett, Sylvia Ann, and Cornel West. 2001. "Caring for Crib Lizards." *American Prospect* 12 (1): 17–19.

Hirsch, Paul M., and Mark Shanley. 1996. "The Rhetoric of Boundaryless—Or, How the Newly Empowered Managerial Class Bought into Its Own Marginalization." In *The Boundaryless Career*, ed. Michael B. Arthur and Denise M. Rousseau, 218–238. New York: Oxford University Press.

Holzer, Harry. 2004. Encouraging Job Advancement among Low-Wage Workers: A New Approach. *The Brookings Institution Policy Brief* (May): 1–8.

Holzer, Harry, and Margy Waller. 2003. *The Workforce Investment Act: Reauthorization to Address the Skills Gap.* Washington, D.C.: The Brookings Institution Center on Urban and Metropolitan Policy.

Howell, David. 1994. "The Skills Myth." *American Prospect* 5 (18): 81–90.

Huxley, Mary Pat. 2004. *The History, Current Status, and Future Direction for the California Community Colleges Biotechnology Initiative: Helping Meet the California Biotech Industry Need for an Operational Workforce.* California Community Colleges Economic and Workforce Development Program White Paper. http://www.cccbiotech.org/pdf/white_paper.pdf.

Huxley, Mary Pat. 2002. "Operational Review Document." Applied Biological Technologies Initiative, California Community Colleges Economic and Workforce Development Program.

Jacoby, Daniel. 1991. "The Transformation of Industrial Apprenticeship in the United States." *Journal of Economic History* 52 (4): 887–910.

Javar, J., and S. Wandner. 2002. "Use of Intermediaries to Provide Training and Employment Services: Experience under WIA, JTPA, and Wagner-Peyser Programs." In *Job Training in the United States: History, Effectiveness, and Prospects*, ed. G. O'Leary, R. Straits, and S. Wandner. Kalamazoo, Mich.: Upjohn Institute for Employment Research.

Jenkins, Davis. 1999. *Beyond Welfare-to-Work: Bridging the Low-Wage Livable-Wage Employment Gap.* Chicago: Great Cities Institute, University of Illinois at Chicago.

———. 2003. *The Potential of Community Colleges as Bridge to Opportunity for the Disadvantaged: Can It Be Achieved on a Large Scale?* Paper presented at the Seminar on Access and Equality, Community College Research Center, Teachers College, Columbia University.

Jenkins, Davis, and Nik Theodore. 1997. *Hiring Needs and Practices of Chicago Manufacturers.* Chicago: Great Cities Institute, University of Illinois at Chicago.

Jenkins, Davis, and Richard Florida. 1999. "Work System Innovation among Japanese Transplants in the United States." In *Remade in America*, ed. Jeffrey Liker, Mark Fruin, and Paul Adler, 331–360. New York: Oxford University Press.

Kaiser Commission on Medicaid and the Uninsured. 1999. *Long-Term Care: Medicaid's Role and Challenges.* Washington, D.C.: Henry J. Kaiser Foundation.

Karoly, Lynn A. 1993. "The Trend in Inequality among Families, Individuals, and Workers in the United States: A Twenty-Five-Year Perspective." In *Uneven Tides: Rising Inequality in America*, ed. Sheldon Danzinger and Peter Gottschalk, 19–98. New York: Russell Sage Foundation.

Katz, Lawrence, and Kevin Murphy. 1992. "Changes in Relative Wages, 1963–87: The Role of Supply and Demand Factors." *Quarterly Journal of Economics* 107:35–78.

Kazis, Richard. 2004. "Opportunity and Advancement for Low-Wage Workers: New Challenges, New Solutions." In *Low-Wage Workers in the New Economy*, ed. Richard Kazis and Marc Miller, 1–18. Washington, D.C.: Urban Institute Press.

Klemanski, J. S. 1989. "Tax Increment Financing: Public Funding for Private Economic Development Projects." *Policy Studies Journal* 17 (2): 325–328.

Klineman, Jeffrey. 2003. "Training as Uncertain as Drug Approvals." *Mass High Tech: The Journal of New England Technology.* http://www.masshightech.com/ls_05.asp (accessed March 5, 2004).

Knauss, Jody. 1997. *The Low-Road Threat: Briggs and Stratton and the Transformation to Modular Mass Production*. Madison: Center on Wisconsin Strategy.

Knoke, David, and Arne L. Kalleberg. 1994. "Job Training in U.S. Ogranizations." *American Sociological Review* 59:537–546.

Kuttner, Robert. 1997. *Everything for Sale*. New York: Knopf.

Lafer, Gordon. 2002. *The Job Training Charade*. Ithaca, N.Y.: Cornell University Press.

Lautsch, Brenda, and Paul Osterman. 1998. "Changing the Constraints: A Successful Employment and Training Strategy." In *Jobs and Economic Development*, ed. Robert Giloth, Thousand Oaks, Calif.: Sage.

Laverty, Kassin, Alice Burton, Marcy Whitebook, and Dan Bellm. 2001. *Current Data on Child Care Salaries and Benefits in the United States*. Washington, D.C.: Center for the Child Care Workforce.

Lawler, Edward E., III. 1994. "From Job-Based to Competency-Based Organizations." *Journal of Organizational Behavior* 15:3–15.

Lederer, John. 2002. *Broken Promises: Lifelong Learning, Community Colleges, and the Sad State of Incumbent Worker Training*. Seattle, Wash.: Shoreline Community College.

Leigh, Duane. 1989. *Assisting Displaced Workers*. Kalamazoo, Mich.: The W. E. Upjohn Institute for Employment Research.

Leighton, Mary S., Eileen O'Brien, Karen Walking Eagle, Lisa Weinger, George Wimberly, and Peter Youngs. 1997. *Roles for Education Paraprofessionals in Effective Schools: An Idea Book*. Prepared for the U.S. Department of Education by Policy Studies Associates. http://www.ed.gov/pubs/Paraprofessionals/roles2.html.

Lenberg. C. B. 1997. *Nursing Education Mobility Action Group Project (NEMAG), Evaluation Research Final Report*. Cleveland, Ohio: Center for Health Affairs.

Leonard, R. 2001. "Policy Considerations for Nursing Home Quality Improvement." *Harvard Health Policy Review* (spring): 48–57.

Levitan, Sar A., and Isaac Shapiro. 1987. *Working but Poor: America's Contradiction*. Baltimore, Md.: Johns Hopkins University Press.

Lidman, Russell. 1995. *The Family Income Study and Washington's Welfare Population: A Comprehensive Review*. Olympia: Washington State Institute for Public Policy.

Luria, Dan. 1996. "Why Markets Tolerate Mediocre Manufacturing." *Challenge* 39 (4): 11–16.

Luker, Bill, Jr., Gary Layden, and Robert C. Turner. 1997. *On the Road to High Performance: Three Case Studies of the Wisconsin Regional Training Partnership in Action*. Milwaukee: Wisconsin Regional Training Project.

Lynch, Lisa M., and Sandra E. Black. 1998. "Beyond the Incidence of Employer-Provided Training." *Industrial and Labor Relations Review* 52:64–81.

MacDuffie, J. P. 1995. "Human Resource Bundles and Manufacturing Performance: Organizational Logic and Flexible Production Systems in the World Auto Industry." *Industrial and Labor Relations Review* 48:197–221.

Marano, Cindy, and Kim Tarr. 2004. "The Workforce Intermediary: Profiling the Field of Practice and Its Challenges." In *Workforce Intermediaries for the Twenty-first Century*, ed. Robert Giloth, 93–123. Philadelphia: Temple University Press.

Marcelli, Baru, and Donald Cohen. 2000. "Planning for Shared Prosperity or Growing Inequality? An In-Depth Look at San Diego's Leading Industry Clusters." San Diego: Center for Policy Initiatives.

McGahey, Richard. 2004. "Workforce Intermediaries: Recent Experience and Implications for Workforce Development." *Workforce Intermediaries for the Twenty-first Century*, ed. Robert P. Giloth, 124–154. Philadelphia: Temple University Press.

McGroarty, Daniel, and Cameron Humphries. 1995. "Milwaukee's Gullible Corporate Donors." *Wall Street Journal*, August 22, A11.

McNally, Margaret. 1999. *Ladders in Nursing Careers Program*. Princeton, N.J.: Robert Wood Johnson Foundation.

Mead, L. 1992. *The New Politics of Poverty: The Working Poor in America*. New York: Basic Books.

Meares, Carol Ann, and John F. Sargent. 1999. *Infotech Skills at the Speed of Innovation*. Washington, D. C.: U.S. Department of Commerce, Office of Technology Policy.

Meisenheimer, Joseph R., II. 1998. "The Services Industry in the 'Good' Versus 'Bad' Jobs Debate." *Monthly Labor Review* (February): 22–47.

Meléndez, E. 1996. *Working on Jobs: The Center for Employment Training*. Boston: Economic Development Assistance Consortium.

Meléndez, Edwin, and Bennett Harrison. 1998. "Matching the Disadvantaged to Job Opportunities: Structural Explanations for the Past Successes of the Center for Employment Training." *Economic Development Quarterly* 12 (3): 3–11.

Meyerson, H. 1999. "Caretakers Take Charge." *LA Weekly*, February 26–March 4. http://www.laweekly.com/ink/99/14/powerlines-meyerson.shtl.

Mezey, Jennifer, Rachel Schumacher, Mark H. Greenberg, Joan Lombardi, and John Hutchins. 2002. *Unfinished Agenda: Child Care for Low-Income Families since 1996: Implications for Federal and State Policy*. Washington, D.C.: Center for Law and Social Policy.

Miller, R. H., and H. S. Luft. 1994. "Managed Care Plan Performance since 1980: A Literature Analysis." *Journal of the American Medical Association* 271:1512–1519.

Mills, Jack, and Radha Roy Biswas. 2003. *State Financing Declines for Job Training: Need for Federal Funding Increases*. Boston: Jobs for the Future.

Millsap, M., M. Moss, and B. Gamse. 1993. *The Chapter I Implementation Study: Final Report*. Washington, D.C.: U.S. Department of Education.

Millsap, M., B. Turnbill, M. Moss, N. Brigham, B. Gamse, and E. Marks. 1992. *The Chapter I Implementation Study: Interim Report*. Washington, D.C.: U.S. Department of Education.

Military Family Resource Center. 2002. "Overview of Military Child Development System." http://www.mfrc-dodqol.org/MCY/mm_cdc.htm.

Mishel, Lawrence, and Jared Bernstein. 1994. *The State of Working America, 1994–95*. Washington, D.C.: The Economic Policy Institute.

Mishel, Lawrence, Jared Bernstein, and Sylvia Allegretto. 2004. *The State of Working America, 2004–2005*. Ithaca, N.Y.: Cornell University Press.

Mishel, Lawrence, Jared Bernstein, and Heather Boushey. 2003. *The State of Working America 2002–2003*. Washington, D.C.: Economic Policy Institute.

Mishel, Lawrence, Jared Bernstein, and John Schmitt. 1999. *The State of Working America: 1998–99*. Washington, D.C.: The Economic Policy Institute.

Mitchell, A., L. Stoney, and H. Dichter. 1997. *Financing Child Care in the United States: An Illustrative Catalog of Current Strategies*. Philadelphia: The Pew Charitable Trusts and the Ewing Marion Kauffman Foundation.

Mitnik, Pablo A., Matthew Zeidenberg, and Laura Dresser. 2002. *Can Career Ladders Really Be a Way Out of Dead-End Jobs? A Look at Job Structure and Upward Mobility in the Service Industries*. Madison: Center on Wisconsin Strategy, University of Wisconsin.

Moses, E. B. 1994. *The Registered Nurse Population: Findings from the National Sample*

Survey of Registered Nurses, March 1992. Washington, D.C.: Division of Nursing, Bureau of Health Professions, Health Resources and Service Administration, U.S. Department of Health and Human Services.

Moshoyannis, Thalia, Anna Lou Pickett, and Len Granick. 1999. *The Evolving Roles and Education/Training Needs of Teacher and Paraprofessional Teams in New York City Public Schools.* New York: Center for Advanced Study in Education, City University of New York.

Moss, Philip, Harold Salzman, and Chris Tilly. 2000. "Limits to Market-Mediated Employment: From Deconstruction to Reconstruction of Internal Labor Markets." In *Non-Standard Work: The Nature and Challenges of Changing Employment Arrangements,* ed. Françoise Carré, Marianne A. Ferber, Lonnie Golden, and Steve Hertzenberg, 95–121. Champaign, Ill.: Industrial Relations Research Association.

Moss, Steven. 2001. *Child Care and Its Impact on California's Economy.* Washington, D.C.: National Economic Development Law Center.

National Academy of Sciences, Institute of Medicine. 1996. *Nursing Staff in Hospitals and Nursing Homes.* Washington, D.C.: National Academy of Sciences, Institute of Medicine.

——. 2000. *Improving the Quality of Long-Term Care.* Washington, D.C.: National Academy of Sciences, Institute of Medicine.

National Association for Home Care. 2000. "Basic Statistics about Home Care." http://www.nahc.org/Consumer/hcstats.html.

National Association for the Education of Young Children. 2004. http://www.naeyc.org/accreditation.

National Association of Manufacturers. 2003. *The Facts about Modern Manufacturing.* Washington, D.C.: National Association of Manufacturers.

National Center on Education and the Economy. 1990. *America's Choice: High Skills or Low Wages.* Rochester, N.Y.: National Center on Education and the Economy.

National Child Care Information Center. 2000. "The Child Care Partnership Project: Georgia's Voluntary Pre Kindergarten Program." http://www.nccic.org/ccpartnerships/cases/georgia.htm.

——. 2004a. "Threshold of Licensed Family Child Care (August 2004)." http://nccic.org/pubs/cclicensingreq/threshold.html.

——. 2004b. "Child Care Licensing Requirements (August 2004): Minimum Early Childhood Education (ECE) Preservice Qualifications, Orientation/Initial Licensure, and Annual Ongoing Training Hours for Family Child Care Providers." http://nccic.org/pubs/cclicensingreq/cclr-famcare.html.

——. 2004c. "The Effects of Quality Child Care on Young Children." http://www.nccic.org/poptopics/effectsqualitycc.html.

National Council of Jewish Women. 1999. *Opening a New Window on Childcare.* http://www.ncjw.org/programs/NCJWfinal.pdf.

National Manufacturing Association, the Manufacturing Institute, and Deloitte and Touche. 2003. *Keeping America Competitive: How a Talent Shortage Threatens U.S. Manufacturing.* Washington, D.C.: National Manufacturing Association.

Needleman, Jack, Peter I. Buerhaus, Soeren Mattke, Maureen Suewart, and Katya Zelevinsky. 2001. *Nurse Staffing and Patient Outcomes in Hospitals.* Boston: Harvard School of Public Health.

Neighborhood Capital Budget Group. 2002. "What Is TIFWORKS?" http://www.ncbg.org/tifs/tif_works.htm.

——. 2004. "How TIF Funds Are Spent in Chicago." http://www.ncbg.org/tifs/tif_spend.htm.

Nelson, Julie. 2001. *Why Are Early Education and Care Wages So Low? A Critical Guide to Common Explanations*. New York: Foundation for Child Development.

North Carolina Community College System. 2003. "NCCC System 2003–05 Expansion Budget Request." http://www.ncccs.cc.nc.us/News_Releases/03–05_Budget_Request.htm.

North Carolina Division of Facility Services. 1999. *Comparing State Efforts to Address the Recruitment and Retention of Nurse Aide and Other Paraprofessional Aide Workers*. http://facility-services.state.nc.us/recruit.pdf

——. 2000. *Results of a Follow-Up Survey to States on Wage Supplements for Medicaid and Other Public Funding to Address Aide Recruitment and Retention in Long-Term Care Settings*. http://facility-services.state.nc.us/survy.pdf.

Olson, Lynn. 2002. "Starting Early' in Quality Counts 2002: Building Blocks for Success." *Education Week* 21, no. 17 (January 10): 10–14, 16–21.

Osterman, Paul. 1993. "Why Don't They Work? Employment Patterns in a High Pressure Economy." *Social Science Research* 22 (2): 115–130.

——. 1995. "Skill, Training, and Work Organization in American Establishments." *Industrial Relations* 34 (April): 125–146.

Paraprofessional Healthcare Institute. 2000. *National Survey on State Initiatives to Improve Paraprofessional Healthcare Employment: October 2000 Results on Nursing Home Staff*. Bronx, N.Y.: National Clearinghouse on the Direct Care Workforce.

Park-Jadotte, Jennifer, Stacie Carolyn Golin, and Barbara Goult. 2002. *Building a Stronger Child Care Workforce: A Review of Studies of the Effectiveness of Public Compensation Initiatives*. Washington, D.C.: Institute for Women's Policy Research.

Parker, Eric, and Joel Rogers. 2003. *Milwaukee Jobs Initiative: Five Years of Better Jobs*. http://www.cows.org/pdf/projects/mji/ov-accompshmts.pdf (accessed July 13, 2003).

Parker, Eric, and Joel Rogers. 1996. *The Wisconsin Regional Training Partnership: Lessons for National Policy*. Berkeley: University of California, Berkeley Institute of Industrial Relations.

Pavetti, LaDonna, and Gregory Acs. 1997. *Moving Up, Moving Down, or Going Nowhere? A Study of the Employment Patterns of Young Women and Their Implications for Welfare Mothers*. Washington, D.C.: Urban Institute.

Pearce, Diane. 2000. *The Self-Sufficiency Standard for California*. San Francisco: Equal Rights Advocates.

Phillips, D., M. Mekos, S. Scarr, K. McCartney, and M. Abbott-Shim. 2001. "Within and Beyond the Classroom Door: Assessing Quality in Child Care Centers. *Early Childhood Research Quarterly* 15 (4): 475–496.

Pickett, Anna Lou. 1986. "Certified Partners: Four Good Reasons for Certification of Paraprofessionals." *American Educator* 10 (3): 31–34, 47.

——. 1995. *Paraprofessionals in the Education Workforce*. Washington, D.C: National Education Association. http://www/nea.org/esp/resource/parawork.htm (accessed November 8, 2002).

Pink, Daniel. 2001. *Free Agent Nation*. New York: Warner Books.

Piore, Michael, and Charles F. Sabel. 1984. *The Second Industrial Divide*. New York: Basic Books.

Popkin, Joel. 2000. *Producing Prosperity: Manufacturing Technology's Unmeasured Role in Economic Expansion.* McLean, Va.: Association for Manufacturing Technology.

Rademacher, Ida, ed. 2002. *Working with Value: Industry-Specific Approaches to Workforce Development.* Washington, D.C.: Aspen Institute.

Rangarajan, Anu, Peter Schochet, and Dexter Chu. 1998. *Employment Experiences of Welfare Recipients Who Find Jobs: Is Targeting Possible?* Princeton, N.J.: Mathematica Policy Research.

Rapson, Mary Fry. 2000. "Statewide Nursing Articulation Model Design: Politics or Academics?" *Journal of Nursing Education* 39:294–301.

Rapson, Mary Fry, and R. B. Rice. 1997. "Colleagues in Caring." *Journal of Nursing Administration* 38:197–202.

———. 1999. "Progress and Outcomes of the Colleagues in Caring Program." *Journal of Nursing Administration* 29:4–8.

Recruiting New Teachers, Inc. 2000. *A Guide to Developing Paraprofessional-to-Teacher Programs.* Belmont, Mass.: Recruiting New Teachers, Inc.

Reich, Robert. 1991. *The Work of Nations.* New York: Knopf.

Reidy, Chris. 2004. "Losing Biomanufacturing Business to Lower-Cost North Carolina." *Boston Globe,* January 23.

Reynolds, Arthur J. 2000. *Success in Early Intervention: The Chicago Child-Parent Centers.* Lincoln: University of Nebraska Press.

Reynolds, Arthur J., Judy A. Temple, Dylan L. Robertson, and Emily A. Mann. 2001. "Long-Term Effects of an Early Childhood Intervention on Educational Achievement and Juvenile Arrest." *Journal of the American Medical Association* 285 (18): 2339–2346.

Rice, R. B., and Mary Fry Rapson. 1997. "Overview of Regional Collaboratives." *Journal of Nursing Administration* 27:11–15; 38:197–202.

Rintell, Ellen M., Michelle Pierce, and Jaime Wurzel. 2002. *Biennial Report: Title VII Project PET Para Educators to Teachers.* Salem, Mass.: Salem State College.

Rintell, Ellen M., and Michelle Pierce. 2002. *Becoming Maestra: Latina Paraprofessionals as Teacher Candidates in Bilingual Education.* Salem, Mass.: Salem State College.

Rose, Steven. 1995. *The Decline of Employment Stability in the 1980s.* Washington, D.C.: National Commission on Employment Policy.

Rosenfeld, Stuart, et al. 2003. *Meeting the Long-Term Skill Needs of North Carolina's Biomanufacturing Industries and Biotechnology Cluster.* Carrboro, N.C.: Regional Technology Strategies, Inc.

Rubin, Jerry, Marlene B. Seltzer, and Jack Mills. 2003. "Financing Workforce Intermediaries." In *Workforce Intermediaries for the Twenty-first Century,* ed. Robert Giloth, 293–313. Philadelphia: Temple University Press.

Rubinstein, S. 2000. "The Impact of Co-Management on Quality Performance: The Case of the Saturn Corporation." *Industrial and Labor Relations Review* 53 (1): 197–220.

Sakai, M. L., and Carolee Howes. 1997. *NAEYC Accreditation as a Strategy for Improving Childcare Quality: An Assessment by the National Center for the Early Childhood Work Force.* Washington, D.C.: National Center for the Early Childhood Work Force.

Salzman, Harold, Philip Moss, and Chris Tilly. 1998. *The Corporate Landscape and Workforce Skills.* Stanford: National Center for Postsecondary Improvement, Stanford University.

Salzman, Jeffrey, Susana Morales, and Aaron Dalton. 2003. "Statistical Picture of Participants in the Quality Child-Care Initiative: Apprentices, Journey Workers, Sponsors." *Social Policy Research Association Final Report.* http://www.spra.com/pdf/Statistical_Picture_of_Participants_in_the_QCCI_1371b.pdf.

Sawhill, Isabel. 2001. "From Welfare to Work." *Brookings Review* (summer): 4–7.

Sawhill, Isabel, and Adam Thomas. 2001. *A Hand Up for the Bottom Third.* Washington D.C.: Urban Institute.

Saxenian, Annalee. 1996. "Beyond Boundaries: Open Labor Markets and Learning in Silicon Valley." In *The Boundaryless Career,* ed. Michael B. Arthur and Denise M. Rousseau, 23–40. New York: Oxford University Press.

Scanlon, Willam J. 2001. "Nursing Workforce: Recruitment and Retention of Nurses and Nurse Aides Is a Growing Concern." Testimony before the Committee on Health, Education, Labor, and Pensions, U.S. Senate, May 17.

Schrammel, Kurt. 1998. "Comparing the Labor Market Success of Young Adults from Two Generations." *Monthly Labor Review* (February): 3–9.

Schulman, K. 2000. *Issue Brief: The High Cost of Child Care Puts Quality Child Care out of Reach for Many Families.* Washington, D.C.: Children's Defense Fund.

Schweitzer, Sarah. 2002. "Vision of Biotechnology Corridor Lacks Allure in Boston Neighborhood." *Boston Globe,* March 18.

Scrivener, Susan, et al. 1998. *Implementation, Participation Patterns, Costs, and Two-Year Impacts of the Portland Welfare-to-Work Program.* New York: Manpower Demonstration Research Corporation.

Seeley, J. 1999. *A Gray Area: Governor Stands in Way of Decent Wages for Health-Care Workers. LA Weekly,* October 8–14.

Shaiken, Harley, Stephen Herzenberg, and Sarah Kuhn. 1986. "The Work Process under More Flexible Production." *Industrial Relations* 25:167–183.

Shonkoff, Jack P., and Deborah A. Phillips, eds. 2000. *From Neurons to Neighborhoods: The Science of Early Childhood Development.* Washington, D.C.: Children's Defense Fund.

Silvestri, George T. 1993. "Occupational Employment: Wide Variations in Growth." *Monthly Labor Review* (November): 58–86.

Smith, Kristen. 1995. *Who's Minding the Kids? Child Care Arrangements, Current Population Reports.* Washington, D.C.: U.S. Census Bureau.

Snyder, T.D., C. M. Hoffman, and C. M. Geddes. 1998. *Digest of Education Statistics. 1997.* NCES 98–015. Washington, D.C.: U.S. Department of Education, National Center for Education Statistics.

Stone, Katherine V. W. 2001. "The New Psychological Contract: Implications of the Changing Workplace for Labor and Employment Law." *UCLA Law Review* 48:519–661.

———. 2004. *From Widgets to Digits.* Cambridge: Cambridge University Press.

Strawn, Julie, and Karin Martinson. 2000. *Steady Work and Better Jobs.* Washington, D.C.: Manpower Development Research Corporation.

Sugalski, Thomas D., Louis S. Manzo, and Jim L. Meadows. 1995. "Resource Link: Re-establishing." *Human Resources Management* 34 (3): 389–403.

"Summary and Impact of the Medicare, Medicaid, and SCHIP Balanced Budget Refinement Act of 1999." 1999. http://www.ppsv.com/issues/mmdoc.htm.

Swartz, Thomas R., and Kathleen M. Weigert. 1995. *America's Working Poor.* Notre Dame, Ind.: University of Notre Dame Press.

Thomas, William. 1996. *Life Worth Living: How Someone You Love Can Still Enjoy Life in a Nursing Home—The Eden Alternative in Action.* Acton, Mass.: VanderWyk and Burnham.

Twombly, Eric C., Maria D. Montilla, and Carol J. DeVita. 2001. *State Initiatives to Increase Compensation for Child Care Workers.* Washington, D.C.: Urban Institute.

Uchitelle, Louis. 2001. "How to Define Poverty. Let Us Count the Ways." *New York Times*, May 26, A15–A17.

U.S. Department of Commerce. 2003. *A Survey of the Use of Biotechnology in U.S. Industry*. http://www.technology.gov/reports/Biotechnology/CD120a_0310.pdf (accessed September 2004).

U.S. Census Bureau. 1997. *1997 Economic Census: Health Care and Social Assistance, United States*. http://www.census.gov/epcd/ec97/US_62.HTM#N624.

U.S. Census Bureau, Administrative and Customer Services Division. 2002. *Statistical Abstract of the United States*. Washington, D.C.: U.S. Census Bureau.

U.S. Department of Education. 1997. *Roles for Paraprofessionals in Effective Schools*. http://www.ed.gov/pubs/Paraprofessionals/summary.htm (accessed November 8, 2002).

U.S. Department of Health and Human Services. 2000. "New Statistics Show Only Small Percentage of Eligible Families Receive Child Care Help." Press release, December 6. http://www.acf.dhhs.gov/news/ccstudy2.htm.

U.S. General Accounting Office. 1999. *Child Care: How Do Military and Civilian Center Costs Compare?* Washington, D.C. http://www.mfrc-dodqol.org/pdffiles/gaostudy.pdf.

———. 2000. *Child Care: State Efforts to Enforce Safety and Health Requirements*. January. http://www.mfrc-dodqol.org/pdffiles/gaostudy.pdf.

USA Child Care. 2000. *Conducting Market Rate Surveys: How Does Your State Rate?* http://www.usachildcare.org/programs/kidsrate/market_rate_report.pdf (accessed September 2004).

Vandell, Deborah Lowe, and Barbara Wolfe. 2000. *Child Care Quality: Does It Matter? Does It Need to Be Improved?* Madison: University of Wisconsin–Madison, Institute for Research on Poverty.

Wallace, Michael, and Arne E. Kalleberg. 1982. "Industrial Transformation and the Decline of Craft: The Decomposition of the Printing Industry." *American Sociological Review* 47:307–324.

Whitebook, Marcy. 1998. *Worthy Work, Unlivable Wages: The National Child Care Staffing Study Revisited, 1988–1997*. Washington, D.C.: Center for the Child Care Workforce.

Whitebook, Marcy, and Laura Sakai. 2003. "Turnover Begets Turnover: An Examination of Job and Occupational Instability among Child Care Center Staff." *Early Childhood Research Quarterly* 18:273–293.

Whitebook, Marcy, and Abby Eichberg. 2002. *Finding a Better Way: Defining and Assessing Public Policies to Improve Child Care Workforce Compensation*. Center for the Study of Childcare Employment. Paper 2002–002.

Whitebook, Marcy, Laura Sakai, Emily Gerber, and Carollee Howes. 2001. *Then and Now: Changes in Child Care Staffing, 1994–2000*. Washington, D.C.: Center for the Child Care Workforce.

Whitebook, Marcy, and D. Berlin. 1999. *Taking on Turnover: An Action Guide for Child Care Center Teachers and Directors*. Washington, D.C.: Center for the Child Care Workforce.

Whitebook, Marcy, Carollee Howes, and Deborah Phillips. 1998. *Worthy Work, Unlivable Wages: The National Child Care Staffing Study Revisited, 1988–1997*. Washington, D.C.: Center for the Child Care Workforce.

Whitebook, Marcy, Laura Sakai, Carollee Howes. 1997. *NAEYC Accreditation as a Strategy for Improving Child Care Quality: An Assessment*. Washington, D.C.: Center for the Child Care Workforce.

Whitebook, Marcy, Carollee Howes, and Deborah Phillips. 1990. *The National Child Care*

Staffing Study Final Report: Who Cares? Child Care Teachers and the Quality of Care in America. Washington, D.C.: Center for the Child Care Workforce.

(The) White House. 2004. *A New Generation of American Innovation*. April. http://www.whitehouse.gov/infocus/technology/economic_policy200404/chap3.html.

(The) White House Office of the Press Secretary. 2000. "Why Manufacturing Matters to the U.S. Economy." Statement, February 5, Washington, D.C.

Wiener, Joshua M., and David G. Stevenson. 1997. *Long-Term Care for the Elderly and State Health Policy*. Washington, D.C: Urban Institute.

Wilson, Randall, Susan C. Eaton, and Amara Kamanu. 2002. *Extended Care Career Ladder Initiative (ECCLI) Round 2: Evaluation Report*. Boston, Mass.: Wiener Center for Social Policy, Harvard University and University of Massachusetts, Boston.

Wisconsin Regional Training Program. 2000. *Annual Report*. Milwaukee: Wisconsin Regional Training Program.

———. 2002. *Annual Report*. Milwaukee: Wisconsin Regional Training Program.

Wolfe, Barbara, and Deborah L. Vandell. 2002. "Welfare Reform Depends on Good Child Care." Special supplement. *The American Prospect* (summer): A19–A22.

Wolff, Edward N. 1996. *Top Heavy: A Study of the Increasing Inequality of Wealth in America*. New York: Century Foundation.

Wright, Eric Olin, and Rachel E. Dwyer. 2002. *The Patterns of Job Expansion in the United States, A Comparison of the 1960s and 1990s*. Madison: University of Wisconsin, Department of Sociology.

Wunderlich, Gooloo S., and Peter Kohler, eds. 2001. "Improving the Quality of Long-Term Care." Washington, D.C.: Committee on Improving Quality in Long-Term Care Institute of Medicine, National Academy Press.

Zellman, Gail L., and Anne S. Johansen. 1998. *Examining the Implementation and Outcomes of the Military Child Care Act of 1989*. Santa Monica, Calif.: Rand Corporation.

Index